THE HOME BOOK

A Guide to *Safety, Security and Savings* in the Home

SELECTED READINGS

INTRODUCTION BY
Ralph Nader

PREPARED WITH THE ASSISTANCE OF
Elizabeth Hax

DESIGNED BY
Kathleen Glynn

Center for Study of Responsive Law
P.O. Box 19367
Washington, D.C. 20036

ISBN 0-936758-26-0
LIBRARY OF CONGRESS CATALOG NUMBER 89-060153

Table of Contents

Introduction

BY RALPH NADER

THE HOME SO FAMILIAR, yet so unknown. So much time is spent there, yet so little discovery is brought to bear on ways to make the home safer, secure and less expensive to maintain— in short, more pleasant and liveable.

Years ago, as a small child, I read a comic book about the adventures of two people who were shrunken into microscopic size and placed in a home flower pot. The tiny world of tinier bugs came alive as if it were a seething jungle of wild animals. In their homes people cannot see this miniature world of intense change and activity. But so too are the many facets of the home, and all that sells to, connects with, and pollutes the home, very often invisible either because they escape the naked eye or the uninformed mind.

This collection of materials has an overarching goal to whet your appetite with a panorama of information, advice and leads so that you —male, female, young and old—develop a zest for a home reconnaissance. Once this journey is underway, delight and duty merge toward action. The delight is seeing your home accumulate greater value by preventing hazards to your children and yourselves, forestalling expensive repairs and cleanups and in banding together with your neighbors for savings and security. The duty is in defending your home, be it a house, apartment, condo or coop, from the commercial predators and burglars who daily prey on their unknowing victims.

At school, little is taught about the home. This vacuum becomes apparent whenever people chide themselves with "if only," as: "Why didn't I put that non-skid tape on the stairs before the fall?" or "Why didn't I get in writing what the repairmen promised?" or "Now I know quite late how to detect the indoor pollution to which my children have been sensitive ," or, "Gee, I could have reduced that noise which was irritating my elderly parents and could have made their residence a safety zone," or, "I should have known there was asbestos in the cellar all these years," or "Why didn't I ask the right questions before our lawn was doused with herbicides or our house sprayed by the exterminator company," or, "Look at the money I could have saved every year by making my home more fuel efficient."

These are examples of a neglected learning which can be remedied with some practical self-education.

The Home Book provides an introduction to such "home savvy" or "home skills" and encourages you along a lighted path to obtain more applied knowledge from other mentioned resources, materials and toll-free hotlines. In practical terms, the more you know, the fewer worries and pain you and your family will experience and the more money you will save. The correlation is unassailable; for household ignorance is exactly what unscrupulous businesses feed off. And procrastination is nourished by not knowing what to do to make your home a safer environment for all ages.

Every American can recount stories about home accidents, fires, and other tragedies. In total the National Safety Council reports that for 1987, 20,500 people died in household accidents and 3,100,000 suffered disabling injuries. These casualties also cost over $17 billion a year.

There is an additional enhancement of the quality of household living envisioned by *The Home Book*— such as spreading Neighborhood Crime Watches and more people joining local home buying groups. This is a trend with an important future. Already, home fuel group buying associations are spreading on the east coast and through negotiated volume discounts from dealers, they are saving around 20 cents per gallon. In the Washington, D.C./Baltimore area, Public Citizen's Buyers Up provides for its over 12,000 members, who pay dues of $20 a year ($5 for energy assistance qualifiers), with discounted oil, regular credit, oil furnace maintenance, and energy conservation when selected area distributors agree to service the members. On the horizon one can see coming along coop buying of home insurance, home owners repair coops, and other networking for consumer protection and benefit. This networking can have the most interesting consequences for resurgent civic involvement in City Hall decisions and other municipal policies. At least such banding together will give greater bargaining power to the buyers versus the sellers and replace presently atomized households huddling together physically, with households that work together for health, safety and community betterment through strength.

The Home Book is a reference guide as you need it, which makes it advisable to read it first so you can follow up later. ❖

Section One
SAFETY AND SECURITY

SAFETY AND SECURITY almost go with home dwellers' most natural expectations. After all, if not in the home, where? The facts describe an increasingly different situation, especially as more and more products go into the home and are part of the home's very fabrications.

This section starts with advice about how to discourage would-be burglars from entering your residence and making it very difficult for them to stay if they do break and enter. Also emphasized is the need to make an inventory of your home's major contents to serve as evidence when you take a casualty loss or make an insurance claim.

Next comes a subject which causes more preventable and noisy pain than any other category of perils— a child-perilous home, full of sharp edges, traps, attractive nuisances and badly designed equipment and products. An overview of the "child-safe" home aspiration leads into some concise checklists and advisories relating to nursery equipment, toxic household products, infant falls, flammable fabrics, the horrible lead paint poisoning problems and other harms peculiar to children, from ill-designed toys to baby rattles to children's TV.

Stopping the fire next time is treated in general and specific ways including the problems with fireplaces and chimneys if care is not taken and not so common information on the choice of smoke detectors. More is being discovered about carbon monoxide poisoning in the home from backdrafting of combustion appliances located inside houses such as "conflicts" between a fireplace and a furnace or an air conditioner and a gas water heater. (See *Mother Earth News*, Nov./Dec. 1988).

For millions of people near atomic power plants there is a sober article on what you should know about emergency planning in case a major radioactive leak or meltdown occurs. Then comes a topic which will affect you intimately in the coming months as states rush to follow New Jersey's example and require households to separate their garbage for pickup. Household toxics programs are bursting out all over as landfills become clogged and dreaded incinerators are proposed to transform solid wastes into toxic gases which you can breathe. These programs spell recycling of wastes and someday will encompass waste reduction at the source.

Electrical systems, appliances and the kitchen are given the alerts in ways that will probably invoke some unpleasant memories of what has happened and could happen again. Several pages are devoted to forestalling home hazards and common frauds affecting the elderly. This section concludes with advice on what to do when a natural disaster such as a flood or hurricane is approaching (it's not that obvious), how to reduce noise in and around the home and an overview on making your home a "safety zone." If it all sounds like a lot to absorb, remember it will take you far less time to learn than to deal with the aftermath of just one moderate fall or injury that this applied knowledge could have prevented.

There follows an advisory on detection, rights and remedies when your drinking water is contaminated— unfortunately, a not infrequent condition in our USA. ❖

Take a Bite Out of Crime
How to Crimeproof Your Home
THE ADVERTISING COUNCIL, INC., 1979

Outside Your Home

Protect your home by starting where the burglars usually start—outside.

Landscaping

Look around. Are there large trees near the house? Prune lower limbs that could help a thief climb in second floor windows. Don't forget to trim trees and bushes so doors and windows are visible to neighbors. Think twice about installing high wooden fences— criminals can slip in and work unobserved with little fear of being caught.

Remember to lock up ladders and tools. Ask your neighbors to do the same. Trellises look great, but place them where they can't be used as ladders to second floor windows.

Lighting

Criminals avoid the spotlight. Porches, yards, and all entrances to your home and garage should be well lighted. Check with your police or sheriff's department for suggestions about lighting. A spotlight may be best for your needs but other kinds of lights can work as well at lesser cost.

Your House Number

Make sure law enforcement or fire agencies can locate your house in an emergency: your house number should be clearly visible from the street—day and night. Use numbers made of reflective materials that are 6 inches high or black numerals against a white background. Avoid script letters for the number—they can be confusing. If your house is some distance from the road, post the number at the driveway entrance. If you live on a corner, make sure the number faces the street named in your address.

Doors

You wouldn't put a padlock on a paper chain...so, don't put good locks on a hollow wooden door. If the door is flimsy and weak, or doesn't fit securely into the frame, locks won't help.

Take a good look at your doors. Do you keep them locked? Can a shove or a quick twist of a crowbar pop the door open? Make it tough to jimmy your lock or pry open the door, and you reduce the opportunity for crime. If doors and locks delay a burglar for several minutes, chances are he'll get discouraged and leave.

Hinged Doors

Entry doors should be solid core wood (and at least 1 3/4 inches thick) or metal. Most hollow core doors can be easily broken through. They offer little protection, no matter what locks you use.

Your door should fit its frame tightly—with no more than a 1/8-inch clearance between the door and frame. Too big a gap? Replace the door. If that's too expensive, bolt a sturdy metal strip to the door edge. You boost your protection—and save energy, too. Any hardware dealer can show you the kind of strip to use.

Doors with decorative glass panels or windows are an easy mark. It takes only seconds to break the glass and unlock the door. If you don't want to replace the door, install a break-resistant plastic panel or decorative grille over the glass. Attach the grilles with special non-removable screws.

Sliding Glass Doors

Burglars look for sliding glass doors because they are easy to open. Several types of locks are made especially for sliding glass doors. Or bolster the existing lock by placing a solid strip of wood or a broom handle in the track of the closed door. That helps block the door even if the lock is jimmied.

Determined thieves may lift the door off its tracks. Try one of these preventive tips:

1. Adjust rollers so the door cannot be pushed up enough to lift it off the track.
2. Insert screws along the upper track of the door. Leave enough room for the door to slide, but not enough space to lift the door out.
3. Drill a hole and insert a nail through the inside frame and part way through the metal door frame. You can remove the nail but a burglar can't.

Hinges

Most door hinges are on the inside, safe from a burglar's tools. If hinges are on the outside, it's not hard to remove the hinge pins and take the door out of the frame. To protect such doors:

1. Replace hinges with new ones that have non-removable pins.
2. Adjust existing hinges. Remove the middle screw on each hinge plate, and insert a metal pin or headless screw on one side. When the door is closed, the end of the pin will fit into the opposite hole. That way, even if hinge pins are removed, the door will be "bolted" to the frame.

When people think about securing their doors, they often stop with the front and back doors. Don't forget garage, cellar, patio, or other doors that lead out through storage areas or a spare room. You can be sure the burglar won't. Make sure those doors are strong, equipped with good locks—and always locked.

Locks

Chances are your locks were installed with economy—not security—in mind. Most houses and apartments have inexpensive key-in-knob locks. They are easy to slip open with a credit card or break open with a screwdriver. Night latches mounted on the surface of your door aren't much help. And don't rely on a chain lock—even one with a key. An average man pushing against them can easily break most chain locks.

Deadbolt Lock

A deadbolt lock can provide good protection. When you turn the key, the lock mechanism slides a strong metal bolt from the door into the frame.

When you buy a deadbolt lock, make sure:

- The bolt extends at least 1 inch from the edge of the door (has a "1 inch throw").
- The connecting screws that hold the lock together are on the inside of the door.
- The strike plate is attached to the door frame with screws that measure at least 3 inches.
- The cylinder has a steel guard—a ring around the key section. The cylinder guard should be tapered or rotate around the key section (if twisted) to prevent wrenching.

Auxiliary Rim Mounted Lock with a Deadbolt

Another good lock is an auxiliary rim mounted lock with a deadbolt. It is attached to the door's surface with long sturdy screws. The locking device on the door fits into the plate on the frame. When you turn the key, strong metal bars join the two parts of the lock. This lock is easy to install but hard to jimmy.

Double Cylinder Deadbolt Lock

Double cylinder deadbolt locks can be placed on doors with glass panels or on all your doors. These locks can be opened only with a key from either side. Keep the key near the door but not reachable from the glass panel. That way intruders can't get in, but you and your family can get out quickly in case of fire or emergency. It's best to check with your local law enforcement agency or housing officials before you install this lock. Some communities place restrictions on its use.

Police Lock

A police lock works well on rear and basement entrances and in apartments. It is a metal bar bracketed against the inside of the door at an angle, which slides into a small hole on the floor. It prevents an intruder from jimmying the lock or kicking in the door.

Check with your local police or sheriff to see if they can provide tips on the right locks for your doors.

Padlock

Padlocks are typically used for garages, sheds, and workshops. Look for sturdy padlocks that don't release the key until the padlock is locked. Be sure the padlock is in a rugged laminated case with a 3/8-inch shackle so it can resist repeated smashings. A double locking design can prevent the shackle being pried away from its case. Remember that a padlock is only as good as the hasp it is mounted on. The hasp should be secured with bolts and mounted on a metal plate. Be sure bolts are concealed when the padlock is locked.

Remember, always use your locks. Even a 5-minute trip to the store is long enough for a burglar to enter your home.

Did you know that many police and sheriff's departments will do a security check of your home? Specially-trained officers can show you places where a burglar could enter your home. They'll give you a list of recommendations to make your home safer. Check with your local law enforcement agency. It will cost you nothing—and could save you a lot.

Keys

Don't forget—victims report that as many as half of all burglaries take place without forced entry. In many cases, the burglar used a key. Be sure your keys don't fall into the wrong hands:

- Never carry identification tags on your key ring or holder.
- When you move into a new home or apartment have the locks re-keyed or changed. A locksmith can do this, or if you're handy with tools, you can change the locks yourself.
- Know who has every key to your home. Don't give keys to maintenance or delivery people.
- Don't ever hide your key outside; burglars know all the hiding places.

All the hardware in the world won't protect you if you open your door without checking who's on the other side. Buy an inexpensive peephole or wide angle viewer. Tell your kids and their babysitters not to open the door to strangers.

Windows

Windows are another obvious target. Keep them locked—basement and second floor windows, too.

Double Hung Windows

Most standard windows have a small thumb-turn lock in the center. Don't rely on these locks alone. They can be pried open, or easily reached through a broken pane.

You can buy special key locks for windows at a hardware store. Ask for locks best suited to your type of windows and instructions for installing them. Keep the keys away from the windows, but make sure everyone in the house knows where to find them in case of emergency. Be sure to check with your local law enforcement agency or housing officials to see if there are any restrictions on installation of these locks.

An easy, inexpensive way to secure your windows

is to use the "pin" trick. Drill an angled hole through the top frame of the lower window partially into the frame of the upper window. Then insert a nail or an eyebolt. The window can't be opened until you remove the nail. Make a second set of holes with windows partly open so you can have ventilation without inviting intruders. Eyebolts can provide strong resistance against jimmying. If you live in a high-crime area, it might be best to use them.

For especially vulnerable windows—those on street level—consider installing grates or grilles. Make sure grates are equipped with a quick release feature for emergency exits....

Neighborhood Watch

The best crime prevention device ever invented is a good neighbor. When neighbors band together to look out for each other, crime often goes down.

It's easy to organize a Neighborhood or Block Watch program. First, contact your local law enforcement agency. Then invite your neighbors in to discuss the crime problem and how to combat it. Ask you police or sheriff's department to send an officer to the meeting to offer tips on home security, self-protection, and what to report to police.

At the meeting, exchange work and vacation schedules, home and business telephone numbers, and addresses. Keep these near your telephone so you can use them if you need to report a crime. Choose one person or several individuals who are at home during the day to be responsible for Neighborhood Watch activities. Then make arrangements to watch each other's homes and property and to be on the lookout for suspicious activities or persons. Some neighbors form block clubs that meet regularly to discuss community issues and security techniques.

Operation Identification

Most burglars sell what they steal, making it hard for police to trace stolen goods. Once it's left your home, your TV or bicycle looks just like thousands of others. Unless you can prove it's yours, police can't return it. To help protect your property, join Operation Identification.

Here's how:

Borrow an electric engraving pen from your local law enforcement agency, or buy an inexpensive diamond-tipped marking pen from hardware or department stores. Check with your local police or sheriff to learn the identification number recommended by authorities in your state. Then engrave this number on all valuable possessions. Mark TV's, radios, stereos, typewriters, golf clubs, appliances, tools—any portable item that might be stolen. Photograph unmark-

able items such as china, silver, or jewelry...

Finally, let burglars know your goods are marked and can be traced. Put Operation Identification stickers (available from many local law enforcement agencies) on you front window, front door, or on any other clearly visible location. Just be sure that you marked your property before placing the stickers.

Operation ID is free, simple, and can help cut burglary rates. In Phoenix, Arizona, people who didn't join Operation Identification had 18 times as many burglaries as their neighbors who did join.

Don't Invite Trouble

Be cautious about letting strangers know your daily routine or vacation plans. Tell your children, too. If rooms in your home are clearly visible from the street, check to see that valuables are not clearly visible, too—and tempting to intruders. Keep in mind that many burglars aren't "pros"; they're kids from the neighborhood.

Telephone

Telephone surveys and wrong numbers may be legitimate. But burglars also use these methods to "case" your home. Tell your children and babysitters never to give any information to strangers over the telephone. Make sure you establish the identity of your caller before revealing your name, address, or other information. Don't hesitate to ask for a telephone number to verify the identity of the surveyor. Legitimate survey research organizations will gladly give you a home office number you can call (often collect). You may also receive advance notice of such surveys.

Don't let strangers into your home to use the phone. Instead, make the call yourself while they wait outside.

Classified Ads, Social Announcements, and Obituaries

Burglars read newspapers, too. Don't include your address in a classified ad. Announce social events and vacations after they happen—not before. If there's a death in the family, arrange for a housesitter on the day of the funeral. Ask a trusted neighbor to keep an eye on your home whenever you're out.

Vacation Checklist

Going away? An empty house is a tempting target for a burglar. Use this checklist of tips to safeguard your home while you're gone.

• Tell your local police or sheriff's department you plan to be away. Patrol officers may be able to check your home periodically.

- Stop all deliveries, or arrange for a neighbor or friend to pick up your mail, newspapers, and packages.
- Arrange for someone to mow your lawn, shovel snow, or rake leaves to give your home a lived-in look.
- Put in timers to turn lights and a radio on and off at appropriate times. It's another easy way to disguise the fact that you are away.
- Hide garbage cans in the basement or a storage shed. Empty cans when everyone else's are full can tell a burglar you're away.
- Turn the bell on your telephone down low. If a burglar's around, he won't be alerted to your absence by a ringing phone.
- Close and lock garage doors and windows. Ask a neighbor to park occasionally in your driveway. If you leave your car at home, park it in the driveway rather than the garage. Have your neighbor move it occasionally so it looks like you're using it.
- Leave your blinds, shades, and curtains in a normal position. Don't close them unless that's what you do when you're at home.
- Ask a neighbor to watch the house while you're away. It's a good idea to leave your vacation address and telephone number with a neighbor so you can be reached in case of emergency.
- A winter vacation tip—have a neighbor walk up your front steps after it snows to make your house look occupied.

If You Suspect Burglary

Don't go in. Go to a neighbor and call police immediately. Wait outside for them to arrive.

If you confront a burglar, don't try to stop him. Run to a neighbor and call police at once.

After a burglary don't touch anything. Call the police immediately—even a delay of 5 minutes can mean the chances of catching the criminal drop significantly. ❖

Security Systems for Your Home
Some Are Effective; Others, an "Invitation" to Burglars
SYLVIA PORTER'S *PERSONAL FINANCE*, NOVEMBER 1987

LAST YEAR, thieves broke into more than 3 million homes—that's one burglary every 10 seconds. But, according to FBI statistics, the chances of a successful burglary, or even one being attempted at all, drop fifteenfold when a home electronic security system stands guard.

With all the competing claims of effectiveness and the variety of high-tech gadgetry available, how do you pick a system that will protect you? To find out, we spoke to three experts: the marketing manager of the largest burglar-alarm firm in the nation, ADT Inc.; a consultant who specializes in unusual installations; and a reformed convict, who has served time in prison for burglary.

A good home-security system is a balance between making your home impenetrable by a burglar and habitable by you. Explains Robert Butchko, marketing manager of ADT, based in Parsippany, N.J.: "It's easy to make your home practically burglar-proof. The only trouble is that not only will the burglar have a hard time getting in, but so will you."

Homeowners must decide how much security they'd like and how much inconvenience they're willing to put up with. Each step up in security means somewhat more in inconvenience....

Burglar Alarms

"Keep in mind," explains Paul DeMatteis [who heads Counterforce, a New York City firm that consults on building security and installs sophisticated electronic systems], "the alarm has only two functions: to deter a would-be burglar and, failing that, to warn you or the police that an illegal entry is taking place."

The most basic burglar alarm is an electronic device triggered by the unauthorized opening of a door or window. Typically its controls are inside the house. It gives a homeowner a minute or so after opening the door to disarm the alarm by punching in a code.

Such a system can be bought at hardware stores for $100 to $250 and installed by a moderately handy homeowner. All our experts caution, though, that such alarms have serious drawbacks: a professional burglar quickly learns to recognize cheap or poorly installed alarms and usually can disarm them easily.

At best, do-it-yourself-installed systems are usually only effective for thwarting "casual" thieves, such as local children, who are responsible for the majority of burglaries in some neighborhoods.

A Model Alarm

A good basic electronic alarm should cover all doors and windows. Windows above the first floor can go bare if they're accessible only with a ladder. But if a window can be reached, say, from a tree or a porch roof, it should be protected, too.

Old-style window alarms use two detectors: an electronic trigger that responds to any unauthorized opening, and strips of metal tape along the edges of the glass. Although these are relatively effective, a good second-story man would have little trouble cutting the glass without affecting the tape, and then disarming the alarm.

More modern window alarms are computer-controlled and use sound sensors as their principal detectors. If a window is opened or the glass broken, the device picks up the "sound signature" and trips the alarm. The computer is so sophisticated that it will ignore a tapping on the window by a child or even a bird; it will respond only to a sound corresponding to a break-in or unauthorized opening.

Crude security systems trigger a loud warning bell to frighten off would-be burglars. Sometimes they are effective, but typically they're ignored—by neighbors, the police, and the burglar.

In recent years the strategy of alarm installers has changed. "Today," says Counterforce's DeMatteis, "we focus less on alerting the neighbors and more on scaring the burglar—seeking ways to dissuade him from continuing a break-in." Modern systems trigger a small loudspeaker that announces to the burglar that his presence has been detected, the police have been alerted, and he'd better quit the scene as quickly as possible. They then emit an ear-piercing siren of 140 decibels. The alarm can also be connected to lights in the home, blinking them off and on to frighten the thief.

An even more sophisticated system goes beyond such alarms. If it's triggered, it sends a signal via a small wireless radio transmitter (rather than by telephone, in case the crook cuts the lines) to a security firm, which then alerts local police. Such a central security service rents for between $15 and $28 a month.

If you want even more protection, here are some of the extras that can be added to any security system:

- Motion detectors: If the burglar gets past the door and window alarms, his presence will be picked up by a device that looks like an elec-

trical wall outlet, which then sets off the alarm. Such units can be programmed to ignore motions caused by pets or wind.
- Outdoor detectors: Like the indoor motion detector, the outdoor device can scan your driveway, front, or backyard. If anyone enters the area, it can be programmed to turn on lights (inside or outside) or broadcast a warning to the intruder.

DeMatteis says many people love this system, not only as a burglar deterrent, but also to illuminate the front of the house when they come home at night.

- Screen alarms: For the homeowner who wants to leave windows open, there are specially designed screens with built-in detectors that are just as effective as window alarms.

Advertise Your Alarm

Since the idea behind an alarm is to deter a burglar, it's best to announce that your home is "burglar-proofed." Apply warning stickers, provided by security companies, to conspicuous doors or windows.

Caution: Some homeowners, rather than investing in alarms, buy either a bogus sticker or a device that looks like an alarm and is bolted onto a front door. Butchko of ADT warns that such items "may stop a neighborhood teenager from breaking in, but a professional crook recognizes the real ones from the fakes."

In fact, says ex-burglar Michael, there's an extra danger in using bogus warnings: "When a thief spots the fake, he not only knows the house is unprotected, but that the owner may have something of value he's trying to protect."

Oops: False Alarms

A major problem of security systems is false alarms. Older, less sophisticated systems frequently are tripped by wind, dust, or other accidents. Modern systems are not fooled so easily, but problems still occur occasionally. "For example," says Butchko, "if a crook tries to break into a house and the alarm fends him off, the alert will still go to the police. But when they arrive and find no one there, they assume that the security system is at fault—and who's to prove otherwise."

Such "false" alarms cause homeowners problems beyond annoyance. Most communities have so-called false-alarm ordinances: if an alarm is set off more than a certain number of times and the police find no sign of a break-in, not only will the police refuse to respond to future alarms until the unit is fully checked out, but the resident can be fined. The usual fine is $25.

Selecting an Installer

Choosing equipment is only half the problem: finding a good, professional installer is another. Many small, fly-by-night firms hastily do several jobs a day. They usually have the worst record for false alarms, and their bankruptcy rate runs to about 20 percent a year.

It's often safer to pick a large, nationwide firm, but there are advantages to working with a good, small firm. The major plus: a technical person, rather than a salesperson, generally will tailor a system to fit your needs, rather than try to sell you a standard package.

At the least, says DeMatteis, check the firm out. Be sure it's bonded, request a list of recent and past customers, and call the customers to ask if they were satisfied. Also an installer should give you at least a one-year guarantee on installation and equipment.

Should you buy a service contract? Probably not. A good system, after some tuning to get rid of bugs, should work for 10 years or more without problems. If an installer tries to sell you a service contract, ask yourself: is he counting on a breakdown?

Also be sure that the installer has round-the-clock repair service. It doesn't do you any good if the service only operates from 9 to 5 on weekdays. Burglars work extended hours. ❖

Sylvia Porter's Personal Finance *is available for $11.97 a year. 10 issues. Address: 380 Lexington Avenue, New York, NY 10117.*

Taking Inventory of Your Home

SUSAN M. MENKE

CONSUMER'S RESEARCH, MARCH 1985

SIT DOWN RIGHT NOW and make a list of every item in your home—clothing, furnishings, appliances, jewelry—and include descriptions, dates of purchase, prices and replacement costs. Sound tedious and time-consuming? Now imagine doing it after your home has been devastated by fire or hit by burglary. Sound frightening? Well, that's exactly what you would have to do if adequate records of your belongings didn't survive a catastrophe—or if you didn't have any records.

Each year, one out of every 150 American residences has a fire, according to the U.S. Fire Administration. Americans lost $1.1 billion in 1983. Seventy-one percent of the burglaries were by forceful entry, says the FBI, and the average loss was $860.

Here's what you face if a fire or burglary hits your home and you haven't made an itemized account of your household goods or one has not survived:

The bulk of your belongings would be covered—but you would need to make a detailed list of every item for which you expect to be reimbursed, down to can openers and toilet paper. Such a list could run dozens of typewritten pages, say insurance agents. Credibility is crucial. Adjusters study each entry, and a figure that seems out of line will make them scrutinize everything more carefully.

Sometimes it's possible to get assistance in documenting past purchases through merchants and your bank. Any photographs of the inside of the house that survive could help the insurance adjuster form an idea of the extent and quality of your belongings. But even

so, months or even a year might pass before the adjuster is satisfied with this mass of detail and you are finally paid.

The itemizing process is much faster and easier with complete records. Insurance agents shake their heads over the reluctance of policyholders to keep detailed records of their personal belongings in places safe from fire or theft. So, before such a catastrophe occurs, you should record and update everything you own and include dates of purchase, prices, replacement costs and brief descriptions....

There are two modern record-keeping techniques that can replace or supplement pen and paper: the computer and the video cassette recorder. A home computer can be effective if, every time you make additions to your inventory, you remember to make a copy of the inventory disk and then swap the updated copy for the old disk in your safe deposit box. You can categorize your personal belongings by adapting one of many data base management programs now on the market. The computer's automatic sorting and updating capabilities will take the tedium out of keeping detailed records.

Some common software programs for owners of Commodore, Apple and IBM home computers are: pfs:file, retailing at a suggested price of $149; Phi Beta Filer, $39.95; Timeworks Data Manager, $24.95; and pfs:home inventory, $21.00. Experimentation will be necessary to customize any of these programs to fit your purpose.

A video camera/recorder setup allows you to make

a panoramic videotape by walking through the entire household, picking up many items a still camera would miss. Remember, you need detail—not glamor. Open the closet and cupboard doors, and pull out the drawers.

Now that you're keeping accurate and updated records, don't assume you'll be reimbursed for your entire loss: you can't collect more than the maximum amount stated in your insurance policy. If you want full replacement coverage of personal property without deduction for depreciation, for an additional premium you can get "property replacement cost endorsement." But if you don't have cost endorsement and if you haven't studied your policy recently, you might be shocked to discover limitations similar to

these:

- Money, bank notes, bullion, coins and medals might be covered only up to $100 in the aggregate, unless separately listed on a "floater" policy.
- Securities, deeds, manuscripts, stamps, tickets and the like might be covered only up to $500 for all, unless separately listed.

In some states, loss by theft of jewelry, watches, furs, guns and silverware also carries special limitations; appraisals are requested in many instances. ❖

Consumer's Research *Magazine is available for $18 a year. Published monthly. Address: 517 Second Street NE, Washington, D.C. 20002.*

Deducting Casualty and Theft Loss

THE NUMBER OF tax-deductible losses allowed has been subject to great restrictions. For 1988, you may deduct from your federal income tax all or part of each loss caused by theft, vandalism, fire or storm, as well as accidents caused by car, boat or similar agents, according to the Form 1040 instruction manual.

The catch: you can deduct non-business car or theft losses only to the extent that the amount of each separate casualty or theft loss is more than $100 and the total amount of all losses during the year is more than 10 percent of your adjusted gross income.

Not covered by this law: money that has been misplaced or lost, and breakage of glass, china, furniture and similar items under normal conditions. Publication 547 offers more details for non-business casualties, disasters and theft. ❖

A Child-proof Home

You Can't Save Him from Every Tumble, But You Can Prevent Major Mishaps

BY JAN HART SOUSA
PARENTS, FEBRUARY 1985

THERE IS MUCH more to child proofing your home than just keeping poisons out of the reach of children. Child proofing is an ongoing, often annoying process that really gets going about the time your child becomes mobile. If you really want to be on top of things, begin even before. After all, crawlers have been known to get in over their heads. So it's better to put a little too much out of the way too soon than wait until it's too late.

The first order of business is to get down on your hands and knees and take a crawling tour of your house. This should give you a pretty good idea of what evils may lurk at your child's eye level. Open any low cabinets and drawers and figure out what might pos-

sibly cause harm to your baby—a box of dishwasher detergent or perhaps an overloaded extension cord.

Move any potentially dangerous items completely out of sight and store them out of the way. You will probably find yourself raising these items higher as your child grows taller. Pretty soon your house will look humorously redecorated. But don't despair—this only lasts a few years.

Child proofing requires a constant awareness of the different stages of your child's development, says Arlene Stewart, author of *Childproofing Your Home* (Addison-Wesley). Just when you thought it was safe for your baby to crawl around the house, he foils your safety strategies by learning to walk. And when he masters the art of climbing, you'll need to streamline your plan still further to outwit him.

Your reward for a careful, common-sense approach to this process will be far fewer accidents and injuries.

Another advantage to child-proofing your home is that it will greatly reduce the number of times you have to say no to you child. Though one mother reportedly was able to teach her child not to touch certain valuable objects by taking him around the room and teaching him the concept of "antique," a much easier though admittedly less cultured approach seems to be simply to remove any treasured knickknacks from your child's path.

The Kitchen

Since you spend a lot of time in the kitchen, it is likely your toddler is going to want to keep you company there. But the kitchen contains plenty of potential hazards, so never leave your child alone in this area of the house. Some safety strategies for the kitchen: keep all saucepan handles turned toward the back of the stove when you're cooking. First, it removes a possible challenge for youngsters who are testing their reach and, second, it prevents mishaps caused by the handle getting caught on clothing or tipped by your body on a casual pass by the stove. Teach your child that the stove is a no-no, whether it is on or off. Remember to turn the oven off when it's not in use and to keep youngsters well away from the oven when it is in use. Whatever the insulation on the oven door, it's probably not enough to keep a hot oven cool.

Don't leave pans hot from the oven where the baby can touch them. Fry and boil on the back burners—this will keep most splatters on the stove top. Invest in a dry chemical fire extinguisher for the kitchen, but keep it out of your child's reach.

Install safety latches (Kindergard and Safe T-Latch are two nationally available brands) in whichever cabinets or drawers you want to secure. There are also latches available that slide through handles or knobs to keep doors locked. Separate knives and other utensils with sharp blades (like food processor blades) or edges from the rest of the pack.

All breakable items should be placed on high shelves. Small appliances should be unplugged when not in use. If your oven has a storage area for pots and pans, check it for insulation and place heavy items on the bottom so that they don't fall on your toddler.

If your child insists on being with you while you work in the kitchen, try offering him a plastic tub with some unbreakable cups, bowls, and spoons and have him "help" with the dishes. Or keep some safe play toys in a lower cabinet area. And if you need to, save your toughest jobs—like oven cleaning, dishwasher loading, heavy duty canning or baking, or floor scrubbing (eager-to-help babies can slip)—until nap time.

It is also essential to clean out the under-the-sink area. Most of us would rather not know what lurks under our kitchen sinks. But it is critical to take inventory before your child does. Many of your household products are deadly—and many you might not suspect are quite harmful. Store all of these products in a high place, and never store anything without a label. In case of ingestion, you must know what has been swallowed.

Prepare yourself ahead of time about what to do in case any of these is swallowed. Discuss poison control with your physician, and he can tell you what to administer and where to get help. Many poison control centers are open 24 hours a day. To find out the number of the poison control center nearest you, contact the Institute of Education Communications, Children's Hospital of Pittsburgh, 125 DeSoto Street, Pittsburgh, PA 15213. For $1 the network will send you poison stickers, and a home teaching unit on poison prevention is available for an additional $2.

Even though Oscar on Sesame Street seems to do just fine in a trash can, you should steer your child away from garbage cans or wastepaper baskets. Wrap any sharp objects, like razor blades, before throwing them away. Don't clean garbage cans with poisonous sprays, as a baby can get these on her hands or inhale the fumes. Don't store plastic bags where the baby can get at them—they can cause suffocation. Thin plastic, like those used to protect dry cleaned clothes, are particularly dangerous. To be on the safe side, tie knots in these bags before throwing them out.

Wipe up spills off the floor before your child has a chance to slip on them. Get rid of perilous throw rugs for the time being. Clean up broken glass immediately by wiping with wet paper towels and then vacuuming thoroughly. You don't want to miss any glass splinters.

Never leave cords dangling over countertops within your child's reach. Always place hot irons far out of baby's reach, both during and after use. (Remember that irons stay hot for quite a while after using). Wrap the cord around the iron so that it can't be yanked off the counter. And make sure your ironing board is not precariously placed where it might fall on your child.

Replace any frayed electrical cords as soon as you spot them. And make sure any unused refrigerator or freezer out in the garage is either locked or has its door removed. Children can get trapped inside and suffocate. Speaking of the garage, young children should be kept out. It's simply too dangerous.

Microwave ovens should be mounted so there is no

chance of a child manning the controls. A toddler can easily push the button that opens the microwave door while it is cooking, sending hot splatters his way. Your child should not be able to turn on or climb into your washer or dryer either.

Keep boxes of aluminum foil and plastic wrap out of reach, as jagged package edges can cause nasty cuts. Dispose of used clear plastic wraps, too, since kids can choke on them.

The Bathroom

The bathroom is another area that offers plenty of opportunities for disaster. Lock up cleaning supplies and medicines out of reach. You might even consider moving these items onto a high shelf in a closet in another room. Choose nonaerosol products whenever possible. They're safer and, coincidentally, less expensive.

You can keep the bathroom off limits by installing hook-and-eye latches high on the outside of the door. Or put plastic door knob covers on the door making it too difficult for a youngster to open. Make sure, however, that your bathroom locks can be opened from the outside by an adult. This goes for all the doors in the house. Remove a lock entirely if it does not open from the outside, or tape over the bolt to keep it open.

Place nonslip appliques or strips on the bottom of your tub to minimize slippage. Make sure your shower stalls cannot close on your baby. Always check the water temperature before putting your child in the tub. Beware of running faucet water as well—temperatures can change suddenly in hot water systems that are affected by external conditions, like flushing toilets.

NEVER leave a baby alone in the tub even for a tiny second—babies can drown in as little as one inch of water.

The toilet is obviously a less-than-hygenic place for playing and is actually quite dangerous. The Consumer Product Safety Commission reports that children have drowned in toilet bowl incidents. At least one toddler was playing with the water in the toilet and the lid accidentally fell on him knocking him in. Play it safe. Let your child know early on that the bathroom means business.

If you bathe with your baby, never climb out of the tub with the baby in your arms. For obvious reasons this is asking for trouble.

Keep hair dryers and all other electrical appliances up and away. Electrocution results when a plugged in appliance falls or is pulled into water. To be safe, don't use electrical appliances on a wet floor and avoid using them altogether when the baby is present.

Finally, remove any toiletries that don't come in plastic bottles and it's best to use either plastic or paper cups in the bathroom. The less glass there is around to break the better.

Baby's Room

Nowadays, cribs have strict safety standards. However, there is no guarantee that everything you buy or receive as a gift (that old, "it's been in the family for years" crib) meets with the safety regulations. The Consumer Product Safety Commission estimates that over 14,000 infants are treated for crib-related injuries each year. From 50 to 100 infants die each year in crib-related incidents. However, all new cribs should meet these specific requirements; they must have a standard-size mattress that fits snugly into the frame with slats no more than two and three eights inches apart. Rail height must be sufficient even when in the drop position. There must be strong, baby proof devices for locking the drop side. And there must be no hardware that can hurt the child.

Use fabric padded bumpers around the sides of the crib to protect the baby's head, but remove when the child is old enough to use the bumper as a stepping stool out of the crib. Bumpers must tie in at least six places, and you should trim the ties so the baby doesn't choke. A baby can also strangle on decorative gaps and holes build into head or footboards of a crib.

As soon as your toddler shows gymnastic potential, remove all large toys or stuffed animals from his crib that may be used to vault him up and over the rail.

Don't place a crib or other furniture that can be climbed on near a window. Babies have strangled on window cords that have loops just high enough to fit their heads through. Likewise, don't place the crib near fans or heaters.

Store powders, ointments, diapers, toilet paper and safety pins out of your baby's reach. Some mothers suggest hanging three tiered wire baskets (usually used in kitchens) and putting these items safely out of your child's reach but conveniently in yours.

Don't let your baby play with your starch powder, baby powder or talc. He can aspirate the powder and choke. You never know if the top is completely closed. And don't apply powder if you are directly in front of a fan. It's impossible to control the amount or the area that will be covered.

Finally, don't leave diapers to soak for long periods of time in diaper pails. Many babies have drowned after playing around and falling into these pails...

Use open, stackable cubes, vegetable bins, or milk crates for storing toys rather than the traditional toy box with a heavy wooden lid. If you do use a standard toy chest, either remove the lid completely or be sure it has a lid support. According to Commissioner Terrence M. Scanlon of the U.S. Consumer Product Safety Commission, the lid support is a device (not a hinged device) that breaks the fall of the lid at various intervals and prevents it from slamming shut. These devices can be installed on older model toy chests. While not readily available at local hardware or toy stores, they can be purchased from the manufacturers: Carlson Capitol Manufacturing Company, P.O. Box 6105, Rockford, Ill 61125.(815)398-3110; Counter Balance Support Company, 4788 Colt Road, Rockford, Ill 61109. (815)874-7211. The cost of the lid supports is $4.50 plus $2 for postage, prepaid. The manufacturers suggest that you include the dimensions and the approximate weight of the lid with your order. There are different-size lid supports for different-size lids. Don't use any toy box that is self-locking—your child could get trapped inside.

Make sure any mobiles and dangling toys are hung out of reach, so your baby cannot get caught in the strings. Plants should be saved for other rooms in the house.

A word on houseplants: entire books have been written on the subject of poisonous houseplants. If you have any questions about a plant's potential danger to your child, call your regional botanical garden, arboretum, or poison-control center. One expert on the subject warns that all plants, when ingested, will cause some kind of physiological reaction. How severe that reaction is depends on that plant's level of toxicity: While some plants cause little more than a mild case of diarrhea, others can bring on nausea, vomiting, convulsions, cardiovascular collapse, coma, and even death.

As for the rest of the house...

You should check the condition and security of all windows and screens in your house. In many cities, landlords are legally bound to provide window bars for every window above the third floor for families with very young children. Window bars fit tightly into the window space and can't be pushed out by the child. Any window above the first floor should have window bars. You can also install ventilating window locks (available at hardware stores) on the sides of the window frame. This prevents the window from opening beyond a certain height.

If you have stairs at home, you should install safety gates at the head and foot of every stairway. (You might want to leave a couple of bottom stairs free so your baby can practice climbing safely). Encourage him to climb down backwards—it's safer. Accordion gates are the wooden diamond-shaped collapsible variety. They attach to one side of the opening and latch onto the other. These are sturdy, but young children can get their heads caught in them, so be sure the gates do not have wide openings. These are also fairly easy to climb.

If you have a fireplace, never leave your baby alone by a fire. Don't even make a fire if you are alone with the baby. Make sure the fire is covered by a secure screen that cannot be opened or pulled down by a child.

Never use a kerosene heater around young children. It's far too dangerous. If you must use an electric heater, make sure it is out of your child's reach.

You should enclose radiators and block them from your child's reach. And young children should not be allowed to play on floor register grates (though these are always inviting).

You can keep young hands out of desk drawers and end tables by turning these pieces of furniture around so they face the wall. You can still use the tops, and you could get into those drawers if you had to!

Pull dining-room chairs flush up against the table so your child won't be as tempted to climb up on them. And banish all tablecloths for a while if you value your china place settings, or even your everyday dishes.

Buy "corner bumpers" for all sharp table corners. Or better yet, move the treacherous coffee table out of the room for a while—especially when your child graduates to walking.

Wedge books tightly into bookshelves, and hope that your toddler leaves them alone. But make sure the shelving unit is sturdy and won't topple over on him if he decides to continue yanking on it. You might reserve a lower bookcase for your child's toys and books. But chances are he will still find the items on your shelves more interesting.

Likewise, keep a bottom drawer in your room filled with a few articles of old clothing and other safe but interesting objects. Such a diversionary tactic can go a long way when you're trying to get the bed made.

A big help to parents needing to child-proof their homes is the injury prevention program (TIPP) developed by the American Academy of Pediatrics' committee on accident and poison prevention. TIPP enables parents to obtain free literature on the subject of child-proofing and accident prevention from their pediatricians. Especially useful are the series of age-related safety tips that give parents an idea of what their child will be getting into as he grows older.

No home can be guaranteed accident-proof, so don't kick yourself when your toddler manages to trip and fall all on his own with no help from any hazardous household item. Bumped noses and scraped elbows are an inevitable part of early childhood. But once you know you've done your best to protect your child, you will be less likely to hover over him, and better able to deal with whatever rolls along. ❖

Parents Magazine is available for $18 per year. Published monthly. Address: 6857 Third Avenue, New York, NY 10017.

Nursery Equipment Checklist

FROM: *THE SAFE NURSERY: A BOOKLET TO HELP AVOID INJURIES FROM NURSERY FURNITURE AND EQUIPMENT*
U.S. CONSUMER PRODUCT SAFETY COMMISSION, FEBRUARY 1988

	Yes	No
Back Carriers		
1. Carrier has restraining strap to secure child.	❏	❏
2. Leg openings are small enough to prevent child from slipping out.	❏	❏
3. Leg openings are large enough to prevent chafing.	❏	❏
4. Frames have no pinch points in the folding mechanism.	❏	❏
5. Carrier has padded covering over metal frame near baby's face.	❏	❏
Bassinets and Cradles		
1. Bassinet/Cradle has a sturdy bottom and a wide base for stability.	❏	❏
2. Bassinet/Cradle has smooth surfaces—no protruding staples	❏	❏
or other hardware that could injure a baby.	❏	❏
3. Legs have strong, effective locks to prevent folding while in use.	❏	❏
Carrier Seats		
1. Carrier seat has a wide, sturdy base for stability.	❏	❏
2. Carrier has non-skid feet to prevent slipping.	❏	❏
3. Supporting devices lock securely.	❏	❏
4. Carrier seat has crotch and waist strap.	❏	❏
5. Buckle or strap is easy to use.	❏	❏
Changing Tables		
1. Table has safety straps to prevent falls.	❏	❏
2. Table has drawers or shelves that are easily accessible without leaving	❏	❏
the baby unattended.		
Cribs		
1. Slats are spaced no more than 2-3/8 inches apart.	❏	❏
2. No slats are missing or cracked.	❏	❏
3. Mattress fits snugly—less than two fingers width between edge of mattress		
and crib side.	❏	❏
4. Mattress support is securely attached to the head and footboards.	❏	❏
5. Corner posts are no higher than 5/8 of an inch to prevent entanglement.	❏	❏
6. There are no cutouts in head and footboards to allow head entrapment.	❏	❏
7. Drop-side latches cannot be easily released by a baby.	❏	❏
8. Drop-side latches securely hold sides in raised position.	❏	❏
9. All screws or bolts which secure components of crib together are		
present and tight.	❏	❏
Crib Toys		
1. Crib toys have no strings longer than twelve inches to prevent entanglement.	❏	❏
2. Crib gym or other crib toy suspended over the crib must have devices that		
securely fasten to the crib to prevent it from being pulled into the crib.	❏	❏
3. Components of toys are not small enough to be a choking hazard.	❏	❏
Gates and Enclosures		
1. Gate or enclosure has a straight top edge.	❏	❏
2. Openings in gate are too small to entrap a child's head.	❏	❏
3. Gate has a pressure bar or other fastener so it will resist forces		
exerted by a child.	❏	❏
High Chairs		
1. High chair has restraining straps that are independent of the tray.	❏	❏

2. Tray locks securely. ❑ ❑
3. Buckle on waist strap is easy to fasten and unfasten. ❑ ❑
4. High chair has a wide base for stability. ❑ ❑
5. High chair has caps or plugs on tubing that are firmly attached and cannot be pulled off and choke a child. ❑ ❑
6. If it is a folding high chair, it has an effective locking device. ❑ ❑

Hook-On Chairs

1. Chair has a restraining strap to secure the child. ❑ ❑
2. Chair has a clamp that locks onto the table for added security. ❑ ❑
3. Hook-on chair has caps or plugs on tubing that are firmly attached and cannot be pulled off and choke a child. ❑ ❑
4. Hook-on chair has a warning never to place chair where child can push off with his feet. ❑ ❑

Pacifiers

1. Pacifier has no ribbons, string, cord, or yarn attached. ❑ ❑
2. Shield is large enough and firm enough so it cannot fit in child's mouth. ❑ ❑
3. Guard or shield has ventilation holes so baby can breathe if shield does get into mouth. ❑ ❑
4. Pacifier nipple has no holes or tears that might cause it to break off in baby's mouth. ❑ ❑

Playpens

1. Drop-side mesh playpen or mesh crib has warning label about never leaving a side in the down position. ❑ ❑
2. Playpen mesh has small weave (less than 1/4 inch openings). ❑ ❑
3. Mesh has no tears or loose threads. ❑ ❑
4. Mesh is securely attached to top rail and floorplate. ❑ ❑
5. Top rail has no tears or holes. ❑ ❑
6. Wooden playpen has slats spaced no more than 2-3/8 inches apart. ❑ ❑
7. If staples are used in construction, they are firmly installed and none missing, or loose. ❑ ❑

Rattles/Squeeze Toys/Teethers

1. Rattles and teethers have handles too large to lodge in baby's throat. ❑ ❑
2. Rattles have sturdy construction that will not cause them to break apart in use. ❑ ❑
3. Squeeze toys do not contain a squeaker that could detach and choke a baby. ❑ ❑

Strollers

1. Stroller has a wide base to prevent tipping. ❑ ❑
2. Seat belt and crotch strap are securely attached to frame. ❑ ❑
3. Seat belt buckle is easy to fasten and unfasten. ❑ ❑
4. Brakes securely lock the wheel(s). ❑ ❑
5. Shopping basket low on the back and located directly over or in front of rear wheels. ❑ ❑

Toy Chests

1. Toy chest has no latch to entrap child within the chest. ❑ ❑
2. Toy chest has a spring-loaded lid support that will not require periodic adjustment and will support the lid in any position to prevent lid slam. ❑ ❑
3. Chest has ventilation holes or spaces in front or sides, or under lid. ❑ ❑

Walkers

1. Walker has a wide wheel base for stability. ❑ ❑
2. Walker has plastic sleeves over coil springs to avoid cuts. ❑ ❑
3. Seat is securely attached to frame of walker. ❑ ❑
4. There are no x-frames that could pinch. ❑ ❑

Poisonous Household Products
Product Safety Fact Sheet
U.S. CONSUMER PRODUCT SAFETY COMMISSION, APRIL 1979

IT'S ATTRACTIVE. Perhaps it's brightly colored. Or maybe it looks like food. It's within reach. And it's poison.

An 18-month-old boy died after drinking floor cleaner containing petroleum distillates. An 8-year-old grabbed a bottle of liniment that he thought was cough syrup and drank it down. A 1-year-old girl spent nine days in the hospital after swallowing charcoal lighter fluid from a can left in the yard after a family picnic.

Every year thousands of children are poisoned by hazardous household substances. Medicines, furniture polishes, lighter fluid, turpentine. They're only a few of the numerous potentially dangerous products commonly found in the home.

Yet most household poisonings can be avoided— if adults take proper precautions with hazardous products. Do you? If you're not sure, the U.S. Consumer Product Safety Commission has a few suggestions to help you poison-proof your home:

- No matter how attractive a hazardous product may be, children usually can't be poisoned by something they can't get their hands on. Therefore, one key to poison prevention in the home is keeping all medicines and other hazardous products locked up when not in use.
- Don't depend on close supervision. It's impossible to watch a child every minute and children can move very quickly.
- Always read the warning labels on hazardous products. These labels will tell you the seriousness of the danger and list all hazardous ingredients. If your child is accidentally poisoned, the first thing a doctor needs to know is the identity of the poison. The label will also tell you what immediate first aid you can give.
- Keep all hazardous products in their original containers. Never store them in cups, soda bottles, or other containers that would normally contain food or drink.
- Avoid taking medicines in a child's presence. Children imitate adults, particularly their parents.
- Call any medicine by its proper name. Never suggest that medicine is "candy."
- When giving medicines to children, give them only the proper dosage. Don't think that because a little medicine gives relief, more would do an even better job.
- Promptly dispose of prescription drugs by flushing them down the toilet once the illness for which they were prescribed is over.
- Do not store any other hazardous products with medicines that are to be taken internally. There are many look-alike containers on the market. You or your child could make a tragic mistake.
- Be careful when using a hazardous product. Always keep it out of children's reach. If you are interrupted while using the product, take it with you.

A wide variety of drugs and hazardous household products are now required to be packaged in containers with safety closures that are very difficult for most children to open. Other hazardous products will soon be added to the list. Child-resistant packaging has the potential to reduce dramatically the number of youngsters poisoned, but only if it is purchased and then properly used. Be sure to:

- Keep the product in its safety packaging.
- Close the container properly after use, resecuring the safety feature.
- Remember that poison prevention packaging is only an additional safeguard. Safety closures can help but they can't do the whole job of protecting your children. Most children cannot open poison-prevention packages, but some can. ❖

TO REPORT A product hazard or a product-related injury, write to the U.S. Consumer Product Safety Commission, Washington, D.C. 20207. Call the toll-free hotline: 800-638-2772. A teletypewriter for the deaf is available on the following number: National (including Alaska and Hawaii), 800-638-8270, Maryland residents only, 800-492-8104. During non-working hours, messages are recorded and answered on the following working day. ❖

Infant Falls
Product Safety Fact Sheet
U.S. CONSUMER PRODUCT SAFETY COMMISSION, FEBRUARY 1980

ACCIDENTAL FALLS are quite common among infants and small children. Most of them are minor. But some falls can be severe, particularly if the baby is only a few months old. The skull of an infant is quite fragile in the first months of life. A head injury at this time could cause permanent brain damage.

A 5-month-old girl fell from a kitchen table while her mother was dressing her. The mother dropped a shirt and the baby rolled off while she was picking it up. The baby's head struck a radiator and she suffered a skull fracture. The mother stated that she usually strapped the baby to a bassinette but that day she was in a hurry.

A 1-year-old boy fractured his left arm after he fell out of his crib onto a carpeted floor. The side rail was half lowered.

How do you protect children from falls from high places? A good way to prevent many falls is to pay close attention to small children anywhere they might fall. Watch infants very carefully when they are on a bed, sofa, counter top, dressing table or similar piece of furniture. Use guard fences at the top and bottom of stairways to block them off to infants too young to use them safely.

The U.S. Consumer Product Safety Commission recommends the following additional precautions in selecting and using furniture designed for babies:

• **Cribs.** Federal safety regulations for full size cribs became effective February 1, 1974; and for non-full size cribs, August 10, 1976. These regulations require that spaces between the slats be no more than 2 3/8 inches to prevent infants from slipping between the slats. They also set a minimum distance between the top of the mattress and the top of the side rail to help prevent children from climbing over the rail.

If you own a crib that was manufactured before the regulations went into effect, be sure to use bumper pads, securely tied in place, to prevent falls between the slats. These are particularly dangerous because an infant's body will usually pass between the slats, but the head will not and the child could be strangled. Remove bumper pads once the child can stand up to prevent them from being used to climb out.

As soon as a child can stand up, set the mattress at its lowest position and lock the side rail at its highest position. Do not put boxes or large toys in the crib that could be used for climbing.

Remove children from cribs once the side rail height is less than three-quarters of their height.

• **Infant Carriers.** (Plastic seat type) If you buy an infant carrier, be sure that it is stable; usually, the wider its base, the more difficult it will be for a child to upset it.

Keep an infant carrier away from the edge of any high surface. Never leave a baby unattended in an infant carrier.

Always use any belts or other restraining devices provided.

Be sure the carrier has a non-skid surface on the bottom. If it doesn't, attach rough-surfaced adhesive strips.

Do not use an infant carrier as a car seat.

• **Dressing Tables.** Always strap your baby in place on a dressing table. Remember, though, that even straps do not always prevent falls. There are no substitutes for close supervision.

A table with guard rails offers some additional protection against infant falls. So would a table with a recessed rather than a flat top.

• **High Chairs.** Select a high chair that is stable—one that cannot be pushed or tipped over easily and that will not fold up while the child is in the chair.

Check the tray to be certain that it is properly locked in place.

Be sure that the child is strapped in properly and that the straps are secure.

Teach children not to stand in high chairs, and caution older children not to climb on them.

• **Baby Walkers.** Select a stable baby walker, one with a wheel base wider and longer than the frame.

Baby walkers can tip over when moving from one surface to another—from rug to floor, over a door threshold, from a sidewalk to a lawn. The ideal play area for a baby walker is a flat, smooth surface.

Always use guard fences at the top of a flight of stairs to prevent falls.

• **Playpens.** Do not leave large toys or boxes inside the playpen that could be used for climbing. Likewise, avoid decorative items which tie or strap across the top of a playpen since children can also use these for climbing.

The playpen should not be used once a child is able to climb over the side. ❖

Baby Rattles
Product Safety Fact Sheet
U.S. CONSUMER PRODUCT SAFETY COMMISSION, AUGUST 1987

EIGHT CHILDREN IN the United States and at least two more in Canada have choked to death on baby rattles, according to U.S. Consumer Product Safety Commission reports. The victims, the oldest of whom was 13 months, either partially swallowed the rattles while sucking on them, or fell with the rattles in their mouths, causing the rattles to be jammed down their throats.

This is one of the actual cases:

> A six-month-old child fell with a telephone-shaped rattle in her mouth. The fall knocked the rattle into the back of her throat, blocking her air passage. She died after her mother and the police were unable to pull out the rattle.

An infant's mouth is extremely flexible and can stretch to hold larger shapes than you might expect. To date, the largest rattle known to have lodged in a baby's throat had an end 1 3/8 inches in diameter.

The Commission has issued regulations requiring that infant rattles be large enough so that they cannot become lodged in an infant's throat and be constructed so that they will not separate into small pieces which can be swallowed or inhaled. It is important, however, to check older rattles which may have been manufactured or sold before the regulations became effective in August 1978 for parts or ends that are small enough to fit in a baby's mouth...

CPSC urges you to be particularly cautious when your child has a rattle and to:

1. Check over your baby's rattles. If you feel that an older rattle may be too small for safety, break the rattle and throw it away.
2. Watch carefully when your baby is playing with a rattle or other small object.
3. Take rattles and other small objects out of the crib or playpen when the baby sleeps. ❖

Flammable Fabrics
Product Safety Fact Sheet
U.S. CONSUMER PRODUCT SAFETY COMMISSION, MAY 1981

EVERY YEAR THERE are thousands of injuries and deaths from burns associated with flammable fabrics, according to estimates by the Consumer Product Safety Commission. Some typical accident illustrations are:

- Six-year-old Tommy found some matches on a coffee table in his home. He lighted one of the matches and dropped it on his shirt, setting it afire. He suffered severe burns over 40 percent of his body and was hospitalized for six months.
- Mr. McIntire, 60, was smoking while cleaning some paint brushes with gasoline. Sparks ignited the flammable vapors. The flames quickly spread to his clothing because some of the gasoline had earlier been spilled on his pants' legs. Burned severely, he was hospitalized for months.
- Several pots of food were being heated on a gas range. Susan reached over a lighted burner to stir something in a pot on a back burner and her long-sleeved robe ignited near the cuff. The flames traveled up her sleeve and burned her arm. Although she quickly dropped to the floor and smothered the flames by rolling, she suffered burns on her arm and part of her face.
- Roberta Smith, 38, was smoking in bed while reading. She fell asleep, dropping the cigarette on the bed. The mattress began to smolder. She awakened and crawled out of the room but she still suffered from severe smoke inhalation.

Recently flame resistant sleepwear has reduced burn hazards to children. But flame-resistant does not mean flameproof, and caution should always be taken to avoid fires.

In recent years the federal government has taken steps to make some fabrics less flammable. Federal standards have been set for the flammability of general wearing apparel, carpets and rugs, mattresses (and mattress pads) and children's sleepwear in sizes 0-14.

CPSC has the following suggestions for the purchase, use, and proper laundering of flame resistant fabrics—and some first-aid suggestions if you do suffer burns.

Purchase

- Flame resistant clothing for your children can reduce the risks of burn injuries. Some stores may sell children's clothing other than sleepwear made of flame-resistant fabric.
- If you sew, buy flame resistant fabrics for the garments you make.
- For all garments, consider the following:

Construction

- Tightly woven, heavy fabrics (such as denim used in jeans) are harder to ignite and burn more slowly than lightweight and loosely woven fabrics (such as cotton broadcloth used in shirts). Sheer fabrics burn quickly.
- Napped fabric (such as cotton flannel) with air spaces between the loose fibers will ignite much faster than a smooth surfaced material (such as denim).
- A fluffy high pile of fabric (as used in some sweaters) will ignite and burn faster than a close knit, low pile fabric.

Design

- Close-fitting garments are less likely to ignite than loose-fitting garments, such as robes, housecoats, shifts, nightgowns or blouses, with loose-flowing sleeves, ruffles and trims.

Use

- Be aware of the hazards of ignition sources and flammable liquids.

Kitchen Ranges

- Teach young children to maintain a proper distance from stoves.
- Don't reach across lighted burners when wearing loose-fitting sleeves.
- Use a potholder—instead of a towel—when removing a pot or pan from a lighted burner. The loose ends of a towel could catch fire.

Cigarettes

- Take care when smoking near upholstered furniture. Check for any cigarettes that may have been dropped inadvertently.
- Smoking in bed is dangerous. The chance of your dozing or falling asleep and dropping a cigarette is too risky.
- Elderly and handicapped persons may be more apt to drop cigarettes on their clothing and they may be unable to react quickly enough to help themselves.

Flammable Liquids

- Vapors of flammable liquids can travel invisibly across a room and can be ignited by any spark or flame.
- Use flammable liquids only in well ventilated areas.
- Store flammable liquids in tightly-capped safety containers and keep them away from living quarters—in an outdoor shed, if possible, and out of the reach of children.

Laundering Procedures for Flame Resistant Fabrics

Flame resistant fabrics should have permanent care labels. To maintain the flame resistant qualities, always follow the care instructions. ...

First-Aid for a Burn

- Cool the burn with cool water; this reduces pain and stops further damage to the skin.
- Cover a large burn with a clean, dry sheet.
- Do not try to clean the burn.
- Do not put grease, butter, or ointments on a burn. Grease or butter can make a bad burn worse.
- Do not pull clothing over the burn.
- Do not try to remove pieces of cloth, or clothing, that may be stuck to the burned area.
- Do not break blisters.
- Get medical attention immediately—even small burns can become serious if they are not treated properly.

Talk to children about the dangers of fire and teach them what to do if their clothing does catch fire;

- Never run. Do not remain standing.
- Drop to the floor immediately and roll—over and back—to smother the flames.
- Plan two exits out of every room, especially each bedroom. This may require the purchase of ladders to escape through upstairs windows.

Plan emergency escape procedures

- Install smoke detectors in your home.
- Close your bedroom doors at night. If a fire does start while you are asleep, a closed door will hold the smoke back longer. If you smell smoke, check the door first to determine whether it is hot. Don't open the door unless you are sure the hallway is not filled with smoke.
- Have all family members, or occupants of the home, meet at a prearranged site outdoors, so that a quick check can be made to see that all are out.
- Know how to call the fire department.
- Save the people first, then the possessions. ❖

Lead Paint Poisoning
Product Safety Fact Sheet
U.S. CONSUMER PRODUCT SAFETY COMMISSION, JULY 1982

LEAD POISONING is a serious crippler and killer of young children. A study by the Center for Disease Control found that of 510,000 children screened, 25,300 had lead poisoning. The Center for Disease Control states in their report: "Lead-based paint remains the most common high-dose lead source for children with lead toxicity." In other words, almost all lead poisoning in children comes from lead-based paint.

Lead-based paint may be found on the windowsills, doors, and walls of older homes. Some children—usually one to six years old—apparently like to eat leaded paint. If the poisoning is not treated early, it can lead to irreversible brain damage and even death.

Children are also exposed to lead paint poisoning by:

1. Chewing or mouthing other objects covered with lead paint, such as children's furniture, toys, and other playthings.
2. Inhaling lead dust during restoration or repair of lead-painted homes. Adults also are susceptible to this type of lead poisoning.

Children who have lead poisoning may show the following symptoms:

- Unusual irritability
- Poor appetite
- Stomach pains and vomiting
- Persistent constipation
- Sluggishness or drowsiness

Many victims, unfortunately, show no symptoms until it is too late. These symptoms also could be indicative of other childhood illnesses. Only a doctor can tell if a child has lead poisoning.

To reduce the danger of lead paint poisoning, CPSC regulations effective January 1, 1973 banned paints containing more than 0.5% lead for household use. To further lessen the danger of exposure to lead, the Commission lowered the permissible lead content in paint to 0.06% for products manufactured after February 28, 1978. The stricter ban applies to consumer product paint itself, and to toys, children's articles, and furniture bearing such paint. Exempted from the ban are mirrors backed with lead-containing paint and artists' paints and related materials. Certain other items are exempted if they carry cautionary labeling.

Despite these laws, a great deal of heavily-leaded paint remains on the walls of older homes. As long as the paint remains in good condition, there is little immediate danger, provided children do not chew on accessible wood surfaces such as windowsills. But when the paint or painted plaster begins to crack and peel, children are in great danger.

The U.S. Consumer Product Safety Commission offers the following suggestions to lessen the danger of lead paint poisoning:

1. Examine carefully the condition of all your painted walls, ceilings, woodwork, windowsills, and doors, especially those areas within the reach of children.
2. If the paint is peeling or cracked, you can have it checked for lead content by your local health department. (Some local health departments may not be able to check for lead content. If that is the case, your state health department may be able to help.) If the paint has high lead content, contact your physician or local clinic and have your children's blood level checked.
3. Lead paint should be removed from all surfaces within the home and the areas repainted with non-lead paint or covered over with other material.
4. If you recondition your home yourself, there are several steps you can take to rid it of lead paint:

- Scrape off chipped and cracking paint on windowsills, woodwork, and doors. Then sand and repaint the area. As a temporary measure, the area can be sanded and covered completely with contact paper. It is very important to avoid inhaling the dust created when leaded paint is scraped or sanded. When removing or sanding old paint, follow these precautions:
- Wear a face mask;
- Clothing worn in the room being renovated should not be worn in other areas of the dwelling;
- Use a wet mop after cleaning up debris;
- Don't eat in the room where work is going on;
- Make sure plates and eating utensils are not exposed to the dust;
- Keep children out of the area;
- If possible, strip and sand walls, and plaster holes before repainting. Or, instead of paint-

ing, cover walls with wallboard, plywood, or paneling.

- At all times, keep paint flakes and chips swept up. Dispose of them promptly so that children cannot eat them. Wet mop the area thoroughly.

5. Examine toys and children's furniture for peeling paint. Strip off the lead paint and repaint toys, cribs and other children's furniture and articles with lead-free paint.

If you know your children have eaten paint or if you even suspect that they may have, you should take them to your doctor or local clinic immediately for a checkup. Lead poisoning must be treated early if it is to be cured. ❖

Colorful Cutouts to Help Prevent Glass-Door Accidents

SUNSET, APRIL 1988

WHEN A PERSON, all too often a child, crashes into a clear plate-glass door that looks as if it is open (but isn't), the results can be tragic.

You can't prevent such accidents, but bold, bright designs...can reduce their chances of happening. More than decorative, these figures, cut from self-adhesive contact paper, stick to sliding or hinged glass doors (and nearby windows), making the glass "visible"....

The paper peels off easily, so you can change graphics to match the seasons or holidays...If you use letters, remember that they'll be seen in reverse from the outside.

Contact paper comes in a wide variety of bright colors and designs. A 1 1/2-by-9-foot roll costs about $2.50.

Start by spreading out the contact paper with the paper backing face up. with a narrow felt-tip or nylon-tip pen, mark your design on the backing. Draw freehand, or, if you find an image you'd like to duplicate, copy it onto tracing paper, then transfer the design with carbon paper to the backing. Cut out your figures.

Apply designs to the inside surface of doors and windows. Make sure glass is clean and dry before you start. Peel off backing, position cutout low enough to catch a small child's eye, and press firmly. Squeeze out any air bubbles with a rolling pin or brayer. ❖

Sunset *Magazine is available for $16 a year in the thirteen western states and $20 a year anywhere else in the U.S. Published monthly. Address: 85 Willow Road, Menlo Park, CA 94025.*

SAFETY GLASS, specially designed to reduce injuries when it shatters, should be installed in all glass doors and adjacent windows in your home.

To find out if you already have this type of glass, look for the words safety glass, or tempered or laminated glass (types of safety glass), etched into the surface or printed on a small decal, usually in a corner...No luck? You probably have plate glass, especially if it was installed before 1964.

Since then, it has been illegal to use plate glass (also called annealed glass) in or adjacent to doors, since it shatters into lone, razor-sharp shards. If you still have plate glass, we recommend replacing it with one of these other types:

Tempered glass. It takes quite a blow to break this glass, and when it does break, it shatters into gravel-size bits. (They still cut, but rarely do as much damage as broken plate glass.) It costs $4 to $6 a square foot, compared to $3 for plate glass.

This glass comes in standard or custom sizes (tempered glass can't be cut to fit). Cost to replace glass in a standard 3/16-inch-thick, 34-by 76-inch sliding door unit ranges from $150 to $250, including labor. Double-pane tempered glass can cost up to twice as much.

Laminated glass. If you collide with this glass, you'll probably shatter it—but not smash through it. However, broken shards can still cut.

Laminated glass can be made or cut to fit any dimension. It costs $5 to $10 a square foot. Standard-size sliding-door units cost $400 to $700, including labor. ❖

Children

EXCERPTS FROM *BUYER'S MARKET*, VOLUME II, NUMBER 8 AUGUST 1986

Taking a Look At Toys

The average child received playthings worth over $150 in 1985, according to the Toy Manufacturers of America. Some toys were boring, some toys broke the second time they were used, some toys were downright dangerous—and some provided hours of entertainment. A little good, old-fashioned consumerism could have eliminated some of the "lemons" from the batch.

Reading labels and examining products before purchase is especially important with toys. While this will help you steer clear of toys that are overpriced or will never be played with, even more important, it will help you avoid toys that are unsafe. According to the Consumer Product Safety Commission (CPSC), the number of toy-related injuries rose from 118,000 in 1983 to 126,000 in 1984. "Besides very frequent cuts and bruises to the extremities and face, there are thousands of burnings, blindings, permanent disfigurements, puncture wounds, fractures, dislocations, poisonings, strains and sprains, and far too many deaths," Edward Swartz grimly recounts in his book *Toys That Don't Care.* "Toys with sharp cutting edges, easily shatterable parts, high explosive potential, lethal electrical hazards, dangerous flammability, unnecessary psychological risks, suffocation or strangulation capabilities, or fatally poisonous potential can be found by the dozens."

With some 150,000 toys on the market, it is difficult for the Consumer Product Safety Commission to keep up. It is up to you to be sure the toys are not hazardous and that your children use them in a safe way (if you find a toy that you believe is hazardous, report it to the CPSC). The CPSC puts out free guidelines on choosing safe toys.

Apart from physical safety, parents should ask themselves if the psychological effects of the toy might be disturbing or damaging. There is a distressing trend in today's toy marketplace: movie "heroes" that children are not even allowed to see in theaters—because the movie industry rates these film stars too violent and profane—are being made into children's dolls and cartoon shows. One example of this is Rambo, who has emerged from killing sprees in Southeast Asia to become a children's cartoon character and a new line of toys.

Taming Television

One of the greatest shapers of popular consciousness—and consumer priorities—in America is the television set. TV dominates our leisure time: according to a report by the National Institute of Mental Health, families spend half of their free time at home watching television. Television is our window on the rest of the country and the world, bringing us not only entertainment, but consumer information. Prime-time hits help define which fashions are "in," advertisements bring us a parade of items new and old, the news tells us of business and product developments.

Television especially shapes our children's view of their society, world, and marketplace. By the time the average student graduates from high school, he or she has spent more time watching television than in the classroom—over 15,000 hours in front of the TV set. Youngsters watch an average of four to five hours of television each day (adults watch even more!)

Aside from its well-known effects—for example, that children with previous aggressive behavior are likely to be affected by TV violence ("If you watch enough violence [on TV]," says Peggy Charren, president of Action for Children's Television (ACT), "you are more used to thinking of violence as a solution to a problem")—television has profound effect on the consciousness of children. Children see 20,000 commercials a year. And while you may tune out the commercials, kids love the catchy jingles and are absorbing the message—young children are more likely to recognize Ronald McDonald than Santa Claus.

"All television is educational," says Representative Tim Wirth, whose Congressional subcommittee oversees children's broadcasting, "but the question is, what does it teach?" What it teaches depends on the hands that control it, however wisely, ignorantly or innocently. It teaches what it shows whether it intends to or not. Many parents conclude that controlling TV use—or stopping it altogether—is necessary for the benefit of their children (It is true that children who watch a lot of TV tend to do worse in school than children who do not). What can a parent do? Charren advises parents to handle the television with "T.L.C."

Talk with your children about television and different shows, and answer questions your child has about specific program content. Point out that TV perpetuates stereotypes, and that most of the role models are white, male and middle class—there are three times as many men on TV as women (and there are more speaking roles for animals and robots on TV than for blacks, Orientals and Hispanics). Talk about ways TV characters could solve problems without violence. Explain that everything advertisements say or imply about a product is not necessarily true; this is especially important with the new children's shows that are program-length commercials, where there is no distinction between the shows' characters and the products being advertised.

Look at the shows with your children. Television's impact is greatest when parents or other adults are unavailable to supply additional information; by watching with your sons and daughters, you can help them understand when a show is unrealistic or irresponsible. You can also explain your personal judgments about shows' contents, including crime, cruelty, violence, sex, sexism and profanity. If you watch television commercials with your children and then take them to the store to examine the items advertised, you can help them decide whether or not the items live up to the advertising promises.

Choose television programs with your children (with young children, you may want to pick programs for them). Develop guidelines for TV use in cooperation with your children—ask why your children enjoy different programs. Teach them to watch television programs, rather than just television—if there are no programs you want to see, turn it off. Some parents decide that their families are better off watching no TV at all.

Project for Young People:The TV Log

Each day for a week, write down how much TV you watch, and which shows. How many hours a week do you watch? Do you watch every day? Which shows are your favorite? Which shows could you cut down on? What else could you do or learn with the time you are spending watching TV? Read books? Play sports? Join the scouts? Learn to play a musical instrument? Help others? A recent study says that by watching TV for 10 hours a week or less, students may actually improve their schoolwork. Try going a week watching no TV at all—can you do it?

Examining Advertising

One of the most powerful influences on children who watch TV is not the shows they watch, but the advertisements. Advertising does what it is intended to do—it gets children to ask for the products advertised. As advertising executive Mel Helitzer said in 1973, "Children can be very successful naggers. By and large parents quite readily purchase products urged upon them by their youngsters...[We] found that a parent will pay 20% or more for an advertised product with child appeal—even when a less expensive, non-advertised product is no different."

Young children "place indiscriminate trust in televised advertising messages" and are "highly susceptible to external influence," according to studies by the Federal Trade Commission (FTC). "Children develop personal and trustful relationships with the animated and imaginary characters often used in television advertisements. Children not only develop affection for these make believe characters, such as Tony the Tiger and Ronald McDonald, but feel that the characters want to help them."

Experts suggest you explain the purpose of advertising to your kids. "They are trying to get money out of your pocket," Flora Williams advises telling your children. "They don't want you to have it, they want it."

A disturbing development in children's TV is the program-length commercial. Before, parents could explain to their children the difference between a show and an advertisement. Today, though, "what parents have to remember," says Peggy Charren, "is that children's programs have become advertising." In 1969, the Federal Communications Commission (FCC) stopped ABC-TV and Mattel from running the "Hot Wheels" show because it was essentially an hour-long advertisement for Mattel. The FCC said the program was "designed primarily to promote the sale of a sponsor's product, rather than to serve the public by either entertaining or informing it."

In 1983, however, in the new atmosphere of deregulation under the Reagan administration, 13 shows based on children's toys sprang up that were basically program-long ads. When these shows were challenged by consumer groups, the FCC reversed is 1969 position and allowed the shows to continue. In 1986, the field of program-length commercials has burgeoned to 58 different shows—some, like "Thundercats," "He-Man and She-Ra," and "Challenge of the GoBots," syndicated every afternoon in many media markets—where toy companies have some modicum of editorial control. The Hasbro-Bradley toy company boasts to its retailers that it has been able to include every character, every vehicle and every accessory available in each of the 90 episodes of their cartoon "G.I. Joe."

In the past, it was not unusual for toys based on characters featured in kid's (and adult) TV programs to appear after the show had become a hit, but now the toy and the television show are released at the same time. And the "shows" work: all of the current top 10 selling action toy figures have their own TV shows. "This merchandising doesn't happen with adult shows," says Charren. "We don't have 'Spencer for Hire's Root Beer.' It is not 'Marriott's Hotel,' it's just 'Hotel.'"

The Children's Television Educational Act calls for an inquiry by the FCC into program-length commercials to determine their effects on children. Sponsors of the bill invite citizen comment to members of Congress; if you are interested, write your Member of Congress (U.S. House of Representatives, Washington D.C. 20515) about H.R. 3216 and your Senators (U.S. Senate, Washington, D.C. 20510) concerning S. 1594.

Project for Young People: Analyzing Advertising

Next time you are watching TV, pay close attention to the advertising. Think about the following:

- To whom is the ad speaking? What kind of person does the advertiser want to attract? Gullible? Thoughtful? Impulsive?
- What does the action in the ad have to do with the product or service the company is trying to sell? Many advertisements, like car and toy commercials, show action scenes but don't tell you much about the price, quality or durability of the product. Are there ads that do tell you about the product? Which type of ads are more useful?
- Take a close look at food ads. What do the advertisements tell you about nutrition? Cost? Convenience? Ingredients? List all the foods advertised on TV, then make a separate list of all the foods you need to eat to be healthy. Compare the two lists.
- What facts do the ads give you? Some commercials don't have any information at all, but just try to be entertaining. What do they tell you about the product?

We have adapted *Penny Power's* breakdown of commercials into different "games" the advertisers play. Can you spot these ad games in the commercials you see?

The star game. Ads in this category show famous people or cartoon characters praising a product or service. They would like you to believe two things: 1)If the star likes the product, it must be good; and 2)If you use the product, you will be like the star—attractive, powerful or well-liked. "Remember," warns

Penny Power, "the star is being paid a lot of money to say that the product is terrific."

The word game. These ads seem full of facts—new ingredients, special features, improved styling—but do not actually tell you very much. They may not explain why the new ingredient, feature or styling is better than the old, or why they are better than those in any other product. Ask yourself if the words make sense, or just sound good.

The everybody's-using-it game. "People want to be popular," *Penny Power* points out; these ads play on that desire, implying that if you use the product, you will belong to the happy, popular crowd that parades across the commercial ("Join the Pepsi generation"). The message is also that if you don't buy the product, you won't gain acceptance. They imply that if you don't use a certain kind of make-up or cologne, you will not be attractive; if you don't drink a certain soft drink you won't be part of the club ("Wouldn't you like to be a Pepper, too?")

The numbers game. Many ads use impressive-sounding numbers to get you to buy their product—"Four out of five doctors recommend..." Listen closely. What do those numbers really mean?

The prize game. To sell a product, some companies offer prizes or bonuses that have nothing to do with the item at all—super-hero glassware from your local fast food joint, free plastic toys in the cereal box, or vacation trips to Hawaii that could be yours if you only buy a certain product. What do the ads say about the product? Not much, except maybe that the company can't sell it on its own merits.

Do the commercials you see offer enough information so you can make an informed decision about the product? Do the commercials give you the facts, or do they just play ad games? Some will give facts and play these games, some will play other games, but if you approach advertising in a way to spot the games then you are well on your way to being a competent consumer. ❖

For a list of back issues, write to: Buyer's Market, P.O. Box 19367, Washington, D.C. 20036. Volumes of 10 are available for $10.00.

Toys
Product Safety Fact Sheet
U.S. CONSUMER PRODUCT SAFETY COMMISSION, SEPTEMBER 1982

DOLLS, TOY TRUCKS and cars, toy wagons, and balls are among children's favorite playthings. But in 1979, according to U.S. Consumer Product Safety Commission estimates, more than 135,000 persons received hospital emergency room treatment for injuries from these and other toys.

Falls on or against toys are a frequent type of accident, but children have also been seriously injured when they have swallowed or choked on small parts, placed tiny toys in noses and ears, and cut themselves on sharp edges and points on children's products.

WHAT THE GOVERNMENT DOES:

Toy Safety regulations

Under the Federal Hazardous Substances Act and the Consumer Product Safety Act, the Commission has set safety regulations for certain toys and other children's articles. Manufacturers must design and manufacture their products to meet these regulations so that hazardous products are not sold.

Some of the Commission's regulations set safety specifications for specific kinds of products, while others deal with hazards such as sharp edges or points which can occur on a wide variety of toys or children's products. The following CPSC toy regulations are now in effect:

Sharp Points: CPSC regulations, which became effective in December 1978, provide manufacturers with testing methods to ensure that toys and other articles intended for children under eight years do not have hazardous sharp points.

Sharp Edges: The Commission has also issued testing methods which manufacturers can use to eliminate hazardously sharp glass and metal edges from toys and other children's articles. These test methods, intended to protect children under eight years of age, became effective in March 1979.

Small Parts: This regulation, which became effective January 1, 1980, is intended to eliminate small parts from toys intended for use by children under three years of age.

Electrically Operated Toys: Safety specifications for electrically operated toys and children's products have been in effect since 1973. These regulations are designed to prevent electric shock and burn injuries which could result from poorly constructed electrical toys.

Pacifiers: Commission regulations specify that pacifiers must be large enough so that babies cannot choke on them. Pacifiers must not come apart into small pieces.

Lawn Darts: Lawn darts must not be sold in toy stores and must have labels to indicate they are not toys and they could cause serious injury if misused.

Clacker Balls: Clacker balls are a novelty toy consisting of two plastic balls connected by a cord which can be "clacked" together by a rhythmic motion of the hand. These toys must be manufactured in accordance with strict performance requirements so that the plastic balls will not shatter or fly off the ends of the cord.

Sound Level of Toy Caps and Toy Guns: To prevent hearing damage, the Commission has regulated the amount of noise that toy caps and toy guns may make.

Lead-in-Paint: To prevent lead poisoning, the amount of lead in paint used on toys and other children's articles is severely limited to less than 0.06 percent. This lead limitation also applies to paint sold for home use and to the paint used on furniture (except metal furniture).

Aluminized Polyester Film Kites: The Commission banned these kites as of September 1979, since they could become entangled in power lines and cause electric shock or electrocution.

Toys with Hazardous Chemicals: The Federal Hazardous Substances Act prohibits the use of poisonous and otherwise harmful chemicals in toys and other articles intended for use by children. Chemistry sets, model rocketry sets, model airplane fuel, and other products designed for older children, which by their very nature must have such chemicals, may be sold if accompanied by instructions and warning labels.

The commission has also issued safety regulations for cribs, baby bouncers and walker jumpers, bicycles, fireworks, and children's sleepwear.

COMPLIANCE WITH THE REGULATIONS

Manufacturers must assure that their products comply with the toy safety regulations. CPSC's investigators inspect firms which make or import these products to ensure that the regulations are being followed. During these inspections, samples of products are collected for testing at Commission laboratories to determine whether they meet the regulations.

Products which violate certain CPSC toy regulations or which may present substantial product hazards may be subject to recall. When a banned toy is recalled, retailers who have sold that toy may be required to post signs in their stores advising consumers that the product may be returned for a refund.

Here are Ten Toy Purchasing Tips for Consumers from the Toy Group

From *The 1988 Toy Report on Safety, Quality and Price*

CONSUMER AFFAIRS COMMITTEE OF AMERICANS FOR DEMOCRATIC ACTION

- Safety First. Be aware of sharp edges, small parts that can come off; of projectiles. Potential danger lurks in a broken toy.

Look for the words:
- flame retardant/flame resistant on fabrics;
- non-toxic on painted toys;
- machine surface washable on stuffed and cloth toys;
- Buy the TOY, not the BOX. Try to see the contents of an expensive boxed toy, so you will know that it's the same as the picture on the box. Most good merchants keep a sample on display.
- Consider play value. Can a child get enjoyment from the toy for a long while, or will he/she get bored after 15 minutes and never bother with it again?
- Batteries make the toy cost more. Don't forget this additional expense. This year, one "hot" toy we tested required 8 batteries!
- Save sales receipts. Some stores will meet the price of the competition!
- Don't throw away toy directions. Always read them, and avoid overcomplicated ones.
- Consider how messy or destructive a toy may be.
- Check newspaper ads right before Christmas. Sometimes the really hot toys are shipped then; sometimes there are special sales.
- Look for toys your child can play with safely on his or her own. A good toy of appropriate age level should not need constant supervision to insure safety or correct use.
- Try not to buy this year's "hot" TV toy. It may be cheaper next year! And remember: that TV ad often glamorizes the toy.

For a copy of the 17th annual toy report, send $10.00 to: ADA, 815 15th Street NW, Suite 711, Washington, D.C. 20005.

WHAT THE CONSUMER CAN DO

Not all toy-related injuries can be prevented by government regulations. New and old toys around the house should be checked for possible hazards.

Teach children to put their toys safely away on shelves or in a toy chest after playing to prevent trips and falls.

Toy boxes, too, should be checked for safety. Use a toy chest that has a lightweight lid that can be opened easily from within. The lid should stay open when raised and not fall unexpectedly on a child. For extra safety, be sure there are ventilation holes for fresh air. Watch for sharp edges that could cut and hinges that could pinch or squeeze.

The Commission has the following suggestions for toy safety:

- Toys should suit the skills, abilities and interests of the individual child. Avoid toys that are too complex for young children.
- Remember that a toy that is safe for an 8-year-old may be hazardous for a younger child.
- Avoid hand-me-down toys with small parts for children under three years of age.
- Look for labels that give age recommendations such as "Recommended for Children Three to Five Years Old." Also use your own judgement in deciding whether a toy may be hazardous for a youngster.
- Avoid toys that shoot objects that can injure eyes.
- Arrows and darts used by children should have blunt tips made from resilient materials such as rubber or plastic suction cups. Make sure these tips are secure.
- Avoid toys for infants and very young children with long strings or cords. The cords may become wrapped around an infant's neck and cause strangulation. Never hang toys with long strings, cords, loops or ribbons in cribs or playpens where children can become entangled.
- Explain to the child how to use toys properly and safely.
- Encourage children to put their toys away so they do not get broken and so that no one else trips or falls on them.
- See that toys used outdoors are stored after play—rain or dew can rust or damage a variety of toys and toy parts creating hazards.
- Examine toys periodically; watch out particularly for sharp edges and points that may have developed. Repair broken toys and discard toys that cannot be fixed.

REMEMBER, THERE IS NO SUBSTITUTE FOR ADULT SUPERVISION.

Children and Pool Safety Checklist

U.S. CONSUMER PRODUCT SAFETY COMMISSION
SPRING 1988

How Child Drownings Happen

In 1986, the Commission studied drowning and submersion accidents of children under age five in Arizona, California and Florida to document the events leading and contributing to the accidents. Some important statistics were uncovered during the investigations. For example,

- 75 percent of the victims were between 12 and 35 months of age.
- 65 percent were male.
- 65 percent of the accidents occurred in the pool owned by the child's family.

These children are at the highest risk of a drowning accident. Their capabilities change daily and they are always doing something unexpected.

- 46 percent of the children involved in the accident

WERE LAST SEEN IN THE HOUSE prior to being found in the pool.

Doors that exit to the pool should be locked, not just latched, at all times. Locks should be out of reach of young children.

- 23 percent of the children were last seen in the yard, porch or patio prior to the accident. In all, 69 percent of the children were not expected to be at or in the pool, yet they were found in the water.

Complete fencing around the pool, with a self-closing, self-latching gate or door, and with the latch out of children's reach, could prevent many accidents.

- 31 percent of the children were in or around the pool just prior to the accident.

Children at poolside must be watched constantly. Adults should not allow themselves to be distracted by household chores. Flotation devices should not be relied upon to protect children.

- 77 percent of the children had been seen 5 minutes or less before being missed and subsequently discovered in the pool.

Drownings happen quickly and without warning. There is no cry for help.

- Survival depends on rescuing the child quickly from the pool and restarting the breathing process.

Minutes count in preventing death or brain damage. Know CPR and begin resuscitation immediately. A poolside telephone showing emergency numbers will let you summon help after CPR is started.

Many communities have enacted safety regulations governing in-ground and above-ground residential swimming pools. Homeowners should obtain a current copy of these regulation to make certain their pool complies with the law. Apart from these ordinances, pool owners should carry out their own safety precautions to reduce chances of drownings or submersion accidents. Check the following safety features to make sure your pool meets the test:

Barriers

Fencing

- There is a fence on all four sides of the pool.
- The fence is at least 5 feet high.
- No vertical opening in the fence is more than 4 inches wide.
- Young children cannot climb the fence.
- The fence allows a clear view of the pool from the house.

Gate

- The gate is self-closing.
- The gate has a self-latching mechanism in proper working order.
- The gate latching mechanism is out-of-reach of young children.

Doors

- All exit doors from the house to the pool are routinely kept locked.
- All exit doors from the house to the pool have a lock at least 5 feet above the floor.

Pool Covers

- Pool covers are always removed, completely, when the pool is in use.
- Standing water is always removed from pool covers.

Steps

- Steps leading to an above-ground pool are removed when the pool is not in use.

Supervision

- Young children are never left alone in or around the pool. They are always supervised by an adult.
- Babysitters and guardians are always instructed about potential hazards to young children in and around the pool.
- Caretakers never rely on flotation devices or swimming lessons to protect a child. Young children are always supervised. ❖

Drinking Water

BUYER'S MARKET, VOLUME I, NUMBER I, JANUARY 1985

Destination—Cleanup

America is faced with a contaminated drinking water gap. From coast to coast, rivers, lakes, groundwaters and other essential water supply sources are polluted with industrial, agricultural and municipal wastes. Yet, water treatment technologies, safety standards and public education programs continue to reflect concern about 19th century infectious disease rather than the growing array of chronic ailments cause by 20th century toxic pollution problems, including cancer, birth defects, nervous system damage and other irreversible diseases. As a result, most Americans are essentially unprotected from the insidious public health consequences of consuming a staggering variety of toxic chemicals in their water.

Evidence of an exotic spectrum of toxic chemicals in U.S. drinking water supplies was first discovered in the 1970s. At about the same time, a series of epidemiological studies detected a link between toxics consumed in drinking water and elevated cancer risks. In the ensuing uproar, Congress recognized the shortcomings of antiquated drinking water protection programs and adopted a Safe Drinking Water Act in 1974. This landmark law gave the U.S. Environmental Protection Agency (EPA) a clear mandate to prevent water-borne potentially toxic chemicals in drinking water. After more than a decade of opposition by both public water supply and industry lobbies to this law's implementation, many chemicals in water are more prevalent than ever. The health risks suffered by Americans demand strong citizen awareness and action.

Your Rights

Under the Safe Drinking Water Act, as amended in 1986, you and every other citizen have the right to obtain the following information about your drinking water from your local water supplier:
- where it is from (its source);
- how it is purified;
- the contaminants for which the drinking water has been tested;
- past and present contamination problems;
- contamination levels that violate current federal drinking water standards; and
- how the public was notified about the violations.

Further protection under the Safe Drinking Water Act of 1974 includes:
- the right to bring civil suits against your local

water system, your state, or your federal officials if they fail to do their job. Civil penalties of up to $25,000 per day can be assessed by the courts depending on the seriousness of the violation and the danger to public health.
- requirements of the public water system to chemically treat contaminated water or install clean-up equipment to remove the contaminant(s) to concentrations below the standard when a violation occurs. If contamination is serious, wells are sometimes closed until the pollutants can be removed.
- public notification of maximum contaminant level violations must now, under the 1986 amendments, occur within 14 days of their detection and at least once every three months if the contamination continues. For minor violations of standards, public notification must be made once a year.

Public notification should include:
- a clear explanation of the violation;
- any potential adverse health effects;
- the steps being taken by the system to correct the problem; and
- the need, if any, to seek alternative water supplies.

Where Does Drinking Water Come From and How Does It Get Contaminated?

Drinking water comes from two major sources, ground water and surface water. Half of the population is served by ground water, which includes underground aquifers and artesian wells or springs. The other half of the population gets their supply from surface water, which includes lakes, ponds and rivers. Both sources are contaminated by the dumping of contaminants onto soil, which is carried either throughout the soil to the underground source aquifer, or throughout the runoff of the contaminated soil into lakes and rivers. Contamination is also caused by natural degradation of vegetation and animal matter and by pollutants carried by air and rain. Surface water is also contaminated by direct dumping of pollutants in lakes, rivers and ponds.

How Is Water Made Safe to Drink?

Once ground and surface water are contaminated they have to be treated to be safe to drink. The standard system for purifying water is called rapid sand filtration and is used in combination with chlorine for disinfection. This process involves the following:

- Water is moved from the surface and ground-water sources to storage areas.
- Copper Sulfate is sometimes added to control the growth of algae.
- Chemicals such as chlorine, lime, and alum are added to coagulate particles, disinfect, and sometimes to soften water.
- Water is allowed to sit in sedimentation basins until solid particles sink to the bottom and is then strained to remove debris.
- Water then flows through beds of gravel and sand for final filtering.
- Chlorine or other disinfectants are added as a final treatment to kill bacteria.
- Water is then tested to ensure that it does not obtain any quantities of pollutants in excess of EPA's or the state's maximum contaminant levels.
- Treated water goes to reservoirs or holding tanks. In some cases, it goes directly into the water system.

Other methods of cleaning water for drinking purposes such as granular activated carbon filtration (GAC) and packed tower aeration (PTA) more effectively eliminate hazardous substances but are not commonly employed in water treatment systems in the United States. If used, these two systems would remove the majority of the 83 contaminants to be regulated by EPA over the next three years as well as many of the 2,100 contaminants that have been found in the random drinking water tests.

What Can You Do About Contamination at the Source?

Proper disposal and storage of contaminants is vital to our ground and surface water source and to ensure an adequate supply of drinking water. Stricter regulation and enforcement of existing standards, together with greater consumer awareness of methods dealing with toxic products can significantly improve drinking water quality. Common methods of disposal such as pouring products down the drain, putting them out with the trash and burning and burying, can only compromise water quality. For example, as Clean Water Action Project's (CWAP) *Guide to Toxic and Non-Toxic Household Products* points out, "drain disposal causes pipes to corrode, fumes to back up into the home, and septic and sewage systems to break down.... Disposal with the trash ultimately results in the release of chemicals into the soil, groundwater and air." CWAP's guide provides a list of common household products which are harmful to the environment and a

list of alternatives. When alternatives cannot be utilized, however, proper disposal is essential. Clean Water Action Project recommends the following:

- Waste oils and batteries should be taken to recycling centers or the place of purchase.
- Banned pesticides should be returned to the manufacturer.
- Acids corrosives, pesticides and their empty containers, flammables, outdated medicines, paints, paint removers, and wood preservatives should be taken to a hazardous waste collection site.

Contamination During and After Treatment

The more contaminated ground and surface water becomes, the greater the need for more treatment to make it safe. However, contamination not only occurs at the source but also during and after treatment. According to the September 1986 *EPA Journal*, contamination can occur as follows:

- During treatment
- By disinfectant by-products and other additives.
- After treatment

By corrosion of piping materials, including lead and asbestos; bacteria and dirt from leaking pipes; and cross connection (incorrect pressure gradients that can suck polluted water into pipes instead of pushing it out).

Contamination by chlorination by-products and lead contamination are two such problems which occur during and after treatment.

Chlorination: A Dangerous Tradition?

Since the early 1900s, chlorination has been used as the primary disinfectant in water systems across the United States. In the mid-1970s, a group of chemicals called trihalomethanes (THMs), recognized as by-products of chlorination, were found to present serious risks of causing cancer and birth defects. This finding prompted the EPA to set a limit of 100 parts per billion (ppb) on the amount of trihalomethanes allowed in drinking water.

Trihalomethanes comprise only 30 percent of the by-products that result from chlorination. Recent studies have identified other chemical by-products of chlorination which may cause cancer. Testing has already proven that some of these chemicals have a high potential to cause birth defects.

What are the alternatives to chlorine? Ozone is a more effective, safer and less expensive disinfectant than chlorine or chlorine based disinfectants. Currently, only 30 water systems in the United States use ozone to disinfect drinking water. More than 1,300 water treatment plants outside the U.S. use ozone for disinfection. Although ozone is a less expensive method of disinfecting, there are initial costs for switching over to an ozone system. While ozone does not disinfect pipes in a system as well as chlorine, this shortcoming could be remedied by adding a small amount of chlorine at the end of ozone disinfection. As more testing of chlorination by-products is completed, more water systems operators may make an economic and safety decision and switch to ozone.

- Heavy chlorine tastes and odors will dissipate if water is kept for several hours in an uncovered pitcher.
- Use a blender or mixer for several minutes to force air into the water which will reduce the level of chlorine and other volatile chemicals.

Lead in Drinking Water: A National Health Hazard

Background:

Lead occurs naturally at very low levels in drinking water sources, but as water passes through the pipes of the distribution system from the treatment plant to your house and then through your household plumbing, it can dissolve minute amounts of metals present in the piping. Distribution systems widely use lead piping and connectors and almost all household plumbing in this country, whether copper or galvanized piping, is connected with lead solder. Consequently, lead is one of the main metals that leaches into drinking water.

Lead is a known toxin, causing damage to the nervous system, the blood-forming processes, the gastrointestinal system and kidneys. Recent studies show that lead can cause cognitive damage, stunt children's growth and raise blood pressure in adult males at concentrations as low as 10 ppb. At higher levels of exposure, lead can cause severe retardation or even death. Young children and fetuses are most at risk of damage from exposure to lead. By drinking water at or above 10 ppb, you are at risk of raising the lead content of your blood to unsafe levels. The Maximum Contaminant Level is presently at 50 ppb but the Environmental Protection Agency has proposed a guideline of no greater than 10ppb.

A recent EPA report documented the extent and effects of lead contamination of drinking water nationwide. At least 42 million people are exposed to dangerous levels of lead in their drinking water in the United States.

Why are we just hearing about the problem now? Studies have confirmed lead contamination in numerous states over the past 20 years. However, water suppliers are not required to test tap water samples for lead content. Since the contamination often occurs in household plumbing, the extent of the problem has remained largely unrevealed by present testing methods.

As part of the 1987 amendments to the Safe Drinking Water Act, a federal ban on the use of lead piping, solder and flux (a substance applied during soldering to prime the surfaces to be joined) in plumbing systems was enacted and came into effect in June 1988. If enforced strictly, this ban will help to protect future generations from the health hazards of drinking water. In addition to lowering the Maximum Contaminant Level, EPA has proposed changing testing requirements for lead so that tap water samples will be more frequently tested. However, the problems posed by existing lead piping and solder remain.

What can you do about lead in your drinking water?

Check to see if lead pipes, solder, and flux are used in plumbing that provides your tap water. Plumbing made of lead is dull gray and relatively soft. Scratching piping with a key to check for softness is a good way to determine if your pipes are lead.

A greenish discoloration and unpleasant taste of tapwater are indications that copper pipes are corroding and most likely lead corrosion is also occurring.

For More Information

CONSUMER'S RESEARCH, JULY 1988

- Environmental Protection Agency, Drinking Water, 401 M Street, S.W., Washington, D.C. 20460.

- Water Quality Association, 4151 Naperville Road, Lisle, Illinois 60532.

- National Sanitation Foundation, 3475 Plymouth Road, P.O. Box 1468, Ann Arbor, Michigan 48106

- Clean Water Action Project, 317 Pennsylvania Avenue, S.E., Washington, D.C. 20003.

- Concern, Inc., 1794 Columbia Road., N.W., Washington, D.C. 20009.

- "Test of 29 Home Water Treatment Systems," *Protect Yourself: A Magazine for Consumers*, July 1988. 5199 Sherbrooke St. E., Montreal, Quebec H1T 3X1 Canada.

Contact your local drinking water supplier and your public health department to find out if the water is corrosive, is known to have a lead problem, and if lead is used in the distribution system.

Get your water tested for lead content. Your local water supplier or public health department may be willing to test water from home taps or should be able to provide testing labs in your area. Make sure samples are collected in the morning before the tap has been used since this is when the highest levels of lead are usually found.

Run the water from the kitchen tap for three to five minutes in the morning and evening and after several hours of disuse before drawing water to drink or cook. Running the water will flush out water that has had extended contact with lead pipe or solder and should significantly reduce exposure.

If you find high levels of lead in your water, a blood test for you and your family can determine how much lead has entered your system.

Don't use hot tap water for drinking, cooking or preparing baby formula. Just as hot water dissolves a lump of sugar much more quickly than cold water, hot water tends to dissolve more lead from pipes and solder. When you need hot water, use cold water from the tap and heat it on the stove.

Make sure that new plumbing and plumbing repairs use lead free materials. Tin-antimony solder is a safer and less expensive substitute for tin-lead solder.

If you find lead levels that violate the federal standard of 50 ppb, call your water supplier, state health department or regional EPA office and request that enforcement action be taken. Though the lead contamination may be restricted to your home, it could be indicative of a community wide problem. If this is the case your water supplier may offer free testing of tap water for lead and can treat the water for corrosivity.

Contact your local and state officials, as well as your Senators and Representatives in Congress if you find high levels of lead in your drinking water. Inform them of all correspondence with your water supplier and health departments.

Investigating Your Water Quality

WITH ALL OF these possible sources of contamination and with the limited regulations and enforcement, an investigation of the quality of water in your community and in your home is a good idea. Testing for Toxics, a 1986 publication of the United States Public Interest Research Group (see Resources section), recommends studying the records of your monitoring agency for past and present compliance with the Safe Drinking Water Act standards and testing water samples yourself for contaminants which are either never or infrequently monitored under federal standards.

Follow these guidelines to conduct your own drinking water investigation:

Free testing of your tap water may be provided by your state or local health department, particularly if you have specific cause for concern. However, these agencies will often test only for bacterial contaminants, not toxic substances.

If you cannot get free or thorough testing, the agencies should be able to provide you with a list of certified water testing labs in your area. Private tests vary in price depending on the laboratory used and on the number of substances the analysis covers. At one commercial lab prices range from $15 for a lead test to $175 for a thorough testing for 59 contaminants.

Remember that test results from a certified lab that find contaminants exceeding the limits of the federal drinking water standards may mean the federal law is being violated.

If you find that your tap water is contaminated above allowable federal levels, contact your local water supplier, who is responsible for maintaining water quality at the federal standards, and your local and state health departments, who are responsible for enforcing the standards. Request that they comply with the law.

If your tap water is contaminated by substances that do not yet have standards, contact your state health department to find out if there is a health danger and if you should stop drinking your water. Your water tester should be able to provide information about any contaminants found.

Send copies of all correspondence with your water supplier and health department to your local and state government officials, and your Senators and Representatives in Congress.

Know your rights under the Safe Drinking Water Act.... and be persistent in exercising them. ❖

Bottled Water: Do I Need It?

The ample evidence of the widespread contamination of drinking water in this country has encouraged many people to turn to bottled drinking water. Approximately one in 17 Americans drink bottled water. In some areas of southern California, drinking bottled water has become part of the lifestyle for a third of the population. In 1986, it was a one billion dollar industry that produced over 450 different domestic brand labels and sold over 1.1 billion gallons of water.

Before you turn to bottled water, consider these facts together:

The average price of one gallon of domestic water is 80 cents. The average price of one thousand gallons of tap water is $1.28, over 600 times less than for bottled water. Bottled water is, as an EPA representative termed it, "a tricky beast." Regulated as a "food" by the Federal Food and Drug Administration (FDA), only bottled water that is marketed over state lines must meet federal drinking water standards. The FDA has declined to define "mineral water" which remains exempt from regulation.

Water bottlers are not allowed by law to make health claims on their labels unless there is compelling evidence to support them. Claims made by some water bottlers that their water relieves dehydration better than tap water are false.

Recent studies have found that showering and washer and dryer vents can expose us to far greater amounts of a certain group of chemicals called volatile organics than the water we drink. If these chemicals are present in your water, they turn to gases at high temperatures (such as in a shower or dryer) and contaminate the household air. Some drinking water contaminants are also absorbed through the skin while bathing. Bottled water will not protect you from this kind of exposure.

If you decide to turn to bottled water, carefully investigate its contents. Bottled waters should be low in sodium, disinfected with ozone rather than chlorine to improve taste, and uncontaminated by any toxic chemicals or harmful substances. *Consumer Reports* magazine tested 50 brands of bottled water and reported the results in their January 1987 issue. This is a good source of basic information on the differences in brands.

Ask you water bottler to provide you with regular results of tests completed for a wide range of drinking water contaminants. Ask for test results for chemical contamination, chlorination by-products (if chlorine is used as a disinfectant), heavy metal content, and sodium content to ensure the purity and safety of the water. If your bottler doesn't do the tests, find a bottler that does. You pay a premium price for bottled water because it is supposed to be safer than tap water; make the water bottler guarantee the safety of their product. Obtain copies of their tests.

Beware of water bottlers that use the word "spring" in their brand name but do not necessarily sell spring water. Water bottled from natural sources is not necessarily pure—natural sources are often unprotected from contamination.

Legally acceptable sources for bottled water are wells, springs and even public water right from your tap. Companies are not required to identify on their product labels the source of their water or the type of purifying treatment used.

Ask them to tell you the source in writing.

Home Water Treatment Systems May Be Hazardous to Your Health

Many different home water-treatment systems are available as an alternative to drinking water straight from the tap. The different types include activated carbon filters, reverse osmosis filters, ion-exchange resin filters and distillation units. The choice of which system to use depends on the particular contaminants in your water; it is essential to get your water tested before you even consider buying a home water-treatment system.

Activated carbon filters:
- Can improve the taste of and remove the odor from water;
- Are very effective in removing chlorine and pesticide residue and many organic chemicals such as chloroform and THM's (known carcinogens), many of which are currently unregulated by the federal standards, and
- Will not remove toxic metals, nitrates and salts, or expressive minerals.

The carbon must, however, be replaced frequently to avoid bacterial contamination.

Reverse osmosis filters:
- Remove toxic metals, and
- Remove radiological contamination.

Ion-exchange resin filters:
- Remove toxic metals, and
- Usually replace minerals with sodium, which may be undesireable.

Distillation units:
- Remove toxic metals,
- Remove radiological contamination, and
- Remove some organic contaminants but they also soften the water by removing minerals, some of which are essential nutrients. This also makes the water flat tasting.

It is important to remember that all of these systems need to be well maintained or you can end up actually adding pollutants to your water. As organic matter present in the water is trapped by the carbon filter, the moist habitat provides an ideal breeding ground for bacteria. If the filter is not in use for several days, the growth of bacteria can increase significantly. This build-up of bacteria is common when one goes on weekend outings or extended vacations. Unless a disinfection process is built into the unit, the bacteria in the filter can become dislodged and pass through the filter when it is used again.

To counter the bacterial problem, some manufacturers make carbon filters that contain metallic silver. Though silver may effectively retard bacterial growth, it adds a significant new contaminant to the water supply. Water leaving filters has been found to contain up to 76 ppb silver, a level which could cause health problems.

If you are thinking about buying a home treatment system, take the following steps first:

Get your water tested. The results will tell you whether you actually need to invest in a home treat-

ment system. Many unscrupulous home treatment companies prey on national concern about drinking water quality in order to attract customers.

Make sure the manufacturer can supply you with information on: how the system works, what contaminants it will remove, installation and maintenance costs and difficulty, and whether or not problems are covered by a warranty.

Find out if you can replace filters yourself. One consumer wrote to tell us that his $500 home water-treatment system needed its filters changed every 18 months at a cost of $55 each time.

Read the February 1983 issue of *Consumer Reports* on water filters. This is a good first step to get background on different home treatment systems.

At present, home treatment systems are not regulated or tested by the government. In California and Iowa, legislation has been passed that will require water filter manufacturers to be certified and have their products tested by the state. These laws have not been implemented yet. In New York, Washington and Connecticut similar legislation may soon be passed. ❖

What You Should Know About Home Fire Safety
U.S. CONSUMER PRODUCT SAFETY COMMISSION, OCTOBER 1983

Flammable Materials In Your Home
Your home is filled with materials and products that will burn if ignited. Upholstered furniture, clothing, drapery fabrics and liquids such as gasoline and volatile solvents are involved in many injury-causing fires each year. Most of these fires could be prevented.

Flammable Liquids
These liquids include gasoline, kerosene, lighter fluid, some paints and thinners, plus alcohol-based products. We use many of them each day without a thought about the fire hazard. And that's the problem! A moment's thought should remind us that the strong smell of most of these liquids is proof that they produce invisible vapors.

It's actually these vapors that can catch fire, sometimes from a distant or out-of-sight spark or flame. When this happens, the flames often flash back to the liquid itself, setting it afire. If vapors from some of these volatile liquids become concentrated in a con-

fined space, a violent explosion can occur!

Gasoline - The fuel we use daily in our cars and trucks is the biggest culprit in fire injuries involving flammable liquids. It is extremely hazardous when used in the home environment. It gives off vapors which are heavier than air, which means they can flow along the floor or even down stairs. If they come into contact with an ignition source, such as a water heater pilot light or even a spark in a refrigerator motor, a flash of flame can result.

Other substances which produce flammable vapors include many glues (such as model airplane cement) which contain volatile ethers, ketones, or esters; the acetone-type solvents in nail polish remover; and rubber cement.

For Safety With Flammable Liquids Choose Them Carefully
The Federal Hazardous Substances Act, which is administered by the U.S. Consumer Product Safety

Commission, establishes three labeling categories for liquid consumer product which will burn:

- Extremely flammable liquids produce ignitable vapors at room temperature, and even when relatively cold (below 20 degrees F.). Gasoline, white gas (often used in camping stoves and lanterns), contact adhesives, and some wood stains are in this category.
- Flammable liquids also produce ignitable vapors, but they do so at higher temperatures. Among these liquids are paint thinners, some paints, and automotive products such as brake fluid.
- Combustible on a label tells you that the fluid will burn once ignited, but it is less likely to catch fire than those with more ignitable vapors. Combustible liquids often include furniture polishes, oil-based paints, fuel oil, diesel oil, and kerosene.

When you select a liquid for a specific job, always look for the one that is least likely to ignite.

Some products are not labeled "flammable" because they are not flammable in liquid form as they come from the container. But some paint strippers, for example, become quite flammable once they are spread out, because the flame-suppressant chemicals evaporate. Always use solvent-based products of any kind with adequate moving air ventilation, and when in doubt assume they are flammable. The ventilation will help protect you from any toxic effects of the vapors, as well as lessening the chances that fumes will build up and ignite.

Use Them Wisely

1. Use flammable liquids away from any flame or source of sparks. This includes hidden ones like pilot lights, heaters, or electric motors.
2. Gasoline is not a safe cleaning fluid for clothing, metal parts, or anything else. Use it only as a fuel, in equipment designed for it.
3. Never refuel power mowers, chain saws or other gasoline-powered equipment without shutting them off and waiting for hot parts to cool to the touch. Always fuel up outdoors.
4. Use only liquids labeled "charcoal starters" to get charcoal fires going—and never add starter fluid after fire has been lit. Of course, both charcoal and charcoal starter fluids should only be used outdoors.
5. Always pour and use flammable liquids outdoors or in a very well ventilated space, away from fire or sparks.

Store Them Properly

Always store gasoline and other extremely flammable liquids outside your house or apartment. Never store gasoline in the trunk of a car. Keep stored fuels locked up, or else out of the reach of children. Many flammable liquids carry an additional hazard—they're poisonous too.

Use the proper storage container. Never keep gasoline (especially) in glass bottles, plastic jugs or other unsuitable containers. You may want to consider a container with certain safety features such as a pressure release valve and/or a flame arrester. These containers cost more than ordinary cans, but the added safety they provide is worth the expense.

Flammable Fabrics

The many natural and synthetic textiles we wear and use to decorate our homes vary widely in flammability. The thin, light-weight fabrics often used in blouses, dresses, and shirts seem to ignite more easily than heavier weaves found in coveralls and pants. Adult sleepwear, including pajamas, nightgowns, and robes, is involved in a large proportion of the fire injuries and deaths reported annually. The Flammable Fabrics Act standards, administered by the U.S. Consumer Product Safety Commission, require that all children's sleepwear be flame resistant, but it is a good habit to keep all fabrics away from ignition sources.

Many garment-related fires cause injuries when a loose-fitting portion of a garment, such as a sleeve or skirt hem, comes in contact with a stove burner, lighted candle, space heater, or fireplace fire. Flaming liquids also cause serious injuries when they splash onto a garment and ignite its fabric, or when the textile is already wet with a flammable liquid (such as spilled lighter fluid) which is then ignited by a nearby spark or flame.

Select Fabrics for Flame Resistance

1. Look for "Flame Retardant" or "Flame Resistant" on labels when you buy clothing, especially for children. By law, children's sleepwear up to size 14 must be flame resistant.
2. If you sew, shop for flame resistant fabric to use in the clothing you make.
3. Among fabrics which are not labeled "Flame Retardant" or "Flame Resistant," dense, tightly-woven fabrics (such as denim) are harder to ignite than lighter, more loosely-woven materials, including many blouse and shirt fabrics. Some fabrics with a fuzzy or fluffy surface (such as cotton flannels) may also be easier to ignite, and may burn faster than smooth, tightly-woven or knit fabric.
4. Even the style of a garment affects its potential for ignition. Loose, flowing clothing, like

many nightgowns, shifts, and robes, requires extra vigilance to keep it away from ignition sources. If part of a loose-fitting garment catches fire, you may not be aware of it until the fire is burning strongly.

Care for Flame Resistant Fabrics Properly

Follow the washing instruction label on the garment. In general, wash flame resistant garments in warm water. Some flame resistant fabrics require a phosphate-based detergent or a heavy-duty liquid detergent. Also, some flame-resistant fabrics should not be bleached.

Know What to Do If Garments Catch Fire

Don't run! Drop to the floor and roll over or back and forth to smother the flames. Be sure to teach your family this simple procedure and encourage them to practice it.

Upholstered Furniture

Many people don't recognize that upholstered chairs and sofas contain flammable materials. Fabric and filling material produce smoke and toxic gases when they burn or smolder, even if no flame is visible. Smoke, carbon monoxide, and other harmful gases can kill or injure persons sleeping nearby.

A lighted cigarette can fall between the arm or back of a chair and the cushion, where it may start the upholstery smoldering unnoticed. Comfortable furniture often makes people drowsy - a potential hazard for smokers. Cigarettes, sleepiness, and often alcohol are factors contributing to many furniture fires.

If You Must Smoke, Do It With Care

1. Use a deep, wide-rimmed ashtray, and set it on a table, not on the chair arm or in your lap. Extinguish smoldering butts before you go to bed.
2. If you drop a lighted cigarette into a chair or sofa, get up at once, find and remove the cigarette, and make certain the fabric and filling are cool to the touch.
3. Smoking demands extra care when you're sleepy, when drinking alcoholic beverages, or when taking some medications. Of course, never smoke in bed or when lying down.

Arrange Furniture with Fire Safety in Mind

1. Place upholstered furniture well away from stoves, space heaters, fireplaces, and other heat sources.
2. Keep your family's fire escape route in mind when arranging furniture. Don't put heavy pieces where they could trip a person escaping from a fire through a dark or smoke-filled room.

What To Do If A Burn Occurs...

Cool the burn with cool water to reduce pain and stop skin damage.

Don't put butter, grease, or ointments on a burn.

Protect the burn; don't try to clean it or to remove cloth that may be stuck to the burn. Don't break blisters. Cover large burns with a clean, dry sheet or towel.

Ignition Sources in Your Home

Fire, one of mankind's oldest tools, is all around us in obvious and helpful forms such as stove burners, fireplaces, and heating equipment. It's also nearby in less evident forms like the pilot lights that burn continuously in gas ranges, water heaters, and similar appliances.

Many fire accidents happen when people take these fires for granted, forgetting the potential danger. For example, volatile liquids that give off flammable vapors should be kept away from appliances since a gas burner or pilot in the appliance or the sparks produced inside an electric motor may act as a source of ignition for those vapors. Even light switches may ignite these invisible vapors.

Space Heaters

A CPSC regulation for unvented gas-fired space heaters requires that they have an oxygen depletion sensor (ODS). An ODS device detects a reduced level of oxygen (in the area where the heater is operating), and shuts off the heater before a hazardous level of carbon monoxide is accumulated. The rule also requires that these heaters have labels warning of the hazards of carbon monoxide.

General Safety Tips for All Space Heaters:

1. Read the label and follow the instructions for installation and operation.
2. Keep papers, clothing, draperies, furniture, and especially children, away from space heaters. Refer to the manufacturer's instructions for proper clearances from combustible material.
3. Keep the heater in safe working condition. Replace missing guards and controls at once.

Safety Tips for Electric Space Heaters:

1. Free-standing electric heaters should have tip-over switches to shut off the current if the unit is knocked over. This helps prevent ignition if the heater happens to fall against fabric or other flammable materials.
2. There must be a guard around the coil of your heater. A wire grille or other protection is essential to keep fingers or fabrics from touch-

ing the hot element.

3. If you must use an extension cord, make sure it's marked with a power rating at least as high as that on the label of the heater itself.

4. Keep it away from water! Don't use a portable electric heater anywhere in a bathroom or near a sink.

Safety Tips for Gas Space Heaters:

1. A vented gas space heater must be properly vented. This means it must have a properly sized vent pipe that is free of leaks and blockages. Joints must be tight and both the heat exchanger and the vent pipe must have no cracks through which carbon monoxide might leak out. An undersized or clogged vent is equally hazardous. If you're not absolutely certain that your heater and vent are in good condition, have them checked by your gas supplier or a recommended qualified service person.

2. When you use an unvented heater, keep a door or window slightly open in the room in which the unit is operating. Good ventilation during use is crucial!

3. Light the match before you turn on the gas to the pilot, to avoid the possibility of a flare up which could occur if you allow gas to accumulate before you bring the match near.

4. Remember that a space heater can ignite flammable liquids and vapors. Never use a space heater in the same room where gasoline is stored, or where paint thinners, kerosene, or other volatile liquids are being used.

Safety Tips for Kerosene, Oil, Or Woodburning Space Heaters:

1. Improper installation or maintenance of a wood stove causes many fires. Follow manufacturers' directions carefully and have your stove inspected by a local fire safety official. Clean your chimney regularly.

2. Use only the fuel for which the heater was designed. Most kerosene heaters require a pure grade of kerosene. Never use gasoline. Never burn coal in a stove designed only for wood.

3. Never use flammable or combustible liquids such as gasoline or kerosene to get a wood stove started; use only paper or kindling.

4. These heaters have open flames and hot surfaces; keep furnishings and small children away!

Matches, Matchbooks, and Lighters

Some residential fires begin with a match dropped

into a wastebasket before it is fully extinguished. Injuries can even be caused when matches fragment and throw off flaming particles while being struck.

Children lack the knowledge to use matches responsibly, yet many people leave matches or lighters in purses, on tables, and in other places where they may be reached by the inquiring hands or small children. Older persons, even with decades of experience, may lack the dexterity to use matches carefully.

Lighter fluid is obviously highly flammable. Great care should be taken when filling lighters to avoid or wipe up spills, and of course it is unsafe to smoke while filling a lighter.

Safety Tips for Matches, Matchbooks, and Lighters: Look for Safety when You Buy

Avoid matches that appear discolored or damaged. They may have been exposed to dampness, which can make them more likely to fragment or fall apart when struck.

Use with Care

1. Close cover before striking - old, but very good, advice.

2. Strike away from yourself and others. Flaming particles can fly off of matchheads. Hold the match well away from faces and fabrics.

3. Discard damaged or discolored matches, which are more likely to split or throw off flaming particles when struck.

4. Pay attention! Lighting a match while you're driving or using tools or machinery is inviting both accident and fire. You might not notice a flaming particle dropped from a matchhead until it has started a serious fire.

5. Before you light up, look around. Use your eyes and your nose to check for flammable liquids or vapors. Never smoke around gasoline, paint thinners, or other volatile fluids.

6. Be sure it's out. Hold that match long enough to make sure it's cold. And even then don't throw it in with flammable trash.

Carrying and Storing Matches and Lighters

1. Children are fascinated with fire and lighters; keep them out of reach! This includes not only stored matches and lighters, but those carried in pocket or purse.

2. Don't store them near flammable materials, or in damp places. Check the pockets of clothing going into seasonal storage, and dispose of old matches and matchbooks safely. It is especially important not to pack matches in luggage with other flammable materials,

such as clothing. The movement of items in a suitcase might rub matches against a surface and cause them to ignite.

Surviving A Fire In Your Home

If a fire occurs while you are awake, get yourself and all others out of the building. Call the Fire Department from a phone or alarm box outside the building. Don't go back inside until the Fire Department has determined that the fire is completely out and that the building is safe.

But most fires occur during sleeping hours. . .

Many deaths and injuries are actually caused by smoke and gases often produced before flames appear. This means that survival depends on being warned as early as possible. The safest warning method is one or more smoke detectors, correctly placed and in good working condition.

Choosing Smoke Detectors

Ionization or photoelectric? Most detectors on the market fit into one of these categories, which describe the way in which they detect minute amounts of airborne smoke. Well designed detectors of either type should give warning in time to escape.

Another difference between some models has to do with whether they get the electrical energy they need to operate from a battery or from the house's electrical circuits. Battery-powered detectors will operate for about a year, and most will give you an audible warning that the old battery should be replaced. You can also test your detectors (bi-weekly, with a candle) to prove that the battery is still good.

Many people prefer battery-powered units because they are easy to install, especially where there is not a hand electrical plug. Also, they cannot be disabled by an electrical power blackout. Other people have more confidence in a detector that gets power from the house's electrical circuits, perhaps because they won't ever have to change the battery. Either type will significantly increase fire safety in your home.

It's important to select detectors that meet acceptable performance requirements. Look at the package or the label on the detector itself for the seal or stamp of a recognized national testing laboratory. This shows that particular design to have been tested and found to operate within the performance limits established by the laboratory.

Installing Smoke Detectors

Place detectors close to where people sleep, so that an alarm will be heard. If you have just one detector, put it in the hallway just outside the bedrooms. Be-

cause smoke travels slowly between floors, a multi-story building really should have a detector on each level.

Don't put a smoke detector in the kitchen, since airborne grease and cooking fumes may cause it to give false alarms. Also avoid putting detectors close to heating or air conditioning vents, since these may blow smoke away from the detector while it is spreading through the rest of the house.

Two detectors offer more safety potential than one. Having two also lets you choose both the ionization and photoelectric types. One detector can also be battery powered while the other runs on home current. Some new detectors offer both ionization and photoelectric sensors in one unit.

Caring for Smoke Detectors

1. Replace batteries annually. Most detectors warn you when a fresh battery is needed, but if more than a year goes by with no apparent battery failure, change it anyway. Failure, when it comes, could be sudden.
2. Replace the light source in photoelectric detectors as soon as it burns out. Have an extra on hand, so that delay won't lead to forgetting.
3. Test regularly with real smoke. Hold a freshly-extinguished candle a few inches under photoelectric detectors (a puff of cigarette smoke will also work). For ionization detectors, use a lighted candle. The alarm should sound within 20 seconds, and should shut off quickly when the smoke is removed. If there is no alarm, check the battery or power cord, or replace the light source (if appropriate). Some authorities suggest testing every two weeks, or after you've been away for more than six days, since the battery or lamp may have failed during that period.

Escape!

Have two exists from each part of the house. If bedroom windows are too high above the ground for safe jumping install rope or chain safety ladders. These provide an alternative way out, in case the stairway or first floor is blocked by fire or smoke.

If you live in an apartment, look for escape instructions that have been posted by the building management. If none are posted, check with your local fire department.

Practice escape. Fire drills help make certain that each member of your household knows the escape routes. Small children should be part of this rehearsal and discussion, and it is especially important to make sure they understand that they must escape—they can't hide from fire under a bed or in a closet.

Learn the "tricks" of safe escape.
1. Stay low. Most smoke rises, so to pass safely through a smoke-filled hall or room keep down, even crawling on hands and knees if necessary.
2. Feel the door before you open it. If the knob or door panels are hot to the touch, fire may be just outside. Escape by the window instead.
3. Agree on a place to meet after escaping. In your fire drill, choose a place safely outside the home where you can all meet to "count noses," to be sure everyone got out safely. ❖

The First Line of Defense
BY MIKE MCCLINTOCK
WASHINGTON POST, APRIL 9, 1987

Smoke Detectors Can Save Lives, but Only if Properly Installed and Maintained

For about $15 you can buy the most effective, reliable, long-term protection against fire, one of the most lethal threats to life and property. Fifteen dollars is the average cost of a smoke detector, a modest price for the key to residential fire safety and about $10 less than the average cost when smoke detectors were introduced in the early 1970s.

Most consumers know how important this protection is. Close to 75 percent of American homes already have at least one smoke detector. But the U.S. Fire Administration (USFA) and other groups estimate that one-third to one-half of all smoke detectors do not work. Some units may be worn out or clogged with dust. Others may have dead batteries. Many have purposely been disabled to stop the occasional shrill blast brought on by a piece of burned toast or a brief puff-back from a fireplace.

Whatever the cause, such gaps in residential fire safety are partly responsible for about 6,000 deaths (more than three-quarters of which occur in the home), 100,000 injuries and $7 billion of property damage from fires every year. (The United States has the highest fire death rate per capita of all industrialized Western Countries, according to the USFA.)

Typical smoke detectors are simple to install, requiring only a screwdriver and about five minutes for the job. They are simple to maintain, requiring only a push on the test button once a month and a battery check once a year. But easy installation and easy maintenance may be part of the problem: Smoke detectors are easy to forget about.

But the $60 cost of buying four new detectors (enough to protect most homes) pales next to the cost of replacing the average house. And detectors protect lives that cannot be replaced. A number of studies by the National Fire Protection Agency (NFPA) the USFA and other groups have shown that smoke detectors are one of the best ways to prevent fire deaths.

In fact, many states and counties now require that all housing include smoke detectors. They are required by law in the District and in Maryland, and on houses being sold in Fairfax and Arlington counties in Virginia. But if you are in the minority and still do not have smoke detectors, consider this finding from a NFPA study: People in homes without smoke detectors are twice as likely to die in a home fire than people in similar circumstances who have them.

If you have one or more operating smoke detectors, the ear-splitting sounds they emit are likely to be the first and most important warning of a fire. The International Association of Fire Chiefs (IAFC) reports that detectors provide the first warning of a fire 60 percent of the time when a fire erupts at night. Night fires tend to be the most deadly, since these blazes are often slow-developing, smoldering fires that break out after everyone is asleep.

Early warning is critical because the longer the delay in discovering a fire, the more deadly the consequences. One NFPA study shows that 63 percent of overnight fire fatalities occur when it takes more than 20 minutes to discover the fire. And two-thirds of those fatalities occur when it takes more than 40 minutes to discover the fire.

Smoke detectors have another built-in benefit. Of the three consequences of a home fire—loss of life, loss of property and personal injury—detectors are best at saving lives (sprinkler systems, which are about 20 times more costly than smoke detector systems, are best a protecting property). The NFPA has found that smoke detectors cut property loss by only 20 percent, and reduce the risk of injury by only five percent. This small risk reduction seems to be the only shortcoming of an early warning system, which also provides occupants with a chance to fight the fires, a dangerous activity that increases the chance of injury.

But the life-saving potential of smoke detectors can be short-circuited by mechanical problems and old age. Like everything else, smoke detectors can simply wear out. The NFPA reports a failure rate of between 16 and 30 percent for detectors bought since 1974. Many units can be tested by pushing a button mounted on the detector surface. Some may have to be triggered by holding a candle nearby. It is easy enough to find out if detectors are working. But the percentage of owners who test their detectors monthly has dropped from 48 percent in 1977 to under 40 percent in the most recent NFPA surveys.

A fresh battery may bring a dead detector back to life. But after five or 10 years of service, springing for a new $15 detector is not an extravagant investment.

New smoke detectors should bear the label of a testing lab such as Underwriters Laboratories. "Hard-wired" detectors may be powered by the house electrical system with battery backup. "Stand-alone" units that do not require wiring are powered by batteries alone. Detectors should be installed on every level of a home, high on the walls or on ceilings in centralized, open areas such as hallways where smoke is most likely to spread from floor to floor. Since most fatal fires occur at night, it is important to locate detectors in halls just outside bedroom doors.

Although smoke detectors are easy to install, it can be more difficult to plan an efficient but effective network of detectors throughout the house. In many areas the best source of fire prevention and safety information is your local fire department, which can offer practical installation advice. Some departments even have personnel who make house calls. ❖

Making a Chimney Sweep
BY MIKE MCCLINTOCK
WASHINGTON POST, OCTOBER 6, 1988

Before Lighting That First Fire, Check Out the Chimney and Fireplace

A masonry fireplace and chimney must contain smoke, ash, coals, flames and exhaust gases, and at the same time radiate heat while providing a view of the crackling logs. Outside—on a brick barbecue, for instance—a few cracks in the mortar won't hurt. Stray sparks and leaking exhaust gases are not likely to cause any problems. But inside the house they could be lethal.

So before you light the first piece of paper under that first piece of kindling in the fireplace this year take a look at its condition—from top to bottom.

• Evaluating the current condition. Homeowners can make general safety checks themselves. For example, while one person ignites a damp piece of paper in the fireplace, another can check for small smoke leaks where the chimney passes through the attic. Where smoke can escape, flames could follow. If the fireplace and chimney have not been cleaned or checked by a professional over the last few heating seasons, a sensible first step is to call in a chimney sweep.

Sweeps can recognize potentially dangerous deposits of creosote, a gummy, brown by-product of incomplete wood combustion that builds up inside chimneys. Creosote can be reignited, starting a chimney fire that is difficult to detect until it is burning fiercely, hard to extinguish and dangerous to the entire house. A sweep can clean away soot and ash in the flue, and use stiff wire brushes on long poles to dislodge the creosote. If you live in an old house, the sweep may inform you that the chimney has no lining—an inner core normally made of clay flue tile that prevents combustion by products or flames from contacting the structural walls of the chimney. Most older chimneys are made of brick, stone or masonry block.

Chimneys without liners may have safely carried away soot, smoke and live ashes for years. But it is wise to have a liner as a second layer of fire protection.

• Relining existing chimneys. If an old chimney is structurally sound, some form of fire-safe relining is almost always possible. There are several patented relining systems. Some consist of pouring a dense, heat- and fire-resistant mortar inside the chimney around a removable form that leaves a new, smooth, central flue opening. Others make a fire-safe lining by snaking flexible, stainless steel tubing down the chimney.

A talented fireplace mason might be able to reline a chimney with clay flue tile. But, as you can imagine, it is a tricky business to fit section after section of easily fractured flue tile down into the dark, unexplored cavern of a chimney.

• Repointing exterior masonry. Masonry exposed to the elements from the outside and heat from flue gases on the inside may need repairs. Usually, the weak link is the mortar between bricks or concrete blocks.

The tedious work of repairing or "repointing" the mortar starts with vigorous scraping to remove loose mortar. Fresh mix must be pressed into the joints to support the brick and seal the chimney. Premixed mortar for projects with concrete block and brick is available in bags, which takes the mystery out of proportioning sand and cement. But the dry ingredients still should be mixed before water is added. This ensures that clumps of sand or cement that could weaken the mortar are broken up and spread throughout the mix.

• Cleaning ash dumps and air intakes. Some fireplaces are built with two convenient, energy-efficient features that require regular maintenance. Built-in ash dumps may be accessible beneath a removable brick or metal trap door in the hearth. Instead of the fireplace being shoveled out periodically, ashes can be pushed into the dump. It's a nice extra. But the ashes don't vanish into thin air. Typically, you have to remove them at least once a year through a larger door near the base of the chimney in the cellar.

Since fireplaces need air to support combustion they draw warm room air into the fire and up the chimney. This can cause air leaks in other parts of the house as air is pulled in through cracks around windows and doors to replace the air that escapes up the chimney.

This energy-wasting syndrome is avoided with a fresh air intake—typically a duct running from an exterior grill to another grill in the hearth. This system can become clogged with ashes. By removing the exterior grill, however, even compacted ash can be dislodged.

• Cleaning smoke stains on brick. Although smoke stains around the fireplace opening normally are not a hazard, they can be unsightly. And excessive deposits may signal inadequate draft—even a blockage in the flue that is retarding the exhaust of combustion by products.

Small "clouds" of smoke deposits respond to several proprietary masonry cleaners. Light stains may be removed by scrubbing with detergent and water. If that doesn't work, try muriatic acid, usually sold in a three percent solution. This liquid (used with rubber gloves and eye protection), has the capacity to pull stains out of the brick.

•Removing lingering smoke odors. If puffbacks last winter combined with excessive humidity this summer have laced the room with a damp, dank, smoky odor, use some of the remaining, almost Indian summer days to air out the room. ... ❖

Ionization-Type Smoke Detectors

HEALTH RESEARCH GROUP LETTER, OCTOBER 1976

Dear Friend,

We have received numerous requests for information on the potential dangers associated with ionization type smoke detectors. We appreciate your interest and concern, and hope the following information will provide answers to questions you might have.

- Ionization smoke detectors contain either americium-241 or radium-226; the majority of these units contain americium-241. Americium, an alpha-emitting radioactive isotope, is similar to plutonium in its toxicity as a cancer-causing chemical at extremely low levels of exposure. The uptake of americium in plants and in the human gastro-intestinal tract is greater than for plutonium. Radium, also known to cause cancer, is only five to ten times less toxic than americium and plutonium. We advise against the use of either type.

- The ionization smoke detector does not present an immediate hazard to your health. However, the claims made by industry that radiation in ionization smoke detectors is "harmless," are misleading. The issue is not how much radiation is released, but whether radioactive exposure of home dwellers is necessary. Since the non-nuclear smoke detectors, the photoelectric type, are just as effective as the radioactive units, there is no reason at all that dwellers should be exposed.

- Photoelectric smoke detectors, the non-nuclear alternative to the ionization type, utilize a small beam of light and a light-sensitive photocell for smoke detection. Photoelectric and ionization units are equally effective in their response to fires which generate varying sizes of smoke particles, but photoelectric detectors are more sensitive than the ionization type in their response to smoldering, smoky fires—which account for most fire deaths. (Seventy-five percent of fires within the home start as smoldering fires.)

- Protection from fires in the home is imperative. Before removing a smoke detector from your home, be certain that it is an ionization unit, and replace it immediately with the safer alternative, the photoelectric type. Once you establish that your smoke detector is of the ionization type, it can be removed in the same manner that it was installed. For example, if it is battery operated and you installed it yourself, removal should not be difficult. However, if you had professional help with installation, and the detector is wired to a junction box in your home, it should be removed professionally, for your safety.

Ionization smoke detectors present an unnecessary risk of exposure to radiation, and we have asked that they be taken off the market. We urge consumers to utilize the photoelectric smoke detectors for protection from fire.

When you shop for a photoelectric detector, ask the salesperson specifically for the photoelectric type, and check the package labelling to be certain the unit is either UL or FM approved.

Sincerely,

Health Research Group

Emergency Planning

BY MICHAEL MARRIOTTE, NUCLEAR INFORMATION AND RESOURCE SERVICE
SEPTEMBER 1986

EMERGENCY PLANNING for nuclear reactor accidents was virtually nonexistent before the 1979 accident at Three Mile Island. Reactors were required to be located in "low population zones" which extended about two miles from the plant site, and safety precautions were required to be taken for plant workers and residents in the zones. The rationale was that a serious accident was simply "not credible," and thus no need for further public protection from the effects of a nuclear accident could ever arise.

Three Mile Island, however, forever exploded the myth of "non-credible" nuclear accidents. Following two tense days and nights in which federal, state and local officials wrestled with the appropriate response to TMI and attempted to develop an ad hoc emergency evacuation capability, pregnant women and pre-school children within five miles of the plant were advised to evacuate.

Following the TMI accident, and under pressure from Congress, the Nuclear Regulatory Commission (NRC) established new emergency planning requirements for all reactor sites. A ten-mile Emergency Planning Zone (EPZ) was created. Utilities are required to have the ability to notify in the event of an accident "essentially" everyone in the zone within 15 minutes. The ability to evacuate everyone in the EPZ is also required, although for some accidents sheltering would be the preferred option.

Emergency preparedness information is to be provided to all within the EPA annually, and regular tests of the emergency plans are to be held. The emergency plans and drills are reviewed by the Federal Emergency Management Agency (FEMA) prior to their acceptance by the NRC.

Emergency plans normally are developed by the utilities in cooperation with state and local governments. In recent years, however, some jurisdictions have refused to submit emergency plans or cooperate with utility plans on the basis that particular areas could not be effectively or quickly evacuated. For example, Suffolk County officials and New York Governor Mario Cuomo object to the idea that Long Island can be evacuated and therefore have withheld support of the plans as a means of halting the licensing of the Shoreham reactor.

A larger, 50-mile zone, called the "ingestion pathway," was established in order to provide the capability for monitoring milk and other foodstuffs which could be contaminated in the event of a major nuclear accident. Underlying the two emergency zones is an assumption that no accident could take place which would directly endanger humans beyond ten miles from a nuclear plant.

The concept of emergency planning to protect people living near a nuclear plant is certainly valid—as long as there are nuclear reactors to be protected against. In practice, however, emergency plans often have been found seriously lacking and may provide a false sense of security to nearby residents. Emergency plans generally will protect the public only in a "best case" accident scenario; at most plants a severe accident will cause far more disruption and damage than any emergency plan can effectively cope with.

Emergency plans, like nuclear reactors, are different at each plant site. Therefore, the criticisms listed below are necessarily broad in nature and discuss problems that have arisen at more than one plant.

EPZs are too small

The fact is, the Emergency Planning Zones are simply too small. A 1982 study conducted by Sandia National Laboratories for the NRC concluded that under adverse weather conditions a severe reactor accident with containment failure could cause early (within one year) fatalities as far as 25 miles from a reactor site. Cancers could occur even further away. A 1980 California study reached similar conclusions.

The 1986 accident at the Chernobyl nuclear reactor caused the Soviet Union to order a total evacuation of an 18.6-mile radius from the plant, and some towns as much as 50 miles away were evacuated—perhaps permanently—due to radioactive "hotspots." The U.S. State Department advised American citizens in the city of Kiev, nearly 80 miles from the accident, to evacuate as well, leaving some with the impression that the federal government is more interested in protecting U.S. citizens abroad than at home. Clearly though, the Soviet experience with a "real-life" severe reactor accident indicates that utilities and governments in the U.S. must be prepared to deal with the consequences of an accident far beyond a mere ten miles. For that reason, a number of state and local governments have begun examining proposals to expand the EPZ to as much as 40 miles.

Further, the ingestion pathway of the Chernobyl accident exceeded the NRC's figure of 50 miles by more than 20 times. Food more than 1200 miles from the Chernobyl reactor was reclassified as low-level radioactive waste and disposed of. In the U.S., a severe reactor accident will require vast regional planning and cooperation to ensure that contaminated food does not enter the marketplace.

Yet nuclear utilities in the U.S.A. recently have been pressing for a reduction in the size of the EPZ to as little as two miles—which essentially would be a return to the pre-TMI situation. The utilities base their stand on new "source term" (the amount and type of radiation that would be released in an accident) research which suggests that the consequences of an accident would be less severe than previously believed. However, the research remains unproven and extremely controversial. Some accidents, in fact, could have greater consequences than once predicted. And, of course, the Chernobyl accident forced evacuations far greater than two miles.

The utilities also argue that for most postulated accidents, only a small evacuation area would be necessary. This is probably true, but it is the less-likely, but far more consequential severe accident that poses the most threat to public health and safety. The mere existence of a 40-mile EPZ does not in itself require a utility to evacuate a full 40-mile radius in the event of every accident. It merely provides the planning basis so if a more severe accident should occur, the utility and the local governments will be prepared to cope with its consequences.

Site-specific EPZs are also recommended by some utilities. In these cases, source term research and other methods, such a Probabilistic Risk Assessments (PRAs), along with geographical and political boundaries, would be used to determine the appropriate size of the EPZ at any given plant. With a minimum EPZ size—and 20 miles should be the absolute minimum—this may be a useful means of establishing exact EPZ sizes.

The Shadow Phenomenon

Another problem inherent in the emergency planning process, and another prominent reason for the necessity of expanding the ten-mile EPZ, is the fact that evacuations cannot be controlled. If only those people within a ten-mile radius of a plant actually evacuated, some plans might have a chance of working. At Three Mile Island however, according to a study done by two respected professors, not only did those who were told to leave their home (about 3445 people) evacuate, but so did many others. In fact, the actual evacuation numbered as many as 200,000, with evacuations taking place as far as 25 miles from the plant.

The authors followed that report with a study of the area surrounding the Shoreham plant on Long Island,

in which they asked area residents how they would behave in the event of a nuclear emergency.[1] Although only 78 percent of the residents within 10 miles of the plant said they would leave during an accident, nearly 50 percent of those within 25 miles of the plant said they would leave also. According to the authors, "only about one out of eighteen evacuating households would originate from within the zone for which evacuation plans had been put in place." A recent survey conducted near North Carolina's Shearon Harris plant found similar views: 65 percent of those living between 10 and 25 miles from the plant said they would evacuate if those living inside the 10-mile EPZ were told to evacuate.

The implications of this so-called "evacuation shadow" are simple: there would be far more people and traffic on the roads than current emergency plans take into account. This could lead to much longer evacuation times than now believed, which in turn could cause higher casualties among those closest to the reactor. EPZs must be large enough to account for this phenomenon.

Emergency Notification

A frequent deficiency in emergency plans is the inability of a utility to quickly notify residents in the event of an accident. Recently, a NRC Atomic Safety and Licensing board holding hearings at the Shearon Harris plant told the NRC that a potential generic defect exists with the siren system used for early notification at most plants. Apparently, such systems have never been tested at night, when in the summer air conditioning is likely to be on, and in the winter, when windows are likely to be closed with the heat turned on. The Board said its findings indicated that the sirens were unlikely to be heard in much of the EPZ under such conditions. A 1982 NRC study also reported that siren systems are not effective at night during adverse weather. One possible solution would be to place a secondary notification system, such as tone alert radios, inside the homes and workplaces within the EPZ.

There are many other problems with individual evacuation plans. A few examples:

- Utilities are only required to list what medical services might be available; they are not required to determine that those medical services are adequate to treat the population. In fact, as Chernobyl demonstrated, it would take a massive, multinational effort to provide medical assistance to a large number of radiation victims.
- There is often a reliance on volunteers to enter high radiation zones to evacuate school chil-

dren, invalids, and others. Yet rarely is there proof that such volunteers are available and willing. Even contracted employees may not prove reliable in a real emergency. At a recent emergency evacuation drill at New Hampshire's Seabrook plant, for example, there were 111 fewer drivers, 45 fewer buses and 8 fewer vans available than was called for in the emergency plan. But one bus company estimated that no more than 10 percent of its drivers would actually work during a real emergency.

- Local governments are often ill-equipped to handle, or even identify, severe radiation cases. Utility-provided training of local officials and volunteers is often inadequate and designed more to ease fears than to provide knowledge.

A few examples of nuclear plants with high populations within a 50 mile radius:

Beaver Valley (Pittsburgh)	3,599,000
Braidwood (Chicago)	4,332,000
Fermi (Detroit)	4,989,000
Hope Creek and Salem (Wilmington, Philadelphia)	4,709,000
Limerick (Philadelphia)	6,808,000
Dresden (Chicago)	6,600,000
Pilgrim (Boston)	4,200,000
Seabrook (Boston)	3,615,000
Shoreham (Long Island)	5,280,000
Zion (Chicago)	7,100,000
San Onofre (San Diego)	4,900,000
Peach Bottom (Philadelphia)	4,900,000
Indian Point (New York City)	17,000,000

[1]"Evacuation Behavior in Response to Nuclear Power Plant Accidents," Donald J. Zeigler and James H. Johnson, Jr., Professional Geographer, 36(2), 1984, 207-215. Available from NIRS, $1.00.

Toxic Household Trash

RODALE'S PRACTICAL HOMEOWNER, OCTOBER 1987

Environmental disasters can start at home

When health officials discovered that the Biscayne Aquifer, Florida's largest source of freshwater, was slowly being polluted, angry residents were quick to point an accusing finger at industry. But a court inquiry turned up some rude surprises for Florida homeowners. While the grand jury did name several messy industries as contributors to the pollution, it found that "individual and...seemingly minute acts of contamination, such as a single can of paint poured in a single backyard, when multiplied thousands of times over," posed the greatest threat to the water supply.

It's that phrase "multiplied thousands of times over" that hits home. You may not think twice about pouring an old can of turpentine down the toilet or sink until you stop to consider there are 82 million other households in America, and each one contains an estimated three to eight gallons of household hazardous waste. Numerous small acts of carelessness add up.

If you shrug all this off and still think the little bit you toss in the garbage bag or pour in a ditch every now and then can't possibly cause a major environmental disaster, then read on:

- *Seattle, Washington.* City officials concluded that a stream filled with dead fish was the result of a homeowner's careless disposal of old pesticides. One investigator said the problem is "not big bad industry. It's normal, urban runoff; people dumping things down the storm drain."

- *Norman, Oklahoma.* "Undesirable organic chemicals" were found in the groundwater near the city dump. Because the dump accepted no industrial wastes, an inquiry concluded that the pollution came from household products that should not have been thrown in homeowners' trash cans.

- *Canton, Connecticut.* A homeowner's well was contaminated with solvents and chlorinated hydrocarbons after a neighbor used a strong drain and septic tank cleaner. The cleaner flowed through the septic field and poisoned the surrounding drinking water.

According to the Environmental Protection Agency (EPA), there are hundreds of hazardous substances at large in our society. Many can be found in off-the-shelf consumer products that end up gathering dust in laundry rooms, bathrooms, basements and garages. When it's time to toss what's left over, these substances become hazardous wastes.

There are six types of hazardous waste. Two of

these, radioactive and infectious, are rarely found in the home. But the other four types, reactive, corrosive, explosive, and toxic wastes, have become common-place in American homes.

Many types of hazardous waste are too dangerous to flush down the drain or haul away in a garbage truck. Local sewage plants and landfills aren't designed to handle items such as gasoline, creosote, and DDT. Garbage trucks have burned and sewers exploded because people were careless in disposing of flammable materials. Similarly, some homeowners have seen their septic tanks stop functioning and the ground around their home become polluted after they poured toxic chemicals down the drain or toilet.

Smart homeowners can reduce the risk to themselves, to their children, and to others by becoming better consumers. When shopping, be conscientious about reading product labels before you get to the cash register. Whenever possible, choose nonhazardous products to do the job. If you must purchase a hazardous substance, try to buy the smallest quantity required for your needs.

"The less of this stuff homeowners purchase, the less they have to dispose of," says Lisa Kistler, a researcher at the Environmental Hazards Management Institute, in Portsmouth, New Hampshire. Kistler, who helped develop the "Household Hazardous Waste Wheel," a consumer tool that provides information on dozens of hazardous substances, says homeowners often overlook safe alternatives. "People forget that baking soda makes a fine cleanser, that lemon juice mixed with olive oil is a good furniture polish, that you can spray a little soapy water on your plants to control spider mites instead of messing with a harsh insecticide."

Reducing the amount of hazardous substances you purchase is a worthwhile goal, but what about those unwanted reactive, toxic, corrosive, or explosive materials already on the shelf at home?

Recycling can be the solution in some cases, but it often takes some thought. For instance, instead of dumping leftover paint in the trash can, pass it on to a neighbor, a cub scout troop, a school, or a theater company. If you're a home photographer with leftover chemical fixer, call a local photo supply house or studio and ask about recycling; there are firms that will reclaim the silver in the chemical. A homeowner in Seattle who was stranded with a pint jar of mercury ended up selling it to a metal reprocessing firm for $200.

Ultimately, however there are certain types of hazardous wastes, such as weed killers, insecticides, paint strippers, and nickel-cadmium batteries, that should be handed over to professionals for high-temperature incineration or burial in a specially designed hazardous waste landfill.

The trick is locating the organization, agency, or business that runs this kind of hazardous-waste collection program in your area, and this takes some effort. Start by checking the Yellow Pages under "waste disposal." You can also call your state environmental protection agency office or health department for suggestions. If you live in rural area, check with the state department of agriculture or your local cooperative extension service agent.

You might also check with your nearby high school or college. Woodworking, auto body, and chemistry classes generate waste that can't be tossed in the trash, so they may be able to suggest disposal options.

If all else fails, consider organizing an area-wide collection project. "In many cases local collection programs get started because a single individual is concerned and is willing to get involved," explains Dana Duxbury, project coordinator at the Center for Environmental Management at Tufts University in Medford, Massachusetts. "It's a movement that's sprung up from the grassroots, a movement that's powered not by government regulation—there are not federal regulations governing household hazardous wastes—but by concerned people who care about the environment."

Collection programs for household hazardous wastes have been carried out in 33 states. Residents bring their wastes to a temporary, centralized collection point, where the toxic trash is tested, sorted, and prepared for transportation to a permanent site or incinerator. Collections are sometimes organized by towns, counties, civic action groups, or progressive-minded businesses. In Massachusetts, where 143 hazardous waste collection days have been held, the League of Women Voters has been the prime mover. In Florida, state environmental quality officials have taken the lead and sponsored collection days in all 66 counties.

Household Waste Disposal

Ideally, any unused quantities of the products listed here should be turned over to a hazardous-waste collection site or the appropriate public health agency. Because that's not always possible, the next-best alternatives are offered. Under no circumstance should any hazardous waste be poured into a storm drain, stream, river, or lake. Also, know your local laws because in some areas it's illegal to pour any hazardous waste—even if it's been diluted—into the sewer system. Above all read and follow label directions, and think before you throw a substance out.

Automotive Supplies

Used motor oil, transmission fluid, kerosene, brake fluid and diesel fuel:

Ask your automotive supply store or gas station if they accept old auto fluids. The highway department or state environmental groups may have information about oil recycling firms. Some auto supply stores sell waste-oil kits containing an absorbent that can be placed in the trash after use.

Antifreeze, coolant:

Check with your local pollution control office first. In some areas it's illegal to pour antifreeze and coolant down the drain, so the fluids must be saved for hazardous-waste collection. Otherwise, flush with lots of water down a drain connected to a sewage treatment plant. Don't pour more than one diluted gallon per week into a septic system.

Auto battery:

Take to a local battery shop for recycling.

Painting, Decorating Supplies

Oil-base paint, enamel, varnish, and other paint that must be cleaned up with thinner:

If air pollution isn't a problem where you live, remove the lid and place the can in a well-ventilated area (preferably outside) away from pets and children. After the contents have solidified, replace the lid and place the can in the trash. If air pollution is a problem in your area, seal the can and hold for hazardous-waste collection.

Paint thinners, turpentine, and mineral spirits:

If used to clean brushes, store in a closed container until particles settle. Filter and store the fluid in a metal or plastic container for reuse and deliver the sludge to a hazardous-waste collection site.

Paint stripper:

If it contains caustics, such as sodium or potassium hydroxide, flush down the drain with lots of water. If it contains methylene chloride, take it to a collection site.

Building, Woodworking Supplies

Broken smoke detectors:

Return to the manufacturer or the retailer because hazardous-waste collection sites won't accept radio-active materials.

Wood preservatives:

If they contain creosote, pentachlorophenol, or arsenic, deliver leftovers to a collection program.

Wood treated with a preservative:

Scrap wood, including sawdust, shouldn't be burned or tossed in the trash. Deliver to a hazardous-waste collection site.

Asbestos:

If it's in pipe insulation or duct wrap, don't attempt to remove it yourself; call a professional because when you sweep or vacuum up the excess, you'll raise clouds of invisible asbestos dust. Household items, such as old ironing board covers, should be put in plastic bags and placed in the trash.

Garden Supplies

Insecticides, fungicides, herbicides (vegetation killer), and poisons for snails, slugs, and rodents:

Give the unused chemicals to a neighbor who can use them or deliver to a hazardous-waste collection program. Some county agricultural extension services will accept unused pesticides, as will some garden clubs, nurseries, botanic gardens, and nature centers. If an insecticide has been sitting on a shelf for a number of years, it may contain ingredients that have since been banned, such as DDT and mirex. If in doubt, take it to a collection site or give to the appropriate public health agency.

Housecleaning, Laundry Supplies

Lye and oven cleaner or drain opener if either contain sodium hydroxide:

If you are connected to a large sewage system, flush down the drain with lots of water. If you have a septic system, either give to someone who can use them or take to a hazardous-waste site.

Rug cleaners and wood-floor polish containing solvents, and furniture polish containing petroleum distillates:

Deliver to a hazardous-waste site.

Cleaners containing ammonia:

Flush down the drain with lots of water, but don't mix with chlorine bleach because a poisonous gas will result.

Spot remover, dry cleaning solvent, moth balls, and shoe dye:

Deliver to a hazardous-waste collection site.

Miscellaneous

Chemistry sets:

Many of the chemicals aren't dangerous, but sorting them requires special knowledge. Take to a hazardous-waste collection site.

Rubber cement thinner:

Deliver to hazardous-waste site.

Aerosol cans:

Only empty cans should be placed in the trash, and never place any aerosol can in a trash compactor.

Rubbing alcohol and cleaners for tile, tub, and shower stall:

Flush down the drain with lots of water.

Disinfectant:

Small amounts can be flushed down the drain with lots of water, unless you're on a septic system. Take industrial-strength disinfectants to a hazardous-waste collection site or agency.

Toilet bowl cleaner (containing caustics such as sodium hydroxide):

Flush down the drain with lots of water. If you have a septic system, take the leftovers to a hazardous-waste site. ❖

Practical Homeowner *Magazine is available for $13.97 a year. Nine issues. To order, call the national toll-free number 1-800-525-0643 or write: 33 E. Minor Street, Emmaus, PA 18098.*

Household Toxics Programs Are Here To Stay

BY ANN H. MATTHEIS
WASTE AGE, APRIL 1988

DESPITE COSTS RANGING as high as $1.00 per pound and low participation rates, these programs are more popular than ever.

In the Sixties, it was "ban the bomb" and "stop the war in Vietnam." The Seventies brought us "Earth Day," long lines at the gas station, and the push for equal rights. What, if any, movement of the current decade will prove as memorable and as historically important?

If you're one of several hundred city, county, or community managers responsible for a household hazardous waste (HHW) collection program, this growing public movement may just win your vote. The most enthusiastic supporters of these programs believe that these community-sponsored events are helping to protect the environment and the public's health by keeping commonly-used household chemicals out of municipal waste disposal facilities.

Criticism of these programs is limited. Someone who seems to be against keeping batteries and toxics out of the landfill would appear to be the type who is against hot dogs, apple pie, and Mom. But the below-the-surface programs serve as little more than an expensive way of dealing with a very small part of the waste disposal problem. Funds needed to develop future wastes disposal facilities are being diverted to one-day collection events that only reach a few people,

they say.

No matter where you may stand on this issue, the HHW collection movement seems to be growing, and will probably be around for quite some time....

Just like the movements of the previous two decades, this one started off small with a lot of good intentions, very little funding, and even less community support. Early programs were plagued with management problems, ineffective publicity campaigns, and community apathy.

But programs pioneers learned from their mistakes. An informal national network of HHW advocates sprouted, its numbers growing, spreading the word from community to community through how-to manuals, pamphlets, and national conferences.

The results, in terms of growth in programs, are impressive: Two HHW programs were held in 1981; at least 288 "Amnesty Days" and other such events were held last year.

A total of 849 local/state HHW programs have been reported, but Dana Duxbury, environmental research analyst at Tufts University, thinks many more have been held. Duxbury has been keeping records on these programs.

Duxbury also notes that the 849 programs include communities that have held more than one collection event. Fairfax County, Va., for instance, has spon-

event in 1984. Other communities, notably San Bernardino and San Francisco, Calif., have established permanent collection sites; still others, like Seattle, Wash., and Cleveland, Ohio, have added HHW collection days to their lists of permanent public services. When all of Duxbury's numbers are tallied by state, an interesting picture of this movement comes through. So far, collection programs have taken place in 43 states. Massachusetts leads with a total of 208 programs, followed by California with 150. Those numbers make sense since both states are densely populated and have passed very strict waste management laws and regulations....

Permanent Efforts Without Sites

Movement leaders have some other ways of providing lower-cost permanent HHW collection programs. One such idea is paint collection days, an area in which San Diego, Calif., has taken the lead. In 1986, the city and county jointly funded 10 paint collection days, using public school parking lots as sites. The paints were mixed together and then reprocessed for sale by a local paint company.

One snag occurred with the program: finding a buyer for the paint. So, says Linda Pratt, a hazardous materials specialist in the San Diego County Department of Health Services, "When we had the paint reprocessed, the colors came out to beige and brown. We chose those colors because we planned to sell the paint to the Navy. But, because the paint didn't meet their specifications, they wouldn't buy it," says Pratt.

After several unsuccessful attempts at selling the paint to local painting contractors and government offices, Pratt says, she decided to auction it off, and "ended up getting $12 a gallon for it!"

In Ingham County, Mich., Robert Ceru runs a permanent HHW collection program on a "shoestring."

With a $10,000 annual budget, the county offers residents a "by appointment only" collection service. Residents calling with a pick-up request are mailed a questionnaire seeking information about the HHW.

Ceru uses the form to control costs. He screens requests, plans collection routes, and organizes loads to prevent accidents. He claims he can keep costs down by recycling much of the waste collected; he's sold the stuff to local theater groups, garden clubs, an auto club, and a low-income housing program.

Legislative Attention on HHW

These are just a few examples of what communities are doing to manage these special hazardous wastes. Are they worth investigating? Well, EPA must think so: In November 1987, it sponsored a three-day West Coast conference on household hazardous wastes, after holding a similar 1 1/2-day event in the Washington, D.C. area in 1986.

And just like its predecessors of the sixties and seventies, the HHW movement is getting a lot of legislative and regulatory attention at the state level. Some states, like Connecticut and Florida, have authorized substantial funds to support local events and programs. Some observers believe household hazardous wastes will also be discussed this year in Washington, as Congress discusses changes that might be made in waste regulation as it considers reauthorization of RCRA.

There seems to be little question, then, that household hazardous waste collection programs have a future. When governments start passing laws and regulations, and spend money to implement them, you can be sure the programs are here to stay. ❖

Waste Age is available for $35 a year. Published monthly. Address: 1730 Rhode Island Avenue, NW, Suite 1000, Washington, D.C. 20036.

Awash in a Sea of Garbage

Practical Steps to Help Stem the Tide of a Growing Crisis

BY NINA KILLHAM

WASHINGTON POST, OCTOBER 19, 1988

"IN THIS WORLD," Benjamin Franklin once said, "nothing is certain but death and taxes."

And garbage.

Face it, human beings are trash machines—incapable of consuming anything without creating a pile of garbage seemingly twice the volume of the product. The United States now produces more than 400,000 tons of trash a day and space is running out—landfills are overflowing, waterways are clogged and beaches are becoming lethal playgrounds.

In 1986, the total solid waste in this country added up to 160 million tons—a full eight percent of which came directly from the kitchen as food waste. There are 16,400 landfills nationally, half of which are expected to close by the year 2000. The one landfill that serves the District, Alexandria, and Fairfax and Arlington Counties, located in Lorton, is expected to be completely filled in the year 2003. Montgomery's landfill in Laytonsville will be filled in May of next year (a new application has been submitted to extend capacity until 2004).

How can you help break the wave of trash?

According to Eric A. Goldstein, senior attorney at Natural Resources Defense Council in New York, three steps can be taken to substantially alleviate food-generated garbage.

First, he says, "to take a nice hunk out of the problem, people should set up composting programs in their backyards." Composting, the degradation process brought about by bacteria and fungus organisms, can effectively turn organic kitchen and garden refuse into a moist black soil conditioner. And, even apartment dwellers with balconies can compost, according to Pegi Ballister-Howells of the Rutgers Cooperative Extension for Middlesex County.

To start composting, the Virginia Cooperative Extension Service suggests laying small twigs or chopped corn stalks down first to aid in aeration and drainage. Then, add both garden (yard waste accounts for a full 18 percent of landfill mass) and kitchen refuse such as husks, coffee grounds, crushed egg shells and canning wastes. Next, add a layer of a nitrogen-rich material such as fresh manure or fresh grass clippings, hay or green weeds (you can buy synthetic nitrogen fertilizer in the form of blood meal or cotton-seed meal). Do not add meat—it will attract rodents. Water the pile to keep the contents moist. If you smell a strong whiff of ammonia, the pile is either too tightly packed or too wet; turn the heap, add some coarser material for aeration and start over. Every three or four weeks, fork over the pile, pushing outside material to the inside so that everything breaks down.

As for the apartment method, here's how: Take a black (color is important because it absorbs heat) plastic bag, fill it three-quarters full with cooking and plant refuse (again only vegetable refuse; meat products could attract rodents), add a nitrogen product and fill with water (it will not decompose if dry). Set out on the balcony—it needs the sunlight—and poke holes in the bag to let the water drain out. "Every once in a while," suggests Ballister-Howells, "when you walk past, you can give the bag a kick, it moves things around and aerates it." If the bag loses its oxygen, she says, anaerobic bacterial will flourish and things will begin to get smelly.

A second trash-reducing idea, according to Goldstein, is to be sensitive to waste in your shopping decisions. According to a report by Worldwatch Institute, an independent nonprofit research organization, packaging accounts for about 30 percent of the weight and 50 percent of the volume of household waste.

"The packaging explosion has gone to far," says Goldstein. "We don't need to wrap something in one layer, then rewrap in a bigger layer, and then put in a plastic bag— this is an area where consumers can make a big difference."

The amount of packaging for food doubled, even tripled, after World War II, says Goldstein. In 1958, the per-capita consumption of packaging material in New York State was 404 pounds per year. By 1986, it had risen to 800 pounds. "Advertisers and marketing experts have assumed, and in some cases it's true that packaging sells." So make sure, he says, that you're buying for the product, not the package.

One obvious answer, says Goldstein, is bulk food shopping. It not only benefits the consumer in price reduction and the environment in waste reduction, he says, it also benefits the producers themselves in overhead reduction—they spend less on packaging, they lose less in the profit corner. "When I'm in the market," says Goldstein, the bulk-food aisle is "the most heavily populated aisle—as the 1990s approach that will be an important trend emerging."

According to a May 1987 article in *Supermarket*

Business News, bulk food is, in fact, declining, as many supermarkets cut back on the number of items available or cut out the program completely. Safeway, which started its bulk-food program in 1983, sees no great increase or decrease in the amount of people who shop from the bins. It has what Ann Cockrell of Safeway calls a stabilized customer base.

A third contribution: Bring a satchel. Follow European shopping fashion and take your own bag to the store. "It's stupid when you go to get something that is already packaged to dump it into another plastic bag. then when you get home you unpack bags, and they're all strewn all over the kitchen, you realize that the products you bought make up just under half of the total volume."

Other shopping decisions might include insisting on recyclable cardboard (rather than Styrofoam) egg cartons, reaching for milk in the paper (rather than plastic) cartons and asking for paper bags when checking out.

Currently both Safeway and Giant offer the choice of paper or plastic. At Safeway in the second quarter of 1988, customers chose plastic over paper three to one. In an effort to do its bit for the environment, Safeway is testing at its Vancouver stores a photodegradable plastic bag that breaks down into fragments when exposed to light and eventually reduces to carbon monoxide and water.

Giant places its plastic/paper bag ratio at 60/40 in favor of plastic. It has not yet incorporated a photodegradable bag in its stores, preferring for the moment to research bags that can decompose without sunlight—something Mark Roeder of Giant says will be more useful in an area served mostly by landfills.

Recycling should come back full force, says Goldstein, to help combat the trash problem. And according to a national poll of 1,000 adults taken by Penn and Schoen Associates, 91 percent said they would be willing to pay a few cents more for products in recyclable or biodegradable material.

"In World War II, we had a lot more recycling because of the need to preserve precious metals for the war." Then as materials returned to abundance, we became extravagant, Goldstein noted. "The legacy of the post-war era, while being a very productive era for us, is that we became a throw-away society."

Olga Sweeney of U.S. Recycling Centers Inc., in Rockville and Hagerstown, says many residents have gotten the message. When she opened the center in 1986 in Rockville, 40 people showing up on Saturdays was considered a good day. In the past few months, the number of people has quadrupled. "Recycling is very suddenly big business. And I think it's because that garbage barge from New York scared a lot of people," she said. (Call your local extension service or look in your local yellow pages for nearby recycling centers.)

Items to separate from your garbage and recycle include glass bottles and jars, aluminum beverage cans, tin foil, aluminum pie plates from frozen foods, cardboard, brown paper bags and newspaper. Recycling of paper is especially important as it is the largest single component in landfill waste—taking up 36 percent.

A word about plastic.

It makes up seven percent of the municipal solid waste. And only one percent of it is currently being recycled. The most widely recycled plastic product is the soft drink container—20 percent of which is being recycled. In an attempt to reduce plastic waste in New York, Gov. Mario Cuomo declared in March that his administration would begin phasing out the use of Styrofoam cups and other unbiodegradable plastic food containers at several of the state parks and beaches.

Of course, food packaging is not all bad—much of it has allowed us longer storage time on certain foods. Says Lenus Barnes, chief of the Solid Waste Regulation and Collection Section of Montgomery County, "I remember when there wasn't a lot of packaging, when my mother would have to throw out things that nowadays we could have stored a longer period of time and have consumed."

But gone are the days of the American Indian who used every last scrap of the buffalo he killed.

Says Goldstein, "Now garbage is excessive and a very expensive proposition. Disposal fees have in some cases doubled because we are running out of landfill space. Incinerators have their own environmental problems and are very expensive—in fact, sometimes the single most expensive decision a community will have to make."

What makes economic and environmental sense in the end, concludes Goldstein, is recycling and waste reduction through responsible buying. ❖

The Home Electrical System
Product Safety Fact Sheet
U.S. CONSUMER PRODUCT SAFETY COMMISSION, DECEMBER 1982

WITHIN YOUR HOME'S electrical system there could be a threat of FIRE! Approximately 60,000 residential fires[1] in 1981 began in the electrical distribution system. The U.S. Consumer Product Safety Commission estimates that about 500 deaths—and another 5,800 injuries—occurred from home electrical system fires.

The electrical distribution system includes the circuit wiring, lighting fixtures, fuses or circuit breakers, receptacles, switches, cords and plugs. When a part of this network fails or is misused, a fire may result.

Need for Inspection of the Electrical System

Wiring and other electrical equipment sometimes does not last the life of the house. There are signs that can indicate your electrical system is beginning to fail, signs such as lights dimming, and fuses blowing or circuit breakers tripping frequently. Other signs often reported by consumers with "old technology" aluminum-wired branch circuits include electric sparks and "glowing" from receptacles, lights flickering, and overheated outlets. These signs are symptoms of a potential hazard.

If any of these signs occur, or if your system has not been inspected for a number of years, CPSC recommends that you have either a licensed electrician or your local power company (if it makes inspections) evaluate the condition of your entire electrical system. Some problems, such as loose connections at receptacles, may be apparent only to a professional. Don't wait until such conditions cause a fire.

The Consumer Product Safety Commission advises that fires can occur in the following home situations:

Deteriorated Wiring

Over the years, the insulation on wiring can deteriorate or be worn away, exposing wires that carry the electric current. You should ask the electrician to look for deteriorated wiring during an inspection.

Electrical appliance cords and extension cords can become damaged or overheat when they are placed under carpeting or furniture, or coiled up during use. Check your appliance and extension cords and replace any that are damaged.

Using Bulbs of Too High a Wattage

Called over-lamping, the use of bulbs of higher wattage than is recommended in light fixtures and lamps may lead to fires through overheating. A homeowner can easily correct over-lamping. If the recommended wattage is not printed on the light fixture, a rule-of-thumb is to use bulbs no higher than 60-watts.

Overfusing

Fuses and circuit breakers are intended to warn when you are overloading the circuit (that is, using so many appliances that their combined current exceeds the rated value of the fuse or circuit breaker) by blowing the fuse or opening the circuit breaker. Thus the power is shut off to the overloaded circuit.

Most fuse boxes are not labeled as to what size fuse to use. In older homes especially, people tend to substitute fuses rated as high as 30 amperes when the 15 ampere size should be used. This is called overfusing.

If you use a higher amperage fuse or circuit breaker than is called for, excessive current will continue to flow, causing the circuit to overheat, which can lead to an electrical fire.

Only a trained person, such as an electrician, can determine which fuse rating is right for your circuit. Branch circuits in most homes are worked with #12 or #14 copper wire; #14 copper wire should be fused with 15 amperes, and #12 copper wire with 20 amperes.

Many older homes use Edison-base fuses, which have the same size base for various amperage fuses, which allows higher rated fuses of up to 30 amperes to be substituted for lower amperage fuses. To prevent overfusing, it is recommended that this type of fuse be replaced with "S"-type, noninterchangeable fuses. Once a qualified person has determined the proper size fuse for the circuit, an appropriate adapter is screwed into the fuse holder, which will then accept only the proper size "S"-type fuse.

Like over-lamping, overfusing is easy to correct once a qualified person has inspected your electrical system and advised you which rating of fuse or circuit breaker is required.

Aluminum Wiring

Homes built between 1965 and 1972, or additions to homes or wiring systems made during that time, may have been wired with "old technology" aluminum wire. Dangerous overheating and fire may occur where this type of aluminum wire connects to an outlet or switch even though nothing is plugged into the

outlet. Signs of trouble with "old technology" aluminum wiring are:
- cover plates on switches and outlets which are warm or hot to the touch
- smoke coming from outlets or switches
- sparks or arcing at switches and outlets
- strange odors, especially the smell of burning plastic, near outlets or switches
- lights which flicker periodically
- outlets, lights, or entire circuits which fail to work.

If a circuit or outlet shows any of these trouble signs, turn off the power to the circuit by either switching off the circuit breaker or unscrewing the fuse. Then call an electrician to inspect and repair the wiring. It would be extremely dangerous for an untrained homeowner to inspect or adjust wiring because of the risk of electric shock or of making an improper repair.

Information on how to obtain the CPSC booklet on "old technology" aluminum wiring appears at the end of this fact sheet.

Summary

Remember, conditions created by deterioration of wire insulation, over-lamping, and overfusing may lead to a fire. If your home wiring system has not been inspected for safety hazards, consider having an electrician or your local power company come in and check your system to make sure it is in safe working condition. You should not attempt to repair any wiring defects yourself.

But you can create a safer home when you:
1. Use only the recommended amperage fuse or circuit breaker
2. Never overload a wall receptacle with too many appliances
3. Use the recommended wattage bulbs.
4. Replace or repair extension and appliance cords at the first sign of wear or damage.
5. Avoid coiling appliance or extension cords during use to prevent possible overheating of the cord.
6. Avoid placing cords under carpets or furniture.
7. Avoid overloading extension cords.

[1]Estimated by applying the proportion of electrical distribution system fires reported to the United States Fire Administration from four states to the estimate of 797,000 residential fires nationwide derived by the National Fire Protection Association. ❖

Extension Cords and Wall Outlets
Product Safety Fact Sheet
U.S. CONSUMER PRODUCT SAFETY COMMISSION, DECEMBER 1982

THE U.S. CONSUMER Product Safety Commission estimates that approximately 4,000 injuries caused by electrical extension cords were treated in hospital emergency rooms in 1981. About one fifth of the injuries involve children under age ten (most under five). Electrical burns to the mouth are the most common injury and the one most frequently suffered by younger children.

In addition, CPSC estimates that about 7,400 fires originated in extension cords in 1979. These fires resulted in 80 deaths and 260 injuries. Common causes of such fires are short circuits and the overloading, damage and misuse of extension cords.

CPSC injury investigation reports reveal the following examples of the kinds of accidents which occur to consumers using electrical extension cords:
- Fifteen-month old Cindy put an extension cord in her mouth and suffered an electrical burn. She required surgery.
- Six-year-old Johnny disconnected a record player from an extension cord by putting the record player plug in his mouth and pulling on the extension cord with his hands. As the two plugs separated, Johnny's lips were burned by the plug's prongs.
- Two young children were injured in a fire caused by an overloaded extension cord in the family's home. A lamp, a TV set, and an electric heater had all been plugged into a single light-duty extension cord.
- An extension cord with an exposed wire was on the floor behind a chair when 23-month-old Mike crawled after the family cat. He touched the exposed wire and was electrocuted.
- A small child pulled an extension cord connected to a coffee pot, causing the pot to tip

over and spill the hot coffee on her. She suffered first degree burns on her leg.

The above incidents illustrate the major accident patterns associated with extension cords. They are: children putting extension cords in their mouths; overloaded cords; worn or damaged cords; and pulling or tripping over cords.

In most areas, electrical contractors are required to follow either the National Electrical Code (NEC) or local electrical codes. The current NEC requires that electrical outlets be not more than 12 feet apart along a wall. Therefore, no point along a wall should be more than six feet from an outlet, thus reducing the need for multiple extension cords.

The current NEC also provides that portable and other types of lamps be equipped with polarized or grounding type plugs. (Polarized plugs have one blade slightly wider than the other and can only be inserted one way into the receptacle.) Polarization and grounding ensure that the part of a lamp into which the light bulb is inserted is connected to the neutral, or grounded, side of the circuit, thereby reducing the risk of shock or electrocution. Such lamps should only be used with polarized or grounded extension cords.

15 Tips on Electrical Safety in Your Home

1. When buying electrical equipment or appliances, always look for the Underwriters Laboratories seal of approval and make sure it applies to the entire appliance, not just the plug or cord.
2. Do not drape electrical cords or wire over radiators or pipes or other metal objects.
3. When working outside, avoid contact with overhead power lines or exposed wires. Be careful when installing CB antennas or towers. Improperly installed antennas might topple and cause power outages, injuries and even death.
4. Check all extension and appliance cords frequently to be sure they are not worn or frayed. If they are, replace them immediately. Don't patch a broken cord.
5. Do not place electrical cords so they run through doorways or under carpets.
6. Do not plug power tools or heavy appliances into a lamp socket. Plug them into a wall outlet. Lamp cords are not made to carry a heavy electrical load.
7. Do not pull a plug from a wall outlet by the cord. Grasp the plug itself and pull it straight out.
8. Do not leave irons or other heating appliances plugged in when not in use or when no one is present.
9. If you have doubts about appliance grounding, cord sizes, or other electrical questions, check with a licensed electrician.
10. Fly kites only in open fields, away from electric wires. Do not use wire, metal or wet string on a kite. If your kite catches in a wire or on a high pole, don't try to remove it—call your electric utility. Don't use metal in making a kite. Don't fly kites on or near a public highway. Don't fly a kite in wet or stormy weather.
11. Be sure tools and appliances are properly grounded. A three-prong plug used in a two-wire receptacle must have an adapter. Connect the "pigtail" wire on the adapter to the metal screw on the outlet cover plate to get grounding protection. Never use a tool or appliance with a two-wire connection outdoors or in a damp location.
12. Water conducts electricity. Be careful when you are using electrical appliances near water. Do not touch an electrical switch while your hands are damp. No electrical cord or appliance should be handled while in water.
13. Improper handling of electrical appliances can cause fire. Don't let wires overheat. Disconnect if there are any sparks. All electrical wires are designed to carry only a certain amount of electricity. Overloading them causes them to overheat, gradually destroys the insulation, and can create a hazard. Turn off any appliance that smokes or stops running.
14. To prevent overheating, make sure the cord is large enough to carry the electricity necessary to operate the tool or appliance. Heavy duty extension cords should be used with portable tools and other heavy duty appliances—never ordinary lamp cords.
15. Never touch, kick, pull or attempt to pick up a fallen wire. Even a telephone wire could be deadly if tangled with a power line some distance away. Notify your electric utility and keep other people away until utility repair people arrive. ❖

Voluntary safety standards, such as those of Underwriters Laboratories Inc. (UL), now require that general-use extension cords have safety closures, warning labels, current rating information and other features for the protection of children and consumers.

CPSC offers the following suggestions for the purchase of extension cords:

- Use extension cords only when necessary.
- Use polarized extension cords with polarized appliances.
- Make sure cords do not dangle from counter and table tops where they can be pulled or tripped over.
- Buy and use extension cords with safety closures and other safety features.
- On cords without safety closures, cover any unused outlets with electrical tape or with plastic safety caps to prevent the possibility of a child's making contact with the electric current.
- Insert plugs fully so that no part of the prongs are exposed when the extension cord is in use.
- Discard any old and cracked, or worn and damaged, extension cords.
- When disconnecting cords, pull on the plug, rather than on the cord, to avoid damaging connections.
- Teach children not to play with plugs and outlets and that they should never attempt to unplug cords.
- Use only 3-wire extension cords for appliances with 3-prong plugs. Never cut off the third (round or U-shaped) prong which is a safety feature designed to prevent the risk of shock or electrocution.
- Inspect frequently at locations where a bed, or other furniture, may be pushed against the wall and against the cord where it is joined to the plug. Special angle plugs are available for use at such locations.
- Watch for any signs of damage to the cord insulation or indication of possible short circuiting.
- Don't place extension cords under rugs or carpets or in any areas where they could be damaged by the weight of heavy furniture or foot traffic.
- Don't use staples or nails to attach extension cords to a baseboard or to other surfaces. This could damage the cords and present a fire or shock hazard.
- Don't overload light duty extension cords by plugging in appliances which draw a total of more watts than the rating of the cord (usually 1250 watts).
- Use special, heavy duty extension cords for high wattage appliances, such as air conditioners and freezers.
- With outdoor tools and appliances, use only outdoor extension cords.

Wall Outlets

Electrical wall outlets also may present a hazard to young children. Most outlets are installed close to the floor within easy reach of crawling youngsters. If children insert metal objects into empty outlets, they may suffer serious burns and severe, possibly fatal, electrical shocks.

Some older houses have wall outlets which only accept plugs with two blades. When using grounding (3-blade) plugs, be sure to use properly installed adapters or have the receptacle replaced with a 3-hole grounding receptacle.

Receptacles with poor internal connections may become overheated. Be careful not to allow receptacles to be covered by draperies, furniture or other items.

A primary rule for reducing the number of accidents involving wall outlets is: if an outlet is not in use, do not leave it exposed.

- To protect young children, insert a plastic safety cap into any unused outlet. Such caps can be purchased at drug, hardware and variety stores.
- Or use rotary cap outlets, which have caps that must be rotated 90 degrees in order to expose the outlet's slots.
- Be sure that a plug is inserted completely into the outlet with no part of its prongs exposed. A poor contact at the wall outlet may cause overheating of the plug and the outlet.
- Never leave an unused extension cord or appliance cord plugged into wall outlets. They present an electrical hazard, particularly to small children. ❖

Kitchen Safety—Advice from the Experts

BY ANN ARNOTT
MCCALL'S, MARCH 1988

HOW CAN YOU make your kitchen a safer place? Here's what 11 food and equipment professionals had to say:

Nancy Nevin, Manager of Consumer Communications, The Quaker Oats Company

- "No bare feet in the kitchen," says Nevin. Shoes protect feet from hot-liquid spills and broken glass.
- A sharp knife is safer than a dull knife. You have to exert more pressure to get a dull blade to cut, thereby increasing the risk of the knife slipping."

Joy Schrage, general manager of Appliance Information Service, Whirlpool Corporation

- "When unloading your dishwasher right after the cycle has ended, don't reach down to retrieve a utensil that's fallen to the bottom; you might touch the heating element and be burned. Instead, allow time for the element to cool."

Richard Vergili, Food Sanitation/Safety Instructor, The Culinary Institute of America

- "Burns are a common injury when people are working together in the kitchen. After all, hot metal looks like cold metal, and someone will often pick up a pot or pan to use or rinse it, not realizing it's burning hot," says Vergili. His advice: Be sure to put hot vessels in the sink or a cleanup area after use.

Linda Smithson, director of the Consumer Center, The Pillsbury Company

- "Don't reuse food packaging designed for the microwave unless the label specifically states that this is safe. A tray designed to crisp a pizza crust, for example, might distort, causing spillage or melting through on second use," explains Smithson.

Annie Watts, director, Borden Test Kitchens and Product Publicity, Borden, Inc.

- "Read through 'old favorite' recipes before preparation, with an eye toward safety. For example, some dessert recipes call for sweetened condensed milk to be heated in its unopened can to caramelize it, but this causes pressure to build up and may result in the can exploding."

Marcia K. Copeland, director, Betty Crocker Food and Publications Center, General Mills, Inc.

- "Don't assume that any item of cookware can withstand tremendous temperature changes. Before taking food from the freezer to the oven, make sure that the container is designed for this type of use. Otherwise, it might warp or break."

Barbara Shinn, director, Creative Food Center and Consumer Nutrition Center, Campbell Soup Company

- "When cooking bacon in the microwave oven, paper plates and toweling are great for easy cleanup, but be sure they're sturdy enough for the job. If they 'give,' hot fat can drip off, causing burns."

Nancy Boyle Levene, manager of Product Development and Training, Sharp Electronics

- "When popping corn in the microwave, use the bag the kernels came in or a utensil designed for this purpose. Popping corn requires alot of energy, enough to break a glass bowl or burn a paper bag.
- Whenever you work with a microwave oven, Levene recommends that you use pot holders.

Sheila Lukins and Julee Rosso, The Silver Palate, a gourmet food company; authors of bestselling cookbooks

- "Wear surgical gloves (available at drugstores) when working with ingredients like chili or jalapeno peppers and even onions. The volatile oils in these foods can be severely irritating if you touch your eyes."

Gretchen Mathers, managing partner of "Gretchen's Of Course," a Seattle-based restaurant and catering company

- "Avoid built-in wood chopping blocks; you just can't clean them well enough," says Mathers. The reason: wood gets deeply scratched, making it difficult to rinse away salmonella organisms, for instance, after you've cut up an uncooked chicken. ❖

McCall's Magazine is available for $9.95 a year. Published monthly. Address: 230 Park Avenue, New York, NY 10169.

Electric Blenders, Mixers, Choppers/Slicers and Grinders
Product Safety Fact Sheet
U.S. CONSUMER PRODUCT SAFETY COMMISSION, APRIL 1979

THE U.S. CONSUMER Product Safety Commission estimates that more than 7,300 persons were treated in hospital emergency rooms last year for injuries associated with electric blenders, mixers, meat and food grinders, choppers and slicers. The following examples of accidents involving these appliances are taken from CPSC injury investigation files:

- Gloria was blending a thick soup when the blender jar came loose from the base. When she grabbed the jar to prevent it from falling, it separated from the collar exposing the rotating blades attached to the motor drive. Her hand was struck by the blades, and she suffered severe cuts on her hand.
- Joanne was stirring a cake mix in her mixer when the blades jammed. She started to push the beaters around, but accidentally turned on the motor. Her thumb was caught in the whirling beaters, and she suffered a contusion and lacerations on the thumb.
- Max was chopping potatoes in his blender. The potatoes at the bottom became slushy, and the blades couldn't reach those at the top. Max poked his fingers into the blender to push down the food when his fingers contacted the blades. The tip of one finger was amputated.

Contact with the blades, beaters, or cutting edges is the major cause of injuries associated with blenders, mixers, grinders, choppers and slicers. The three cases above illustrate the most frequent accident patterns:

- Product defects, such as when a blender jar unscrews in the same direction that the blades rotate so that the jar loosens while in operation and the victim grabs for it.
- Malfunction, such as when the beaters jam or won't insert properly into a mixer and the victim attempts to correct the problem.
- Misuse, when the user puts her finger into or near moving blades or when children play with appliances.

The U.S. Consumer Product Safety Commission offers the following suggestions for the purchase, safer use and maintenance of these kitchen appliances.

1. Purchase
- Look for electric appliances with sturdy construction.
- Check if the appliance stands firmly and level without danger of tipping.
- When buying a blender, look for one in which the jar is screwed to the collar in the same direction that the blades rotate.
- Or, look for a blender that has the blades contained within the jar.

2. Use
- Read the manufacturer's instructions carefully for proper use, care, cleaning and maintenance.
- Always insert the beater into a mixer before plugging it in.
- Do not adjust parts or insert utensils into blades of mixers, blenders or grinders while the motor is on or the power cord plugged in.
- Make sure all parts are connected tightly before operating. For example, see that the jar is tightly screwed onto the base of the blender and that beaters "click" into place on mixers.
- Keep fingers and hands away from the blades of operating appliances at all times.
- Try to avoid handling the appliance with wet hands or when standing on a wet or damp floor.
- Never immerse the motor base of a blender, mixer, chopper/slicer or grinder in water.
- Disconnect appliances by grasping the plug, not the cord. Remove the plug from the wall outlet first, then from the appliance if it is a detachable cord.
- Don't run cords near ovens or other hot objects.
- Unplug the appliance when not in use to prevent danger of fire, electrical shock and injury from moving parts.
- Warn children that these appliances can injure them.

3. Maintenance
- Disconnect electrical appliances before oiling or cleaning.
- Keep parts clean, particularly of food that can rust or clog up the mechanism.
- Immediately replace worn cords and plugs. ❖

SUMMARY
Dangerous Products, Dangerous Places
AN AARP REPORT ON HOME SAFETY AND OLDER CONSUMERS, AMERICAN ASSOCIATION OF RETIRED PERSONS, 1988

WHILE INFORMATION ABOUT the risks of developing cancer, heart disease and other chronic illness is prevalent and available to older persons, not enough attention has been paid to home safety by policymakers or the press. People 65 years of age and older suffer more than half the home injury deaths in this country. Older persons who worry that a heart attack or stroke might debilitate them often fail to realize that they may be involved in an accident involving a consumer product.

Each year, more than 600,000 older persons (age 65 or older) are treated in emergency rooms for injuries caused by products they use every day. They are less likely to sense fire immediately or move quickly, and are more likely to live in older homes which need repairs. The accidental death rate for persons 65 or older is more than three times the rate for the rest of the population.

Following are areas in the home that might cause problems for the older person:

• *Bathtubs and Showers.* A Consumer Product Safety Commission study for the years 1984 and 1985 indicates that bathtubs and showers rank third among products most closely associated with death among persons age 50 or older. Approximately 350 people drown every year in their bathtubs or showers. These accidents can be avoided if designs and fixtures such as grab bars, slip-resistant bathtubs with padding, and bath chairs are installed. Unfortunately, however, such products are not easily available in the marketplace.

• *Farm and Garden Tractors and Riding Mowers.* These vehicles are responsible for hundreds of deaths each year among older persons, when a person is run over, the tractor overturns and pins the driver, the tractor collides with another object, or the victim falls off the tractor. It is unknown whether these accidents are caused by design defects, consumer misuse or a combination of the two.

• *Flammable Clothing.* Out of the approximately 260 annual apparel fire deaths, 75 percent of the victims are age 65 or older. In addition, there are approximately 3,000 injuries from all kinds of clothing fires, with more than one-third of these serious enough to require hospital care. The mortality rate for older persons involved with apparel fires is also high—49 percent for those age 65-80 and 73 percent for those over 80, as opposed to a 17 percent mortality rate for the overall population.

A study prepared for the CPSC indicated that nightwear was involved in slightly more than half of the apparel fires of older persons. The report concluded that increasing the flame resistance of nightwear could eliminate over 50 percent of the injuries and deaths associated with nightwear flammability. This objective may be achieved if the CPSC extends the child sleepwear standard to all adult sleepwear.

• *Hot Water.* If set too high, home water heaters can cause serious or fatal burns. Each year there are more than 150,000 burn cases and 100 associated deaths as a result of hot water. At least one-third of the victims are older persons. By installing protective valves or lowering hot water heating system settings to 120 degrees F, most tap water burns could be eliminated.

Unfortunately, consumers are faced with confusing or non-specific temperature dials. Consumers need additional information on these and other hot water adjustment matters as well as on products (such as protective valves) which interrupt the flow of hot water.

• *Liquified Petroleum Gas Heating Systems.* In 1984, an estimated 20,000 fires were associated with liquified petroleum (LP) gas-fired heating equipment, resulting in an estimated 250 deaths and 900 injuries. LP gas is generally a mixture of propane and butane and is used as a domestic or industrial fuel. Older persons are more at risk of this hazard because they have difficulty in detecting ethyl mercaptan, a commonly used odorant that warns consumers of an LP gas leak. The weight of the LP gas causes it to collect near the floor, further compounding the detection problem. To date, however, research has not identified a stronger odorant which could be more easily detected by older persons. And an LP gas detector capable of warning consumers of leaks has not yet been developed.

• *Ranges.* In 1985, 61 persons age 50 and older died in range-associated accidents and approximately 2,300 persons age 65 and older required emergency room treatment as a result of injuries associated with the kitchen range. Improving the kitchen ventilation system, removing flammable products from stored or hung near a range, and wearing flame-resistant apparel may greatly reduce the frequency of accidents in this area.

• *Stairs/Steps.* In both 1984 and 1985, there were about 120 deaths associated with stairs or steps among older persons age 50 or older, making this area the fourth-ranked hazard associated with deaths among older persons. In addition, there were more than 93,000 injuries associated with stairs or steps that required hospital emergency room treatment among persons age 60 and older.

A CPSC study concluded that this high figure was due to the lack of adequate bone density, in addition to other physical impairments such as vertigo, atherosclerosis and arteriosclerosis. Risk can be reduced in this area with more lighting, better handrails, and improved tread to prevent slipping. Additional research and evaluation on handrail height, shape and distance from the wall, as well as stair tread width and riser height, is needed—changes in building codes nationwide would assure widespread implementation.

• *Swimming Pools.* More than 80 persons age 50 and older die each year in swimming pool-related accidents. A review of swimming pool-related deaths shows drownings of two types: those which occur while people are swimming and those which occur after the victim accidentally falls in the pool. Improved pool alarms, pool edge markings, pool safety education for older persons and lifesaving measures might help reduce the number of accidents.

• *Bicycles.* Approximately 20 persons age 50 and older die on bicycles each year and more than 3,800 persons age 65 or older require hospital emergency room treatment as a result of bicycle-related accidents. Because the older population is growing rapidly, and because bicycles are the consumer product most frequently involved in consumer injury, safety measures might help to counteract the growing accident rate.

Three products can greatly reduce the incidence of injury for older people in their homes.

• *Smoke Detectors.* U.S. Fire Administration statistics show that a working smoke detector in a home lessens the risk of its occupants dying in a fire by 50 percent. Smoke detectors developed for use by people with specific disabilities are also available. Some smoke detectors come with amplifiers, strobe lights or bed vibrators for people with limited hearing. This type of device consists of a smoke detector transmitter, a wrist band one-channel radio receiver and a battery charger. When the detector senses smoke, it sends a signal to the wrist band worn by the hearing-impared person, which in turn causes a warning vibration. The system works when the receiver is within 200 feet of the transmitter detector. This type of smoke detector is designed for the deaf, the hearing impaired or those who are tone deaf and are unable to hear a regular smoke detector signal.

Unfortunately, these alternative methods have not been widely publicized. More public education about smoke detectors is needed, in addition to special projects such as the distribution of free batteries and volunteer projects to assist in installation and maintenance of these devices.

• *Automatic Sprinkler Systems.* Automatic sprinkler systems spray water or other extinguishing fluid in buildings for protection against fires. They are usually triggered by abnormal heat. They are designed to confine the blaze to the room of origin, proving to be about 80 percent effective in protecting property and 95 percent effective in saving lives. There is a need for data that will educate consumers and builders on the importance of sprinkler systems, in addition to providing advice on methods to install the equipment cost effectively.

• *Personal Emergency Response Systems.* (See "Meeting the Need for Security and Independence with Personal Emergency Response Systems (PERS)").

The anticipated growth of the over-60 population during the next 20 years lends additional support to the need for consumer protection legislation. With this growth there will be more people living alone and more people who are frail and less mobile. These consumers will need information and assistance to modify their homes and their behavior in a manner that will increase safety and reduce accidental deaths and injuries. Many older consumers are now changing their daily living habits to reduce the risk of contracting chronic illnesses. They deserve to receive information that will help them adjust their use of hazardous consumer products. With a heightened awareness of these risks, older Americans can then join AARP in demanding from our nation's policymakers and manufacturers the protection they deserve. ❖

SUMMARY

Meeting the Need for Security and Independence with Personal Emergency Response Systems (PERS)

AMERICAN ASSOCIATION OF RETIRED PERSONS, 1987

AS AMERICANS AGE, the need to provide them with security and independence is growing. A major step in this direction has been the Personal Emergency Response System (PERS), a signaling device that summons help when its user is unable to get to a telephone. It is an easy-to-use electronic tool designed to signal a friend, relative or emergency services (police, fire department or ambulance) that help is needed.

Each system has two parts, a small transmitter (portable help button) which the user carries, and a console or receiving base connected to the user's telephone. If a user falls or experiences chest pains, he or she can call for help by simply pressing the transmitter. The portable help button, with an effective range of approximately 200 feet, sends a radio signal from almost anywhere in an average-size home to the console, which automatically calls one or more preselected emergency numbers.

Almost all PERS are programmed to telephone an emergency response center where each incoming call is electronically identified through special coding. Response center staff are then able to quickly review the user's file containing a medical history, list of medications taken, the names and telephone numbers of family, friends and neighbors (responders) who are to be notified in a crisis, local emergency services and other prerecorded information.

The response center will first attempt to determine if there is an emergency and what it is. They will then call the user or, with some systems, communicate directly through a speaker phone built into the console. If they cannot reach the user or determine what is happening, a responder or emergency service are alerted to go to the user's home. In most systems, personnel will monitor the situation until the crisis is resolved. In one system (Lifeline), the console sends a second help-needed message if assistance does not arrive within a specified period of time.

Almost all systems send an electronic message directly to a response center, but two PERS, Newart's Phone Care and AT&T's Emergency Call, relay the help signal through an electronic voice to an emergency response center, emergency services or directly to responders' telephones. Up to five different telephone numbers, which are dialed consecutively, can be programmed by the Phone Care user. An Emergency Call user can program two numbers.

Once the console sends the message, a major concern for any PERS user is what kind of receiving station will be answering the call for help, and whether the service will be prompt and reliable. Some observers have concluded that PERS monitoring is even more important than the equipment itself.

PERS users have two options: Either a local hospital or social service agency maintains a response center, or the PERS manufacturer monitors through a national center. The advantage of the former is that local knowledge is important in some situations. The advantage of the latter is that personnel at national response centers are trained to do nothing but answer PERS users' calls.

A PERS can be rented, purchased or leased, but the consumer almost always pays the charges. A few insurance policies cover these charges when a doctor recommends use of a PERS, and some providers, such as hospitals and social service agencies, subsidize fees for low-income users. However, Medicare will not cover PERS costs.

Rental agreements are available for several years, several months or month-to-month. Read the contract carefully. Rental fees, which include any monitoring costs, can range from $15 to $50 a month, depending on the length of the contract and the type of monitoring services and equipment.

Depending on the type of equipment and additional features (e.g. two-way voice capacity and/or auxiliary transmitter) selected, the purchase price of a PERS can range from $200 to more than $1000. In addition to the purchase price, users may be required to pay a monthly monitoring fee of from $15 to $30. If you decide to lease, review the contract carefully and pay particular attention to any cancellation clauses.

One problem with buying a PERS is the chance that the manufacturer will go out of business. More companies have gotten out of the business than are currently selling. Even AT&T stopped manufacturing their PERS, although they have a large inventory on hand. Should your response center go out of business, it is possible to reprogram some PERS, but it requires contacting a different manufacturer or repair facility and securing another response center. For this reason, AARP recommends that the user rent the PERS for a short period of time rather than buy. ❖

Common Frauds Against Senior Citizens

FACT SHEET, OFFICE OF THE TEXAS ATTORNEY GENERAL

MANY BUSINESSES ARE offering special services to senior citizens. While most of these businesses are legitimate, there are some unscrupulous individuals who attempt to profit at the expense of senior citizens. Some of the common frauds are:

1. Home Improvements (especially those claiming to cut fuel costs)
   - Siding and Storm Windows
   - Insulation
   - Heating and Air Conditioning
   - Roof Repair
2. Business Opportunities (to make money in a short time with little effort)
   - Work at home (envelope stuffing, art work, home assembly)
   - Investment "opportunities"
   - Distributorships and Franchises
3. Self Improvements
   - Dance Studios
   - Health Spas
4. Medical/Health Frauds
   - Miracle drugs or cures
   - Hearing Aids
   - Health Insurance
5. Funeral and Burial
6. Charitable Solicitations

Buying Tips

There are ways you can protect yourself from unscrupulous businesses:

1. Be suspicious of anyone who appears at your door uninvited. Before letting them into your house, ask them to show you identification. If they say they are representing a company, call the company and ask if this person works for them.
2. Don't rush into signing a contract, especially in your home. If the salesman has a really good deal, it will be available tomorrow. If the salesman won't leave a copy of the contract for you or says you have to sign now, it should be a warning to you to not do business with him.
3. Before doing business with any company, call the Better Business Bureau to find out the reputability of the company. It pays to check in advance so you won't have dealings with a known bad business.
4. Shop around before buying. You may be able to save a great deal of money by checking with several companies for price comparisons. This is especially true with home improvements when you are solicited at your home.
5. Deal with established firms. Companies who have been around for years have their reputation at stake and are more likely to satisfactorily take care of complaints.
6. Ask for references of satisfied customers and check them. If the company is unwilling or unable to give references, there may be something they are trying to hide.
7. Remember: Free inspections and expert advice may be available from reliable sources. The fire department may give free advice on smoke detectors, utility companies may inspect your heating and electrical system, and the city or county may have other inspection services at little or no cost.
8. Don't make payment until you are satisfied. Be wary of repairmen who say they need to be paid before the work is completed. Check merchandise such as appliances, televisions, and air conditioners before you pay. If the merchandise is delivered, be sure to see that it works before the delivery person leaves.
9. Be wary of miracle cures or quick ways to make money. Remember that if it sounds too good to be true, it probably is.

By following these few suggestions, you may be giving yourself peace of mind and security. You will be protecting yourself from getting into situations that may be difficult and time consuming to correct.

If you do have problems or more questions, call your local Better Business Bureau or the nearest Attorney General Consumer Protection office in Austin, Dallas, El Paso, Houston, Lubbock, McAllen, or San Antonio. For more consumer information, watch for the Attorney General Consumer Alert in your local newspaper and on radio.

The Attorney General's office is the people's law firm. We're here to help you. ❖

Natural Disasters

BY ALTON L. THYGERSON
SUMMARY OF EXCERPTS FROM THE BOOK, *ACCIDENTS AND DISASTERS*

Natural disasters are the only causes of accidents and property damage which remain completely out of our control. The following information will help you to prepare your home for whatever conditions are most likely to affect your area, and what to do should a flood, tornado, hurricane, earthquake or landslide threaten your life and property.

Floods

Flood warnings are distributed to the public by radio and television and through local government emergency forces. The warning message tells the expected severity of flooding, the affected river, and when and where flooding will begin. Flash flood warnings, the most urgent type of warnings, are also transmitted over public radio, television, and other signals, such as sirens.

If your area is susceptible to floods, you can take several precautions. Find out how many feet your property is above or below possible flood levels. If your property is in danger, locate the closest safe area. Store a stock of food which requires little cooking or refrigeration. Keep a portable radio, emergency cooking equipment, lights, and flashlights in working order. Keep first aid and critical medical supplies at hand. Keep materials like sandbags, plywood, plastic sheeting, and lumber handy for emergency waterproofing.

When you receive a flood warning, store drinking water in closed, clean containers. If flooding is likely, and time permits, move essential items and furniture to upper floors of your house. If forced or advised to leave your home, move to a safe area before access is cut off by flood water. Cut off all electric circuits at the fuse panel or disconnect all electrical appliances. Shut off water service.

Tornadoes and Windstorms

Tornadoes are the most violent of all atmospheric phenomena and, over a small area, the most destructive.

In the event of a tornado warning, you should find an underground shelter or cave, or a substantial steel-framed or reinforced concrete building. If none is available, take cover under heavy furniture on the ground floor in the center of the house, or in a small room on the ground floor that is away from outside walls and windows. When doors and windows on the sides of your house away from the tornado are left open, damage to the building is reduced. But stay away from them to avoid flying debris. Do not remain in a trailer or a mobile home. If it is likely that you are in the path of a tornado, cut off electricity and fuel lines. If you are outside or in open country, drive away from the tornado's path at a 90-degree angle to it. If you don't have time to do this, find the nearest depression, ditch or ravine.

Hurricanes

Hurricanes are tropical cyclones formed over warm ocean areas, in which winds reach speeds of 74 miles per hour or more and blow in a large spiral around a relatively calm center.

As in other weather-related disasters, the vulnerability to hurricane damage of people, property, the economy, and the ecology is far-reaching. Damage to property is caused by rain, flooding and high winds, which uproot trees and shrubs and also do physical damage to the roofs of residential, commercial, and industrial buildings. As a result, rain enters the building and aggravates the damage. Along coastal waterways, storm surges are also responsible for beach erosion and the undermining and collapse of waterfront property.

If you hear a hurricane warning, keep your radio or television on and listen for the latest weather service warnings and advisories. Plan your time before the storm arrives. Waiting until the last minute might mean you'll be marooned. Moor boats securely before storm arrives. Protect windows by boarding them up or covering them with storm shutters or tape. Small windows are threatened by small debris, while large ones may be broken by wind pressure. Secure outdoor objects that might be blown away or uprooted, such as porch furniture, signs, toys, garden tools and garbage cans. Store drinking water in clean, closed containers, such as jugs, bottles or cooking utensils. Your town's water supply may be contaminated by flooding or damaged by the hurricane. Unless advised to evacuate, stay at home if your house is sturdy and on high ground. If it is not or if you live in a mobile home, move to a designated shelter and stay there until the storm is over. Remain indoors during the hurricane. Travel is extremely dangerous when winds and tides are whipping through your area. Beware of the "eye" of the hurricane. Remember, at the other side of the "eye" the winds rise very rapidly to hurricane force, and come from the opposite direction.

Earthquakes

The actual earth movement of an earthquake is seldom a direct cause of death or injury. However, the movement causes buildings to collapse. Most casualties result from falling building materials, toppling furniture, rock slides, sea waves, and fire caused by broken gas lines and spillage of flammable liquids.

If your area is susceptible to earthquakes, check for earthquake hazards in your home. Bolt down or provide other strong support for water heaters and other gas appliances; much fire damage has resulted from toppled appliances and broken gas lines caused by earthquakes. Place large and heavy objects on lower shelves of closets. Brace or anchor high or top-heavy objects. Wire or anchor overhead fixtures. Do not stack glassware or crystal. Slight shaking will topple it.

If you are building a house, follow building codes or other sound practices to reduce earthquake hazards. Build on solid ground or dig down to bedrock. Avoid fill and sedimentary areas as much as possible and do not build below dams that might be destroyed, severely damaged, or breached.

During an earthquake, if you are indoors, watch for falling plaster, bricks, light fixtures and other objects. Watch out for falling bookcases, shelves and other furniture. Stay away from windows, mirrors and chimneys. If in danger, get under a table, desk or bed; in a corner away from windows; or in a strong doorway. Do not run outside. Don't use candles, matches or other open flames during the tremor. Douse all fires.

Landslides

Buildings can be protected from landslide danger by a combination of actions. First, good engineering practices can do much to reduce danger. Methods of slide prevention include removal of unstable materials, selection of a safe slope factor in excavation, provision for both surface, and subsurface drainage between the overburdened material and bedrock, and the installation of retaining walls, bulkheads, pilings and tie rods.

In areas where landslides are expected but for various reasons the above methods are impractical, it may be possible to build debris basins to catch the slide material without damage to property. When the basin becomes full, the material can be removed to provide space to handle future landslides. As the result of 1970 and 1971 brush fires and of the 1971 earthquake, some projects of this nature were undertaken in Southern California.

If Your Home Is Damaged by a Natural Disaster

- Use extreme caution when entering the building, as it may collapse without warning.
- Bring flashlights, rather than lanterns, torches, or lighted cigarettes into the building—there may be leaking gas lines or flammable material.
- Stay away from fallen or damaged wires.
- Check for leaking gas pipes in your home. Do this by smell. If you smell gas, do this:

1. Open all windows and doors;
2. Turn off the main gas valve at the meter;
3. Leave the house immediately;
4. Notify the gas company or the police department;
5. Don't reenter the house until you are told it is safe to do so.

- If any electrical appliances are wet, turn off the main power switch, unplug the appliances and let them dry out.
- Do not use fresh food that has come in contact with flood waters.
- Test drinking water for potability; wells should be pumped out and the water tested before drinking.
- Keep tuned to your radio or television stations for advice and instructions of your local government on: where to go to obtain necessary medical care in your area; where to go for emergency assistance such as housing, clothing, and food; and ways to help yourself and your community recover from the emergency. ❖

Accidents and Disasters was published in 1977 by Prentice Hall, Prentice Hall Building, Sylvan Avenue, Englewood Cliffs, NJ 07632. The book is now out of print, but may be available at your local library.

Make Your Home a Safety Zone

BY TOM SHEALEY

PREVENTION MAGAZINE, NOVEMBER 1985

NO UMPIRE CAN DECIDE if you're safe at home, so you have to catch the "invisible" things around the house that could cause a mishap.

At first glance, it would appear that we are a careless lot. People are accidentally harming, disabling and killing themselves in their home sweet homes at record rates. Yet oddly enough the victims aren't always negligent, unthinking simpletons who beg for accidents by leaving a bar of soap in the bathtub or tossing a loose rug across the stairs. Accidents are befalling careful people who have smoke detectors and sturdy banisters, and who think they've done as much as possible to make their homes safe.

Yet even the most safety-conscious homeowner might be unaware of the more obscure, almost invisible things around the house that aren't readily associated with accidents: aspects of everyday life that could cause serious problems if uncorrected. Sitting in an emergency room waiting to be stitched up is a bit late to realize there should have been a decal or piece of tape at eye level on the sliding glass door you just walked through. And the split second before body meets floor is a poor time to discover there's no grab bar in the bathtub.

The Deceiving Comforts of Home

In the days of dinosaurs, our prehistoric ancestors lived relatively uncluttered lives and mainly had to be careful not to trip over a bone or sit on a spear when puttering around the cave. Today our domiciles are far more complicated, designed for privacy and equipped for our convenience and well-being. Unfortunately, the modern nuances make our lives more hazardous. Preventable incidents involving heating systems, bathing facilities, glass windows, doors, electricity, stairs and a variety of seemingly innocent items, such as automatic garage-door openers are contributing to the rising accident statistics. The National Safety Council reports that an estimated 24.8 million people were injured in their homes in 1984. Accidental deaths in the home increased two percent over 1983, and disabling injuries were up one percent.

"Most people aren't knowledgeable about the accident possibilities around their own houses," says Frank Vilardo, Dr.P.H., of the Indiana University Institute for Research and Public Safety, Bloomington. "People tend to think more about safety in the workplace because there are regulations that must be enforced and supervisors to make sure the standards are followed. When they get home they relax and feel safe in a comfortable environment where they don't feel they have to look for potential accidents."

While some adults apparently feel indestructible in their homes, many realize that their children and grandchildren are anything but superhuman. As a result, great strides have been made to make houses safe for youngsters, says Joseph Greensher, M.D., chairman of the American Academy of Pediatrics Committee on Accident and Poison Prevention.

"The change came about when we did away with the diseases that were claiming so many kids and people realized that accidents were killing children," he says. "The concept of death has also changed. People used to believe that when a person died from an accident, it was an act of God and there was nothing that could be done. Now they realize they have more control over many aspects of everyday life and can do things to reduce the risks."

Avoiding the Falls

Falls are the leading cause of accidental deaths in the home, and head the list of accidents experienced by older adults, according to National Safety Council statistics. More than 80 percent of those killed by falls each year are over 65.

Most falls take place on stairs or steps, statistics show. Many trips and slips occur where there are only a few steps, such as on decks or walkways. Slight, abrupt elevation changes often go unnoticed, and the unexpected rise can throw a person off balance. In older houses, installing a slight ramp with a slip-resistant surface would remove the accident potential.

Stairs inside the house are safer if covered with nonskid material, such as rubber mats or treads. If stairs are carpeted, shag and deep-pile types reduce the width of each step and could make for unsure footing. Carpets and rugs with rich patterns can mask the edge of the steps and make it hard to tell where one ends and another begins.

"Handrails are essential where there are more than three steps, and they should be rounded for the best possible grip," says Ravi Waldon, director of the American Institute of Architects housing program, Washington, D.C. It's also a good idea to install a handrail about two feet above the steps for children.

Banisters can be dangerous for young children.

Since an inquisitive child will often try to stick his head through a railing, openings should be no more than five inches. A similar hazard occurs when a child gets his head caught beneath the bottom rail of a banister that stops a few inches from the floor. One youngster was severely injured when he slid on a marble floor in an East Coast concert hall and jammed his head between the floor and rail. The accident pointed to a safety hazard that had gone unnoticed and codes were modified to alert builders to the potential problem.

Another treacherous area is the bathroom, where most accidents occur when entering or leaving the tub, or while changing positions. The U.S. Department of Commerce estimates that bathtub and shower accidents cost an estimated $78.5 million annually in medical bills and lost work time.

Tubs should have nonslip or textured bottoms or a bath mat. Firm, unbreakable grab bars should be in the bathing area. Don't make the mistake of thinking that a towel rack or soap dish screwed into the wall will stop a fall.

The bathroom floor should also have a nonskid surface, or at least rugs to soak up the inevitable puddles.

To lessen the impact of a fall add-on edges made of a resilient material can be bought or designed for tubs, and a soft seat and cover can be installed on toilets. When designing a house, recessing the soap dish, faucet and controls could reduce the severity of a fall.

Portals to Accidents

Doors and windows that separate the outside from the inside are another source of potential accidents. Garage doors are especially hazardous to both young and old, and even safety experts aren't immune to accidents in the garage as Dr. Vilardo learned.

"I had thought about calling a repairman to fix a spring on my garage door, but then decided I'd save the money and do it myself," he says. "It seemed simple enough, but when I released the spring, there was a lot of tension and it caught my hand between the door and the spring.

"This is a typical approach to a problem around the house. People usually don't have the tools or knowledge to fix something, but they cheat and get away with it a few times. They keep on cheating until they get careless and have an accident. I saved $30 in repair bills but lost $500 in medical expenses and aggravation."

Electric garage-door openers can also be hazardous, especially to children. Two Minnesota children were killed in separate incidents when they were caught beneath closing doors. While newer models spot or reverse the door when an object is encountered,

older models may not have the safety feature, which means the controls should be out of reach of young hands or locked inside the car.

If you open your garage door by hand and it's the type with several folding sections, handles should be on each section so fingers won't be mashed while closing.

Elsewhere in the house, double-action swinging doors should have padding at the doorjamb to minimize injury to pinched fingers. Thresholds on inside doors can cause stumbles, and should be removed unless needed to maintain a level walking surface.

Window walls or sliding glass doors are aesthetically pleasing, but should consist of safety glass, which may be missing in older homes. To keep a child from plunging through the glass, a sill or other guard, such as a planter, decorative railing or furniture, should stretch across the glass about 12 inches above floor level.

Screens can keep bugs out but don't guarantee that children will stay in, so don't arrange furniture in such a way that youngsters can stand in windows. Metal locks can be installed to limit the height a window can be opened. To prevent fingers from being mashed, second stops can be installed.

A Shockingly Current Problem

You turn on electricity with the flip of a switch, forgetting how easily it can turn you on, usually when there's water around.

Electrical hazards are an unending source of danger in twentieth-century bathrooms, which are stocked with hair dryers, razors, curlers, radios, hot lather dispensers and even televisions and tape players. Electrocutions can occur when people in the tub or still wet come in contact with a switch or appliance. The safest preventives are to ensure that electrical apparatuses can't reach the tub, sink, toilet or shower, and that the devices are unplugged when not in use.

Since it's probably impossible to remove all electrical items from the bathroom, ground fault circuit interrupters should be wired into circuits at panel boxes or used to replace ordinary outlets. A GFCI prevents shock by monitoring circuits and shutting off power if leakage to another ground, or source, is detected. Many local building codes now require GFCIs for outdoor receptacles, bathrooms, garages and other applications. Older houses are rarely equipped with GFCIs and an electrician should be contacted about installation. In newer houses, check outlets or the circuit breaker box for little red test buttons that pop out when there's a problem with the circuit.

In bathrooms in many older homes, the light over the sink is turned on by yanking a chain. If a short develops, touching the chain and the metal faucet can

put a person in the middle of an electrical circuit, since the body will lead the charge to the nearest ground—the faucet. To prevent a shock, an insulating link should be installed near the socket, or the chain should be replaced with some type of nonconductive material, such as cord.

Some Like It Hot

The household heating system usually only comes to mind when temperatures drop, but it should be checked before each winter. Homeowners should know where fuel cutoffs are in case of emergency, and fuel lines shouldn't extend into areas where the lines can be easily damaged.

Any stationary fuel-consuming heating device should be vented to the outside, and the vent system should be checked annually for leaks. Older units may require more frequent inspections. The National Safety Council reports that gas heating devices account for 290 of the estimated 340 carbon-monoxide poisoning deaths each year. In spaces that are well insulated, fairly airtight and heated, ventilate by opening a window at least one-half inch.

If a fireplace is used for either heat or aesthetics, the hearth should extend at least 21 to 24 inches into the room to prevent sparks from igniting the rug or nearby materials. Flame-retardant pads can be added if necessary. Outside, the chimney should be in good repair. For a good draft, most codes require that the chimney be at least two feet taller than any point on the roof that is 10 feet or less away horizontally; otherwise, smoke may be sucked into the house. Rather than hiring a brick mason, prefabricated metal chimney extensions can be purchased.

It may be impossible to guarantee a home free of potential accidents since there will always be things to look out for. With your house in mind, consider the following:

• Showers should be equipped with temperature-regulating valves to keep the water in the bath a constant temperature even when the kitchen faucet is turned on to wash potatoes, for example. Otherwise scalds can occur when the chilly bather turns up the hot water just before the potato washer finishes downstairs.
• Cabinet drawers should have catches so they won't pull all the way out and drop on toes.
• Clothes hooks on the back of bathroom and bedroom doors should be above eye level.

Rounded edges on cabinets and furniture are more difficult for the carpenter, "but they are safer," says Jim Presswood, occupational safety and fire-protection officer, University of Texas Health Science Center, Dallas. "You'll get bruised if you hit a rounded edge, but chances are you won't be disabled or killed."

"Accident prevention around the home requires a constant effort because there are so many hidden hazards," says Dr. Vilardo. "There's not the same degree of concern for home safety like there is for highway safety, so it's up to the individual homeowner to be aware that there are things that can be done to make a house safer." ❖

Prevention Magazine *is available for $13.97 a year. Published monthly. Address: 33 E. Minor Street, Emmaus, PA 18049.*

Reducing Noise In and Outside the Home
BY JOHN WARDE
THE NEW YORK TIMES, DECEMBER 22, 1988

REDUCING THE AMOUNT of noise in a house, whether generated from within or from outside, can be challenging. Moderate success can often be achieved rather easily and without great expense. But complete soundproofing is difficult and usually requires costly remodeling.

There are three broad methods of reducing household noise: eliminating the source; containing the sound (reducing sound transmission) and reducing sound reception.

As an example of the first method, noise from a vibrating washing machine can be reduced by overhauling the appliance—tightening loose fasteners and lubricating moving parts.

An example of containing the sound would be placing the appliance on rubber blocks, away from walls, to contain vibration, and paneling the room with sound-absorbent tile or other sound-deadening material.

An example of reducing sound reception would be

erecting sound-deflecting walls in other parts of the house to block the passage of sound from the laundry.

Usually there are only a few noises in a home that can be effectively reduced or eliminated by the first method. These include sounds generated by appliances like washers and dryers, dishwashers, refrigerators and air-conditioners, all of which can be regularly maintained to keep them running quietly, as well as noises from plumbing fixtures and heating pipes.

Plumbing and heating noises generally develop when internal parts wear, air becomes trapped in the system or pipes loosen from the brackets securing them to the building structure. There are ways to silence these noises, and many are easy enough for amateurs to undertake. For professional services or advice, consult a licensed plumbing or heating contractor.

Because most household sounds—conversation, footsteps, normal appliance operation—are unpreventable, containing or limiting the transmission of sound is the more usual method. Look for ways to surround sound-producing items with materials that absorb noise, and try to separate the items from hard, resonant surfaces like walls, ceilings and floors, which can amplify and transmit sound.

Line the walls of rooms where sound is generated with soft or textured surfaces: filled bookcases, textile wall hangings like rugs or thick draperies, and, of course, acoustical tile or cork panels sold at home centers for soundproofing. Other items that will absorb sound are acoustical ceiling tiles, thick floor carpeting with foam or other resilient padding, and upholstered furniture.

Beneath typewriters, computer printers and other noisy office equipment, place rubber vibration-dampening mats, available at office supply and computer stores. Position appliances and vibration-producing items like stereo speakers on resilient mats, and keep them from making direct contact with walls.

These strategies work best to reduce noise levels within the room in which the sound is created. Overall household noise also decreases, because much of the sound emanating from sources is absorbed or prevented from intensifying.

But encapsulating a room with sound-absorbent materials will not prevent noise from entering. Shielding a room against incoming sound requires reducing sound reception through air. It is important to seal any openings that admit air through walls, floors and ceilings, using caulking compound, fiberglass insulation or weatherstripping. Fiberglass insulation strategies work best to revise levels within the room in which the sound is created. Overall bold noise also decreases, because much of the sound emanating from sources is absorbed or prevented from intensifying.

Hollow-core doors filled with material that absorbs and deflects sound are available. Storm doors and windows create a sound-absorbing air space on their exterior sides that reduces the effect of sound waves. Soundproofing can also be achieved by hanging heavy draperies in front of windows.

The best soundproofing is obtained through special construction methods. The simplest way to increase the sound resistance of walls is to cover them with an extra layer of wallboard five-eights of an inch thick, preferably on both sides. More effective, but requiring more effort, is removing the original wallboard layer or layers, fastening resilient metal channel strips (available at building-supply stores) to the framing members and then attaching one or two layers of new wallboard to the strips.

Sound-deadening board manufactured for the purpose can be used instead of the first layers of wallboard. The metal strips interrupt the passage of vibrations between the wall surface and the framing, preventing sound from passing through the wall completely. To prevent noise from passing through a floor into a room below, the only effective solution is to rebuild the floor with a layer of sound-deadening board between the sub-floor and the framing. Unless this is done, soundproofing techniques in the ceiling will have only a moderate effect.

But a "dropped" ceiling consisting of acoustical tile suspended from a hanging framework will muffle noise from above considerably, especially if the space above the tile is filled with fiberglass insulation. Also reasonably effective is rebuilding the ceiling to incorporate resilient metal channel strips as described for walls. ❖

Section Two
INDOOR AIR POLLUTION

THE EMERGENCE OF chemically sensitive people into self-help and advocacy groups, together with greater media coverage of asbestos, lead, radon, formaldehyde and pesticide contamination of the home, are accelerating development of home detection kits, more involvement by local public health departments, stronger regulations, lawsuits and lots of other activity that contrasts with the "home sweet home" image. The movement against indoor air pollution is probably the fastest grass roots environmental drive in the country. Just scan the checklist scorecard early in this section to get an idea of the variety of gases, chemicals, and particulates that could be present in your home. Some can be controlled by the will of dwellers—proper coverings, ceasing tobacco smoking, reduced use of aerosols. Others can be curtailed by using household alternatives for common hazardous products in the home, as simply detailed in one of the following articles.

But there are toxic emissions from the materials that make up the building itself, including asbestos, old leaded pipes leaching into drinking water, or from nature itself such as radon. "I find it appalling that our children can actually be harmed by deleterious substances without ever leaving their homes," wrote London real estate investor, Godfrey Bradman. Unique among his business colleagues, Mr. Bradman sponsored the publication of a book titled *Hazardous Building Materials: A Guide to the Selection of Alternatives* (1986, edited by Curwell and March, E.& F.N. Spon Ltd., London) for builders and repair firms. In our country, *The Healthy House Catalog* (1988, Environmental Health Watch and Housing Resource Center, Cleveland, Ohio) reflects the emerging literature which lists categories of pollutants, testing firms, equipment and other bits and leads. But CAVEAT: just as in the home water filtration business, the indoor pollution detection and treatment business is replete with shady firms and deceptive practices. Presently, the marketing abuses are way ahead of the prosecutors or the standard setting enforcement agencies. *Consumer Reports* and the Canadian magazine, *Protect Yourself*, among others, are striving to keep up with their brand-name testing of such products as humidifiers, portable air cleaners, radon detectors, home water treatment devices and many more. Watch for them, for they may be your only reliable comparative shopping service. In the meantime, absorb the information contained herein which you can apply yourself to diminish these toxics in the home and head off a pesticide or other chemical emergency afflicting a member of your family. ❖

Beware 'Sick-Building Syndrome'
The deadliest pollutants of all may be the ones you breathe at home or at work

NEWSWEEK, JANUARY 7, 1985

THE PARAMEDICS WHO found Eugene Beeman dead in his suburban Chicago home believed that the 54-year-old engineer had been felled by a heart attack. But an autopsy revealed that his blood was laden with carbon monoxide, and an architect discovered a number of sources of the deadly gas in Beeman's home. The verdict: Beeman had been poisoned by the air in his own house.

Over the past decade, Americans have spent nearly $200 billion to win a minor victory in the war against air pollution. But just when we thought it was safe to breathe again, there comes disturbing news. Study after study has discovered that air inside homes, schools and office buildings can be laden with a witch's brew of chemicals, gases, smoke, bacteria and other pollutants sometimes in concentrations high enough to pose serious threats to health. The case of Eugene Beeman is still a tragic exception, since toxic substances are normally detected long before they can reach fatal levels. But scientists warn that the unavoidable act of breathing indoor air may cause or aggravate half of all the illnesses in the nation and may contribute to thousands of deaths a year. What environmental scientists call "sick buildings" pose a problem that cuts across state, social and economic boundaries. They have been found everywhere from trailer parks in Texas to an Environmental Protection Agency office in Washington. "We're just beginning to identify the problem of indoor air pollution," says Hugh Kaufman, EPA hazardous-waste expert and whistle blower. "But everywhere we look, it is worse than we expected."

Assumptions: Recent research has overturned some of the original assumptions about indoor pollution. At first, scientists suspected that indoor levels of chemicals and other contaminants simply reflected their outdoor concentrations. "Our initial thought was that exposure to chemicals would be highest in chemical-manufacturing centers," says EPA environmental scientist Lance Wallace. But when an EPA team sampled air from schools in the shadow of chemical-storage tanks and in relatively pristine suburban settings a few years ago, they discovered that outside air had almost no effect on indoor pollution levels. "It shattered all our preconceived notions," says Wallace. Intrigued, the researchers returned to Bayonne, N.J.,

one of their original test cities, and attached sophisticated air monitors to 350 people. "The results were a big surprise," says Wallace. "Indoor concentrations were always two to five times higher than outside levels. Sometimes they were over a hundred times higher." The lesson: "Even downwind from a chemical plant, it's better to open your windows."

But it does not follow that lack of ventilation is the only problem. Many researchers once thought of unhealthy air as a problem child of the energy crisis, a byproduct of attempts by architects and builders to save fuel by sealing out outside air. It is a notion that dates back to that early environmental engineer Ben Franklin, who once said, "No common air from without is so unwholesome as the air within a closed room that has been often breathed and not changed." Nine years ago, energy experts in the government became concerned enough about potential hazards in tight, energy-efficient buildings to set up an indoor-air-quality program at Lawrence Berkeley Laboratories. But when the LBL scientists actually went out to measure pollutant concentrations, they found that lack of ventilation was rarely the main culprit. Buildings were creating their own forms of pollution.

The home, after all, is a place where oil, gas, wood and tobacco are burned (giving off nitrogen dioxide, carbon monoxide and hydrocarbons); it offers a collection of microclimates ideal for the cultivation of microorganisms (including fungi, nematodes and the bacteria that cause Legionnaire's disease among other ailments); it is a place where countless chemical products invisibly exude their volatile components, including styrene from plastics and benzene from solvents. Manufactured-wood products, such as particleboard and plywood, give off poisonous formaldehyde, and even the very soil beneath the foundation can emit radioactive radon gas. "We're all living in a chemical soup," says Wallace, who gave up after three hours of trying to count all the possible sources of contamination in his own bathroom.

Pungent Odor: No regulations require homes and most office buildings to be monitored for indoor pollutants; as a result, virtually all cases of "sick-building syndrome" are discovered by nature's own imperfect pollution detector, the human body. When Oakland

High School in Oakland, Calif., moved into a new building four years ago, for example, students and teachers alike smelled the pungent odor of formaldehyde. School administrators at first denied that a problem existed. But after nearly half of the 2,000 students began to suffer from headaches, sore throats and fatigue that often mysteriously disappeared on weekends, they bowed to pressure for an inquiry. Researchers discovered formaldehyde concentrations of 1.45 parts per million (ppm), far above the .1 ppm standard used in West Germany and other European countries, and traced the chemical to particleboard shelves in the school's library.

Even the EPA, which critics accuse of neglecting the indoor environment, has had its own bout with indoor air pollution. Three years ago the agency converted part of a parking garage into office space to eliminate overcrowding in its Washington headquarters. Within a year workers began to complain of headaches and other ailments. Testing revealed carbon-monoxide concentrations of 25 ppm inside the offices, almost three times higher than EPA's own outdoor limit of 9 ppm. The agency abandoned the space at a cost of several hundred thousand dollars.

There are hundreds of similar tales. Confined to his condominium in Chicago's John Hancock Center after he broke his foot, businessman Frank Whitmer developed a number of alarming symptoms, including high blood pressure and chest pains. The last thing he suspected was the air in his own apartment. But when doctors could find no cause or cure, Whitmer hired indoor-air-pollution expert Kenneth Woods to investigate. Woods uncovered building-code violations that, he claims, allowed automobile-exhaust fumes from the building's garage to waft up to the residences above. Whitmer is suing the building's owners. Although the owners maintain that Whitmer's ailments were not caused by indoor air, they have already taken steps to improve air quality in the building. In another instance, researchers from the National Institute for Occupational Safety and Health (NIOSH) who were investigating a government building in Washington discovered slime in the air-conditioner drain pans and up to a remarkable 83,700 fungi per cubic meter in the air, "a level," says NIOSH's Philip Morey, "comparable to a chicken coop or swine-confinement facility." During the past several years the Consumer Product Safety Commission (CPSC) has received more than 3,000 complaints about bad air. "If you believe that the air is making you sick," says the CPSC's Sandra Eberle, "it probably is."

Mobile Homes: Investigators have found dangerous levels of pollutants even where there were no symptoms to tip them off. A recent study of 164 mobile homes in four randomly selected Texas trailer parks, for example, discovered that more than half had formaldehyde concentrations about .1 ppm. "Few homes had very high concentrations," says Thomas Stock of the University of Texas School of Public Health, who directed the study. "But a number were above what is considered safe." Scientists at Chicago's IIT Research Institute detected more than 200 different chemicals in a study of indoor air in 35 Chicago-area homes and found that in general, "indoor levels [of the chemicals] are significantly higher than outdoor levels," says IIT senior scientist Sydney Gordon. Other studies have found styrene in 80 percent of sampled homes in Bayonne, and 150 chemicals while monitoring 40 houses in Oak Ridge, Tenn.

The key question, of course, is how serious a threat these indoor pollutants are to health. The clearest danger is posed by radon gas. Produced by the decay of uranium 238, a ubiquitous trace element in the earth's crust, inert radon does not bind to minerals and thus accumulates in the tiny air pockets in soil. From there, it is pulled into houses by pressure differences created by the rising of warm indoor air. Once inside, radon decays into other radioactive elements, such as polonium, that bind to dust and are inhaled into the lungs, where they can cause cancer.

Extrapolating from rates of lung cancer in uranium miners, who are exposed to known amounts of radon and its products, researchers have calculated that 2,000 to 20,000 cases of the disease each year may be caused solely by indoor radon pollution. The geology of Maine and parts of Pennsylvania, Maryland, Oregon and Montana leads to particularly high radon risks.

Passive Smoking: Smoke from other people's cigarettes is another serious health hazard. A continuing study by John Spengler of the Harvard School of Public Health shows that children whose parents light up at home suffer from 30 percent more lower-respiratory illnesses than children in nonsmoking families. British researchers have recently discovered that 85 percent of nonsmokers tested have measurable levels of tobacco substances in their urine, even though only half of the people believed that they have been exposed to smoke. The reason: many building ventilation systems recirculate tobacco smoke instead of removing it. Passive smoking, believes James Repace of the EPA, is responsible for up to 5,000 lung cancer deaths per year, a figure the tobacco industry disputes.

As the case of Beeman demonstrates, carbon monoxide is another killer. A self-employed engineer, Beeman inadvertently increased the number of sources of the gas in his house, while cutting back ventilation to make it more energy-efficient. He built the house with a special bedroom furnace (allowing him to heat only the one room at night) and equipped it with a metal chimney and a flue damper. When the furnace turned off, noxious gases held inside the chimney by the damper cooled quickly and backed down into the room. In addition, carbon-monoxide-laden exhaust from the gas dryer was vented outdoors. Beeman's body tried to warn him about rising concentrations of lethal gases; a week before he died, he came down with the nausea and headache symptomatic of carbon-monoxide poisoning. But, as commonly occurs, the illness was misdiagnosed as flu. Fortunately, Beeman's story is a rare one. But Greg Traynor of LBL warns that cracked furnace-heat exchangers (found in about 5 percent of American homes) and unvented kerosene heaters could cause gases to reach potentially dangerous levels in indoor air.

Links between indoor chemicals and disease are more difficult to prove. Benzene and styrene, for example, which are found in a majority of homes tested, are known carcinogens at moderate doses. But there is still no proof that the lower levels typically found in indoor air pose a human health threat. "We have very few ways to determine if low levels of organic chemicals do cause cancer," says Lance Wallace. Researchers worry both that long-term exposure to low concentrations might lead to cancer and that the mixtures of 30 or 40 chemicals typically found in indoor air may be far deadlier than any one agent alone.

Formaldehyde causes special concern. Found in up to 3,000 different building products, formaldehyde causes nasal cancer in animals, and headaches, nausea and dizziness in humans. Worried that the levels typically found in indoor air posed a significant threat, the CPSC banned one of the major products, urea formaldehyde foam insulation, in 1982. The following year a federal court overturned the ban. Fortunately, believes LBL's John Girman, "it has such a bad rap that no market for it will exist." But there are still thousands of homes that contain the insulation and thousands of other sources of formaldehyde.

No such uncertainty exists about asbestos. A fibrous mineral used everywhere from insulation and floor tiles to brake linings and pipes, asbestos can cause lung cancer, a rare cancer called mesothelioma and asbestosis, a sometimes fatal scarring of the lung.... recent studies suggest that the problem is worse than expected. EPA surveys have discovered that 20 percent of the office and apartment buildings in 10 cities and thousands of schools contain asbestos in an easily crumbled state. In addition, hundreds of thousands of homes contain asbestos-wrapped pipes or air-distribution ducts made of corrugated asbestos paper.

Awareness: The technical cures to indoor air pollution are reasonably straightforward: radon gas, for example, can be maneuvered away from homes with pipes and fans, and increased ventilation alone can often cut concentrations to safe levels. But the economic and social problems are more vexing. Who will shoulder the costs of testing countless buildings and homes for dangerous pollutants or tearing out asbestos and formaldehyde insulation? Who will decide if smoking should be limited to protect the health of nonsmokers? ❖

Newsweek *is available for $39 a year. Published weekly. Address: Newsweek Building, 444 Madison Avenue, New York, NY 10022.*

EXCERPT FROM
Heat Recovery Ventilation For Housing:
Air-to-Air Heat Exchangers
U.S. DEPARTMENT OF ENERGY, MARCH 1984

AN AIR-TO-AIR EXCHANGER is a heat-recovery ventilation device that pulls stale, warm air from the house and transfers the heat in that air to the fresh, cold air being pulled into the house. Heat exchangers do not produce heat; they only exchange heat from one air stream to the other.

The heat transfers to the fresh air stream in the core of the heat exchanger, which is often made of thin sheets of plastic, treated paper or metal. ... Moisture in the stale air condenses in the core and is drained from the machine. Residential heat exchangers come in two basic types: small, through-the-wall units that are the size of a room air conditioner and central, ducted whole-house models, many of which are about the size of a typical water heater.

Small, efficient fans power the two separated air streams, and research indicates that the most efficient residential heat exchangers on the market can recover as much as 70-80 percent of the heat in the stale air.

Although air-to-air heat exchangers are new to the residential market, they have been in use for many decades in large commercial, industrial and hospital applications. Residential air-to-air exchangers were first introduced in North America in the late 1970s, when Canadian researchers built a test house that was so tightly constructed that extra ventilation was needed. Those doing research with superinsulated houses soon focused on the air-to-air exchanger as one way to provide constant, reliable ventilation, thus avoiding potential indoor air quality and moisture problems. ❖

The Walk Through the House Checklist

Excerpt from *House Dangerous: Indoor Pollution in Your Home and Office and What You Can Do About It!*

BY ELLEN J.GREENFIELD

FOREWORD BY RALPH NADER

FOR YOUR HOME'S personal pollution profile, check off all applicable pollution sources for your score. Then add the numbers in parentheses after each item.

The Kitchen

- Unvented gas stove (3)
- Unvented gas oven (3)
- Unvented gas clothes dryer (3)
- Unvented electric clothes dryer (3)

Aerosols (used regularly)

- Oven cleaner (1)
- Air freshener (1)
- Water and stain repellent (1)
- Disinfectant (1)
- Others (add 1/2 point for each additional product)
- Scouring powder (with chlorine bleach) (1/2)
- Ammonia (1)
- General purpose cleaners (e.g. Fantastik) (1/2)
- Spot remover (1)
- Floor wax (self-cleaning, e.g. Wood Preen) (1)

The Living Room

- Fireplace or wood stove (4)
- Coal stove (4)
- Wall-to-wall carpeting (and pads) (2)
- Carpet shampoo (1)
- Decorative paneling or partition walls (new: 3, 1+ years: 2, 3+ years: 1)
- Furniture or shelving made with plywood or particleboard (new: 2, 2+ years: 1)
- Upholstered furniture (1)

Bedrooms and Nursery

- Unvented kerosene or gas space heaters (4)
- Cool-mist humidifier (2)
- Air conditioner (1 each)

The Bathroom

- Enclosed stall shower (1)
Aerosols:
- Hair spray (1/2)
- Deodorant (1/2)
- Air freshener (1)
- Shaving cream (1/2)
- Tub and tile cleaner (1)
- Disinfectant (1)
- Chlorine bleach-based scouring powder (1/2)

Housekeeping

- Do you clean house (dust, sweep, vacuum, shake out sheets and blankets) regularly at least twice a week? (1)
- Portable vacuum cleaner (1)
- Regular use of dusting spray (1)
- Regular use of furniture polish (1)

The Basement

- Gas or oil furnace (2)
- Gas or oil hot water heater (2)
- Asbestos pipe insulation (3)
- Unfiltered forced-air heating system (2)

The Attached Garage

- Motor vehicles (4)
Building Superstructure
- Plywood, particleboard, fiberboard (in new homes) (3)
- Urea-formaldehyde foam insulation (new: 4, 1+ years: 3, 5+ years: 2)
- Glass fiber insulation in attic or below ground floor (2)
- Vapor barrier (e.g. Tyvek) (1)
- Asbestos shingle facade (1)
- Double-or triple-glazed (thermal) windows (2)

Foundation/Subsoil

- Do you live in an area known to have (or suspected of having) high radon content in the soil or bedrock ? (4)
- Have you had your foundation and surrounding soil treated for termites, ants, or flies within the past five years? (3)

Water Supply

In a radon-prone area:
- Is your water supplied by a private well? (3)

Miscellaneous
- Do you or any members of your family smoke? (4 per smoker)
- Are you often visited by smokers? (3)
- Do any furry pets or birds live with you? (1)
- Do you have any house plants? (1)
- Are insecticides or pesticides used indoors? (regularly: 2, rarely: 1)

Hobbies:
- Woodworking, carpentry (2)
- Model building (1)
- Jewelry or lamp-making (soldering) (2)
- Graphic arts (use of spray adhesives, marking pens, etc.) (1)
- Are there pre-1978 fluorescent lighting fixtures anywhere in the house? (1)

Symptoms
- Do you store old, partially used cans of paint, solvents, mothballs, pesticides, polyurethane, paint stripper, etc., in the house? (1)
- Does your house often feel damp, especially in winter? (2)
- Are there any unusual or foul odors in places in your house? (1)
- Do cooking and other odors tend to linger? (1)

Your score to this point _____

Methods of Improving Air Quality
(Subtract the number of points indicated after each item from the above score.)
- Do you use an ion generator, electrostatic precipitator, or effective air filter for indoor air cleaning? (4 points per unit)

- Do you use and maintain an effective air filter in a forced-air heating system? (4)
- Do you open windows for ventilation in all seasons? (4)
- Do you use a heat exchanger to provide ventilation without sacrificing energy-efficiency? (6)
- Do you use a central vacuum cleaning system? (2)

Your total indoor air quality score _____

Understanding Your Score
0-15 Exceptionally high indoor air quality

16-25 Reasonably safe indoor air, with room for improvement, especially if there are unvented fueled appliances or a threat of radon.

26-50 Family members who spend long periods indoors or who tend to be allergic or have other health sensitivities may suffer adverse effects. Acute health effects such as respiratory symptoms, irritability, or fatigue may be apparent. Chronic health problems and long-range illnesses may have their silent beginnings.

50+ Poor indoor air quality which could easily lead to both long-and short-range health problems. With a score this high, however, it should be relatively easy to take steps toward improvement. ❖

House Dangerous was published in 1987 by Blue Cliff Editions (a subsidiary of Random House), 201 E. 50th Street, New York, NY 10022. $7.95.

Purify Air the Space-station Way: With Plants
BY NAOMI J. FREUNDLICH
SCIENCE NEWS, AUGUST 1986

VENTING AIR THROUGH a sun room full of common houseplants could lower indoor pollutant levels, says a NASA scientist who investigates biological methods of keeping space stations healthy. Now he's rigged his own energy-efficient house accordingly.

B.C. Wolverton is breathing easy, now that he's equipped his energy-efficient house with an air-purification system. Maintenance of the system is simple: a good watering twice a week and an occasional dose of fertilizer. The main component of his filtering system is a decorative solarium stocked with plants.

It may sound a little primitive, but Wolverton, an environmental engineer at NASA's National Space Technology Laboratories, developed the plant-based air-purifying system for the proposed U.S. space station. His research shows that some houseplants, especially the spider plant and philodendron, remove formaldehyde and carbon monoxide (potentially dangerous gases that accumulate when there is low air exchange) from ambient air. Energy-efficient houses almost always have low air-exchange rates and occasionally have pollution problems.

Wolverton is not sure, but he thinks that when the plant leaves photosynthesize, they metabolize these gaseous pollutants as they do carbon dioxide, breaking them down into harmless oxygen and water. Intrigued by this, Wolverton built his own solarium and put 15 to 20 houseplants in it, enough, he says, to purify the air for an 1,800-square-foot house. Although Wolverton didn't check gas levels before building the sun room, he did afterward, and reports no measurable formaldehyde in his home. "The plants also put a lot of moisture back into the air that is removed by heat in the wintertime," says Wolverton.

For those who don't have the space or money for a solarium, Wolverton has another idea that takes advantage of the natural filtering abilities of plant roots. He suggests using hanging spider or philodendron plants potted in a mixture of soil and granular charcoal as mini-filters for offices or apartments. A small air pump hidden in the decorative pot pulls air past the roots every hour or so. Organic pollutants are absorbed by the charcoal, where root microorganisms degrade them. ❖

Science News *is available for $29.50 a year. Published weekly. Address: 1719 N Street NW, Washington, D.C. 20036.*

Coping With the Perils of Asbestos
Homeowners Warned That Removal is Not a Do-it-Yourself Job
BY ANTHONY DEPALMA
THE NEW YORK TIMES, MARCH 20, 1988

LILI ELSIS SLUMPED on her cellar stairs and put her head in her hands. "We just moved all this in last Thursday," she said with a sigh.

Mrs. Elsis had just been told that the cardboard boxes, furniture and bulky cabinets she and her husband, Harold, had crammed into the basement of the house they purchased in Montclair, N.J., would all have to be moved back out so that a contractor could begin the tedious and delicate job of removing damaged asbestos insulation from heating pipes. There is also asbestos padding in the radiator covers in their second-story bedrooms, including the nursery of their year old son, Jonathan, and that, too, must be removed.

The work will cost at least $3,500, but the Elsises did not hesitate. "I don't know how bad a hazard this is," said Mr. Elsis, a typographer who works in New York City, "but because of my baby and my wife, I'll have it removed."

The Elsis home is one of millions of structures— among them houses, schools, stores and office buildings—that contain asbestos. The mineral was widely used in insulation and building products until the 70's, when studies showed it could cause lung disease and cancer. While asbestos products are generally no longer used in new construction, untold amounts remain in existing buildings.

The Federal and state governments are increasingly passing laws and issuing regulation on the handling of asbestos material and the alteration or demolition of buildings containing it.

Federal law requires public and private schools around the country to be inspected for asbestos by October and ways of handling it to be presented if it is there.

In New York City, tough regulations enacted last April require that environmental officials be notified any time asbestos material is handled, such as in demolitions of office buildings or large-scale alterations of apartment houses that require city permits.

But private residences are excluded from most regulations, leaving owners to deal with the potential danger of asbestos on their own. In many instances, this has meant that homeowners—scared enough by what they know of asbestos to want it removed, but not knowledgeable enough to realize how lethal the nearly invisible fibers can be—have descended into their basements with putty knives and saws to hack off asbestos pipe coverings and dispose of the material in the regular garbage pickup.

The dangers of asbestos in the home are not fully understood, and there is disagreement on how hazardous it is and what should be done about it. But on one point there is unanimity: asbestos is most dangerous when it is disturbed. And about the most reckless way of handling it is for an untrained homeowner to become a do-it-yourself asbestos abatement contractor.

"I've been dealing with asbestos for three years now and if I had asbestos in my basement I wouldn't remove it myself," said Michael F. Lakat of the Asbestos Control Service of the New Jersey Department of

Health. "Just because asbestos is present in a building doesn't necessarily mean it is a danger."

Mr. Lakat's office operates an asbestos hotline in Trenton that advises homeowners who suspect that their houses contain asbestos. Mr. Lakat said his office receives up to 400 calls a month. He asks callers to describe the potential hazard and the type of material present and its condition and then he seeks to guide them on a prudent course. "It's like trying to read X-rays over the telephone," Mr. Lakat said.

Mr. and Mrs Elsis said they did not need to call the state's toll-free number because they had picked up much of their information about hazardous substances in another way.

For the Elsises, the asbestos in their basement was the return of a nightmare. Three years ago they were told by environmental officials that their home in the southern end of Glen Ridge, just east of Montclair, was contaminated with radon gas.

"They came and took an air sample and we found out we were radioactive," Mrs. Elsis said. "I was shaken by the experience. I was afraid to go out and afraid to stay home."

To their surprise, the Elsises were able to sell their Glen Ridge house, even with the radon problem. They moved in with in-laws for several months and eventually decided to buy the center-hall colonial in Montclair, but not before having a thorough environmental analysis done on the building.

The engineer's report showed there was no radon present. However, asbestos was wrapped around the basement pipes. Mr. Elsis said he told the seller it would have to be removed. The problem was handled in a way similar to many common house repairs: The seller agreed to deduct $3,000 from the sales price to cover the work.

Mr. Elsis said he intended to have the asbestos removed before the family moved in, but the plans went awry. He admitted he did not know how big a job it would be to remove the material.

Early this month, the Elsises called a certified asbestos abatement contractor, Olsen & Hassold of Paterson, N.J. An estimator with the company, David H. Goett, came, not in the lab coat and respirator that might have been expected but in a business suit and tie. Moving slowly through the jumbled basement, he pointed out torn insulation over the gas furnace and cracked and frayed asbestos material, which looks like a crumbly white or gray cement, in areas where the pipes bend. "I won't use the term danger or hazard," Mr. Goett told the Elsises. "What I'll say is that there is a significant exposure to fibers and leave the definitions to the Federal Government." He later told them that while it is not "instant death," it is a "problem you don't want to ignore."

Mr. Goett then explained how the work would be done. After the basement is emptied, it will be sealed off with plastic sheeting to contain loose fibers. Then the workmen from Olsen & Hassold, all with at least 40 hours of training, will enter in jumpsuits and respirators to carefully remove the insulation from around the pipes, misting it first to reduce the release of fibers. The asbestos material will be placed in special plastic bags, which will be sealed and eventually taken to an approved landfill. The pipes will be washed carefully, then sealed with a clear coating to trap any fibers that remain.

Finally, the entire room, every crevice and crack, will be cleaned with a high-efficiency vacuum with a filter dense enough to trap asbestos fibers so thin that 100 bunched together would be narrower than a single strand of human hair.

Before the abatement contractors leave, they are supposed to take air samples that should show there is no more than .01 fibers per cubic centimeter of air, a standard that equals the normal outside air.

The Elsises were surprised to find that the air in the street outside their house contains a certain amount of asbestos. This is true everywhere, officials say. In New York City, the level of asbestos fibers in the air is higher because it has so much demolition work going on.

Scientists know that heavy exposure to asbestos such as occurred in shipyards and factories that made asbestos products caused cancer and lung disease. But they do not know with certainty what level of hazard exists in private houses.

"The chance of developing any disease is extremely small," said Dr. William J. Nicholson, professor of community medicine at Mount Sinai Medical Center in New York and a specialist in asbestos hazards. "But we want to eliminate even that much because the effort of doing so isn't that great."

The Consumer Product Safety Commission has banned the use of sprayed-on asbestos insulation and spackling compound and artificial fireplace logs made with asbestos. The agency is now studying the results of air samples taken inside 45 houses containing asbestos in Cleveland, Philadelphia, and San Francisco, to determine the level of hazard.

According to Sandra Eberle, program manager for chemical hazards at the commission, the level of asbestos fibers inside the houses was roughly equivalent to the levels in the air outside with no measurements exceeding the Federal standard of .01 fibers per cubic centimeter.

Ms. Eberle stressed that the results were preliminary and that it was too early to draw conclusions from them. But John Welch, president of the Safe Buildings Alliance, a trade organization representing companies that used to manufacture asbestos-containing materials, said the study shows conclusively that "because the level of exposure is so low, occupants of houses are really at minimal risk."

On the other hand, James F. Fite, executive director of the White Lung Association, an organization representing victims of asbestos disease, said the Consumer Product Safety Commission tends to underplay the danger of asbestos. He said even the approved Federal standard allows people to breathe in 100,000 asbestos fibers per hour. "Even in the best condition it's a potential hazard," Mr. Fite said.

With such divergent opinions even among the experts, homeowners who know or suspect they have asbestos in their home face a bewildering process of decision making. The risk of litigation also tends to make those involved, such as house inspectors and abatement contractors, reluctant to say clearly whether a dangerous condition exists. But homeowners can expect that the problem, instead of going away, will grow and continue to haunt them.

The Consumer Product Safety Commission's basic advice is simple. Removal of asbestos is usually the last alternative. If it must come out, then a certified reliable contractor who has done that type of work before is the best choice. To be avoided, the commission stresses, are "strip and run" companies promising a cheap, and usually unprofessional (and therefore harmful), job that will make matters far worse than before the asbestos was touched.

Asbestos has become a major issue in co-op conversions and the owners of multifamily buildings have taken to preparing asbestos liability reports to forestall possible lawsuits. Commercial mortgage lenders now routinely require an asbestos inspection before considering a mortgage application; and some banks, such as the American Savings Bank in New York, require their appraisers to notify them when asbestos material is present in a single-family house under contract to be sold.

A few years ago, the New Jersey legislature considered a bill requiring an asbestos inspection before any house could be sold, but the measure was defeated, partly by real estate agents who contended it would lead to wholesale illegal removal by uninformed or desperate house sellers. At present, real estate agents must divulge all information they have about the condition of a building, including whether it contains asbestos.

New York and New Jersey now require that contractors who remove asbestos be licensed by the state, and Connecticut is expected to adopt similar measures soon. The states also maintain information hotlines, as does the Federal Government, and printed material is available. The Consumer Product Safety Commission's booklet, "Asbestos in the Home" is an informative and readable source of information.

But despite that body of knowledge, the final decision lies with the homeowners, like Diane and Alexander Black of Metuchen, N.J. The Blacks, who have three children, bought their neat little colonial two years ago knowing that a sizable amount of asbestos was wrapped around pipes in the basement and completely encased the old furnace. An engineer they hired to check the house told them the asbestos was in poor condition and would probably have to be removed.

"I try not to get hysterical about this but with the kids around I worry," Mrs. Black said. The Blacks have kept the basement clear and Mrs. Black goes there only to do the wash. But now the furnace is on its last legs and will have to be replaced, which means the asbestos will be disturbed.

The Blacks have decided that they now will spend the $2,500 to remove the asbestos. "The motivating factor for us is the kids," Mrs. Black said. "We need a new roof and a new furnace, but this has to be done first." ❖

Asbestos in the Home

HOME MECHANIX, APRIL 1988

FOR NEARLY A CENTURY, asbestos was considered a miracle fiber—used in hundreds of home-construction materials because of its strengthening, fire-resistant and insulating properties. But overwhelming evidence now shows that long-term exposure to asbestos, mainly through inhalation, can cause a variety of debilitating lung diseases including asbestosis, mesothelioma and lung cancer.

Left undisturbed and in good condition, asbestos-containing material poses no immediate hazard. But if it is friable (easily crumbled or crushed into powder) or if it is to be disturbed, such as during a remodeling, it presents a clear health danger. Roy Barnhart, HM's building and remodeling editor, asked William Dundulis of the Rhode Island Asbestos Control Program to provide the answers readers will need before seeking the required professional services from testing laboratories, consultants and asbestos-control contractors. His counsel is particularly valuable because his program has done much to address the types of asbestos problems that homeowners typically face.

HM: Where am I most likely to find asbestos problems in my home?

Dundulis: Most problems occur in the basement, such as in heating-pipe insulation that has degraded or been damaged, or in insulation on boilers and some water heaters. An often-overlooked source is the expansion-joint cloth just above the boiler in hot-air heating duct systems. That type of material can contain up to 70 percent asbestos and may become hazardous if the material begins to deteriorate. Of less concern is asbestos-cement board typically used behind wood stoves. But it is a problem if the board is deteriorating. Vinyl-asbestos tile and sheet flooring (and its felt backing) become a problem during remodeling work...You should know that the standard recommendation would be to cover the flooring with underlayment and your new floor, not to remove it. In older homes, asbestos is found in some acoustical plasters and chopped up with other materials, as insulation in walls.

HM: Does a normal professional house inspection reveal asbestos problems?

Dundulis: Probably only in the most obvious cases, such as deteriorating pipe insulation. If you are buying an old house and are concerned, I'd recommend a specialist consultant.

HM: What asbestos materials present an immediate hazard?

Dundulis: Any asbestos-containing material that is friable or is delaminating, hanging or deteriorating should be taken care of right away. Visible water damage of asbestos materials is a precursor to deterioration. The source of the leak should be located and corrected immediately and the asbestos-containing material should be checked.

HM: Where can I have suspicious materials tested? What does it cost? And how do I gather samples?

Dundulis: The Yellow Pages will list laboratories which will probably analyze materials for asbestos content. If your state has an asbestos-control program, contact it for a list of approved laboratories. If there is no certification program, at least find out if the lab has participated in the Environmental Protection Agency's (EPA) quality-control program. Costs vary widely, but most laboratories would analyze a sample for between $25 and $50, provided that you collect the sample yourself.

To collect a sample, first moisten the material. Then cut a small sample and let it drop into a small plastic or glass container that can be well sealed. There's nothing more disconcerting to a secretary who opens an envelope than to see a dusty clump of plaster fall onto her desk and read a letter asking that the enclosed sample be tested for asbestos content!

If you have a number of suspected asbestos-containing materials, some labs will send a person to collect the samples. This avoids taking unnecessary samples and taking ones that, perhaps, you might have missed in your inspection. Independent asbestos consultants (also recommended by government agencies) can also collect samples, and are more likely to provide impartial advice than an abatement contractor, for example.

HM: I've been exposed to considerable dust while renovating old homes. Are there medical steps that I should take?

Dundulis: My best advice would be to see your doctor and relate your concerns. The doctor may recommend a baseline medical exam—that's what's required for those in the asbestos business—and possible pulmonary-functions tests and chest X-rays.

HM: What are the approaches taken to control asbestos?

Dundulis: Encapsulation, enclosure and removal. Encapsulation seals the offending material with a direct application of a material such as fiberglass cloth, paint, and epoxy. Enclosure usually consists of permanently boxing in the material and caulking all joints for an airtight seal. Removal requires special protection and cleanup and disposal measures.

HM: Which approach is best?

Dundulis: That depends upon the general conditions. Areas that are not readily accessed, such as some crawl spaces, are often enclosed. Areas not easily enclosed, such as water heaters, are encapsulated. Generally, asbestos-containing material probably should be removed if it is extensively damaged. If the damage is extensive, get a contractor's estimate for removal as well as for encapsulation for enclosure. If the cost of the latter is 60 to 70 percent of the cost of removal, or if a problem is likely to crop up again in the near future, I'd recommend removal.

HM: What is the procedure for removing the materials?

Dundulis: In general, the material is most often wetted to limit the creation of dust. Depending on the scope of the project, whole rooms, or just the immediate work area, are sealed off from the rest of the home. Sometimes a machine is used to create a negative air pressure to draw fresh air into the work area. Air contaminated during the work is exhausted after passing through a special filter designed to trap the asbestos fibers.

Pipe insulation is usually cut off with a knife and residual materials are hand-scraped. Bone saws, like those used by orthopedic surgeons, are often used to cut through insulation imbedded with reinforcing wire. Smaller sections of pipe insulation are typically removed in a heavy, clear-plastic bag, called a glove bag. The bag is sealed around a pipe section to contain dust during work, and it also acts as a disposal bag.

There are a few approaches to removing vinyl-asbestos floors. Propane torches can be used to heat floor tiles until they pop free. One particularly ingenious approach for floors on a wood substrate is to push dry ice back and forth over the floor tiles like a hockey puck. It has the same effect as the torch. The least-desirable method involves hand-scraping and sanding. That should only be done by a professional asbestos contractor equipped with a negative air-pressure machine, protective clothing and masks, and a HEPA (high-efficiency particulate-absorbing) filtered vacuum.

Spray-on ceiling materials are scraped off and bagged for disposal by hand. Again, the proper equipment is required.

HM: How much does a typical removal procedure cost? For pipe insulation? For vinyl-asbestos flooring? For acoustical ceiling texture?

Dundulis: Most contractors in the Providence, Rhode Island area that I am aware of base estimates on about $70 to $100 per hour. I'm afraid that there are so many variables that I could not really give a more precise figure. The EPA booklet *Asbestos Waste Management Guidance*, gives some guidelines: $2 to $10 per square foot and about the same for each linear foot of pipe insulation. Once again, my advice is to shop around.

HM: How should asbestos-containing materials be disposed of?

Dundulis: Asbestos-containing materials are in a category defined by the EPA as special waste. As such, they require more regulation than regular solid wastes and less regulation than hazardous wastes. Contact your state environmental agency for disposal information...and shop around. Prices vary widely. Have your asbestos-removal contractor supply you with a receipt from a transporter or landfill showing that the materials (specifically identified) were disposed of properly.

HM: What about cleanup and air testing after work is complete?

Dundulis: To begin, what can be removed from a work area should be. What can be covered should be. After work is complete, the contained area should be west-cleaned and HEPA-vacuumed until it is spotless. Regarding commercial jobs, we at the Rhode Island Asbestos Control Program insist that clearance air testing be done by an independent firm (not the removal contractor). Further, we insist that the test be conducted after the material is thoroughly dry and that blowers be used to agitate the work area during the test. Results should fall below 0.015 f/cc (asbestos fibers per cubic centimeter of air). Though not required, we recommend the same procedures for homeowners.

HM: Do I have to leave my house during the procedure?

Dundulis: Generally not. The work area is normally sealed off. However, some people won't feel safe within three blocks of the stuff, so it's largely a matter of personal choice.

HM: Can renters in single- and small multifamily homes insist that landlords control asbestos?

Dundulis: Many areas don't have regulations or laws for this, but the first person to talk to should be the local building-code official. If local regulations fail to cover the situation, check with your state environmental agency.

HM: I'm afraid that asbestos in my home, though in good shape, will affect resale value, or someday removal may be required by law. It will never be cheaper, or shouldn't I opt for removal now?

Dundulis: Removal is the best approach. It may even

be the cheapest approach—and may be necessary, regardless of cost—but my job, as well as other professionals in the field, is to give proper technical advice that leads to the reduction of immediate risk to safe levels. And if encapsulation or enclosure, typically cheaper procedures, will do, then we recommend them.

HM: How do I know whether an abatement contractor is qualified?

Dundulis: I'd like to emphasize just how important this is. It can cost $10,000, $20,000, $30,000 or more to clean up a home after a botched removal job. So if your state has a certification program, seek only certified contractors. Lacking certification, ask a contractor for proof that workers have been trained at an EPA-approved course or in a formal asbestos course as part of a union apprenticeship program.

HM: Where can I get a complete list of asbestos-containing materials likely to be found in the home?

Dundulis: Wow, that would be quite a list. The EPA estimates that asbestos has been used in about 3,000 products. Their publication, *Guidance for Controlling Asbestos-Containing Materials in Buildings,* lists the most common materials together with the dates when they were typically used in buildings. Or contact your state asbestos-control program. ❖

Home Mechanix is available for $11.94 a year. Published monthly. Address: 1515 Broadway, New York, NY 10036.

Formaldehyde
Excerpt From *The Inside Story: A Guide to Indoor Air Quality*
U.S. ENVIRONMENTAL PROTECTION AGENCY, SEPTEMBER 1988

FORMALDEHYDE IS AN important chemical used widely by industry to manufacture building materials and numerous household products. It is also a by-product of combustion and certain other natural processes. Thus it may be present in substantial concentrations both indoors and outdoors.

Sources of formaldehyde in the home include smoking, household products, and the use of unvented, fuel-burning appliances, like gas stoves or kerosene space heaters. Formaldehyde, by itself or in combination with other chemicals, serves a number of purposes in manufactured products. For example, it is used to add permanent press qualities to clothing and draperies, as a component of glues and adhesives, and as a preservative in some paints and coating products.

In homes, the most significant sources of formaldehyde are likely to be pressed wood products made using adhesives that contain urea-formaldehyde (UF) resins. Pressed wood products made for indoor use include: particleboard (used as subflooring and shelving and in cabinetry and furniture); hardwood plywood paneling (used for decorative wall covering and used in cabinets and furniture; and medium density fiberboard (used for drawer fronts, cabinet doors, and furniture tops). Medium density fiberboard contains a higher resin-to-wood ration than any other UF pressed wood product, and is generally recognized as being the highest formaldehyde-emitting pressed wood product.

Other pressed wood products, like softwood plywood and flake or oriented strandboard, are produced for exterior construction use and contain the dark, or reddish-black colored phenol-formaldehyde (PF) resin. Although formaldehyde is present in both types of resins, pressed woods that contain PF resin generally emit formaldehyde at considerably lower rates than those containing UF resin.

Since 1985, HUD has permitted only the use of plywood and particleboard that conform to specified formaldehyde emission limits in the construction of prefabricated and mobile homes. In the past, some of these homes had elevated levels of formaldehyde because of the large amount of high-emitting pressed wood products used in their construction and because of their relatively small interior space.

The rate at which products like pressed wood or textiles release formaldehyde emissions can change. Formaldehyde emissions will generally decrease as products age. When the products are new, high indoor temperatures or humidity can cause increased release of formaldehyde from these products.

During the 1970s, many homeowners had urea-formaldehyde foam insulation (UFFI) installed in the wall cavities of their homes as an energy conservation measure. However, many of these homes were found to have relatively high indoor concentrations of formaldehyde soon after the UFFI installation. Few, if any, homes are now being insulated with this product.

Studies show that formaldehyde emissions from UFFI decline with time; therefore, homes in which UFFI was installed many years ago are unlikely to have high levels of formaldehyde now unless the insulation is damp and there are cracks or openings in interior walls that expose the foam.

Health Effects of Formaldehyde

Formaldehyde, a colorless, pungent-smelling gas, can cause watery eyes, burning sensations in the eyes and throat, nausea, and difficulty in breathing in some humans exposed at elevated levels (above 0.1 parts per million). High concentrations may trigger asthma attacks in people with asthma. There is some evidence that some people can develop chemical sensitivity after exposure to formaldehyde. Formaldehyde has also been shown to cause cancer in animals and may cause cancer in humans.

Reducing Exposure to Formaldehyde in Homes

Ask about the formaldehyde content of pressed wood products, including building materials, cabinetry, and furniture before you purchase them. If you experience adverse reactions to formaldehyde, you may want to avoid the use of pressed wood products and other formaldehyde-emitting goods. Even if you do not experience such reactions, you may wish to reduce your exposure as much as possible by purchasing exterior-grade products, which emit less formaldehyde. For further information on formaldehyde and consumer products, call the EPA Toxic Substance Control Act (TSCA) assistance line (202-554-1404).

Some studies suggest that coating pressed wood products with polyurethane may reduce formaldehyde emissions for some period of time. To be effective, any such coating must cover all surfaces and edges and remain intact. Increase the ventilation and carefully follow the manufacturer's instructions while applying these coatings. (If you are sensitive to formaldehyde, check the label contents before purchasing coating products to avoid buying formaldehyde-containing products as they will emit the chemical for a short time after application.)

Maintain moderate temperature and humidity levels and provide adequate ventilation. The rate at which formaldehyde is released is accelerated by heat and may also depend somewhat on the humidity level. Therefore, the use of dehumidifiers and air conditioning to control humidity and to maintain a moderate temperature can help reduce formaldehyde emissions (Drain and clean dehumidifier collection trays frequently so that they do not become a breeding ground for microorganisms.). Increasing the rate of ventilation in your home will also help in reducing formaldehyde levels.

The Inside Story is available free from the Environmental Protection Agency, (EPA), Public Information Center, 401 M Street SW, Washington, D.C. 20460.

Letter to Ralph Nader
JANUARY 9, 1988

Dear Mr. Nader:

…I am a 47 year old registered nurse; married and have two children. My husband is an industrial engineer at a local manufacturing plant.

In September of 1979, our family moved to Wooster, Ohio to a new home; very well insulated and air conditioned. In December of that year our family started getting flu-like symptoms. After a long time, the symptoms were still there. The major problems I experienced were: headaches, bleeding under the skin, weight gain, exhaustion, breathing difficulties, nausea, insomnia, and depression. A physician thought it could be "post-viral-syndrome." I was hospitalized for 28 days, had a brain scan, and numerous other tests. I wrote to the C.D.C. in Atlanta, called our local health department and also called the State Department of Health. As a nurse, I of course was upset as I had no definite diagnosis yet. I then wrote to a virologist in Chicago. In his reply he said to look for something toxic: this of course started my search for an answer.

After much work and elimination the Ohio State Department of Health came to my dwelling to measure the air for formaldehyde off-gassing. It was evident in the kitchen—and also the measurement in a china cabinet I owned. They told me at that time it was the highest reading in Ohio (from the Hutch).

The positive formaldehyde readings prompted me to see a physician for chemical testing. From my understanding the formaldehyde has broke my immune system down—it therefore has made me allergic to many, many foods, auto fumes, perfumes, soaps, disinfectants, and news print. The chemical problem has also given me a yeast infection problem in my body. If I am exposed to the above things, I do get many physical problems and symptoms. Of course, I was unable to pursue my nursing career for a long time.

I feel my life has been a nightmare for the past 8 years.

I have had serious thoughts on writing an article or book, hoping to help people that may be having a similar problem.

Thank you for your consideration. ❖

Formaldehyde: An Update

IN A 1981 STUDY, The National Academy of Sciences said that up to 20 percent of the U.S. population is sensitive to low levels of formaldehyde, a toxic gas used in construction material found in homes and buildings. The gas is known to cause memory loss and depression as well as provoke asthmatic attacks in asthmatics. Symptoms from exposure to the gas are more severe in retirees, homemakers and others who spend much time at home. Such sypmtoms as nausea, watery eyes, aching throat and clogged sinuses may be mistaken for an alergy or common cold when in fact formaldahyde gas may be the primary cause.

One source of formaldehyde is urea-formaldehyde foam insulation (UFFI) which has been used as an insulator in homes and schools. However, it is no longer made in this country and most American homes do not contain UFFI as an insulator. An estimated 500,000 homes contain UFFI and any home that has it was most likely built in the 1970s. If you purchased your home before 1970 you probably do not have UFFI in your home.

Although formaldehyde can be found naturally in plants, animals and humans, most health problems occur from exposure to synthetic formaldehyde used as a bonding agent in thousands of consumer products such as countertops, deodorants, disinfectants or cars. Formaldehyde is most likely to leak from consumer products when the product is new.

In 1987, the Environmental Protection Agency reaffirmed that formaldehyde probably causes cancer and found that two in one thousand people living in mobile homes for ten years are likely to get formaldehyde induced cancer. In 1984, the Department of Housing and Urban Development imposed limits on formaldehyde emissions from plywood in mobil homes.

In addition to the home, formaldehyde is also found in the funeral, laboratory, foundry, apparel and furniture industries. The Department of Labor reduced the permissible level of worker exposure to formaldehyde for industries that use the chemical. Currently, worker exposure to formaldehyde must not exceed 1 part per million parts of air, averaged over an 8 hour work day.

The best way to avoid formaldehyde is by avoiding pressed wood products. One may eliminate formaldehyde by spraying the home with a strong solution of ammonia gas, prepared by a laboratory. Close all windows and doors and remove pets, plants and food before spraying; clean the home afterwards.

Although expensive, removing formaldehyde in the home by getting rid of its source is the best measure. For example, removing particleboard sub-flooring or urea-formaldehyde insulation are two effective measures.

Other measures include treating wood that releases formaldehyde with polyurethane or other sealants, varnishes or paints. Using vinyl wallpaper or floor coverings can also be effective.

Many city, county and state health agencies conduct tests in the home for formaldehyde levels in the air, usually at no cost. In addition, commercial laboratories test for the chemical at a cost of about $200. Check the yellow pages under "laboratories" for such companies. The preferred method of testing for the presence of formaldehyde is known as the "chromotropic acid method," recommended by the Occupational Safety and Health Administration (OSHA). Do-it-yourself test kits are available for $50. ❖

Radon

Excerpt from *The Inside Story: A Guide to Indoor Air Quality*

U.S. ENVIRONMENTAL PROTECTION AGENCY
SEPTEMBER 1988

RADON IS A colorless, odorless gas that occurs naturally and is found everywhere at very low levels. It is when radon becomes trapped in buildings and concentrations build up in indoor air that exposure to radon becomes of concern.

The most common source of indoor radon is uranium in the soil or rock on which homes are built. As uranium naturally breaks down, it releases radon gas, and radon gas breaks down into radon decay products (also called radon daughters or progeny). Radon gas enters homes through dirt floors, cracks in concrete walls and floors, floor drains, and sumps.

A second entry route for radon in some areas of the country is through well water. In some unusual situations, houses are made of radon-containing construction materials; in such cases, those materials can release radon into the indoor air.

Studies by EPA indicate that as many as 10 percent of all American homes, or about eight million homes, may have elevated levels of radon, and the percentage may be higher in geographic areas with certain soils and bedrock formations. Radon can be detected only by the use of measurement instruments called radon detectors.

Health Effects of Radon

The only known health effect associated with exposure to elevated levels of radon is lung cancer. EPA estimates that about 5,000 to 20,000 lung cancer deaths a year in the United States may be attributed to radon. (The American Cancer Society estimates there will be a total of about 139,000 lung cancer deaths in 1988 from all causes.)

Reducing Exposure to Radon in Homes

• Measure levels of radon in your home. Two types of radon detectors are most commonly used in homes: charcoal canisters that are exposed for two to seven days; and alpha track detectors that are exposed for one month or longer. (Some states recommend that residents use only the alpha track monitors.)

Your state radiation protection office can provide you with information on the availability of detection devices or services. Ask for materials specifically developed for your state and EPA's *A Citizen's Guide to Radon*. States may also provide you with EPA's Radon Measurement Proficiency Report for your state....

• Refer to the EPA guidelines in deciding whether and how quickly to take action based on your test results. The guidelines are given in the booklet, *A Citizen's Guide to Radon*. The higher the radon level in your home, the faster you should take action to reduce your exposure. EPA believes that radon levels in homes can be reduced to about four picocuries per liter of air and sometimes less.

• Learn about control measures. An effective radon mitigation plan may include one or more of the following actions: sealing cracks and other openings in basement floors, ventilating crawl spaces, installing sub-slab or basement ventilation, or installing air-to-air heat exchangers. The EPA booklet, *Radon Reduction Methods: A Homeowner's Guide*, offers advice about how to select a contractor and how to evaluate proposals for radon mitigation. EPA does not certify contractor competency for planning or executing radon mitigation measures.

• Stop smoking and discourage smoking in your home. Scientific evidence indicates that smoking may increase the risk of cancer associated with exposure to radon.

• Treat radon-contaminated well water by aerating or filtering through granulated-activated charcoal. Contact your state's radiation protection office or drinking water office for more information concerning radon in drinking water in your community. ❖

How is Radon Detected?

Excerpt from *A Citizen's Guide to Radon*

U.S. ENVIRONMENTAL PROTECTION AGENCY
AUGUST 1986

SINCE YOU CANNOT see or smell radon, special equipment is needed to detect it. The two most popular, commercially-available radon detectors are the charcoal canister and the alpha track detector. Both of these devices are exposed to the air in your home for a specified period of time and sent to a laboratory for analysis.

There are other techniques—requiring operation by trained personnel—which can be used to measure radon levels, but such techniques may be more expensive than the devices shown above.

Your measurement results will be reported to you in one of two ways. Results from devices which measure radon decay products are reported as "Working Levels" (WL). Results from devices which measure concentrations of radon gas are reported as "picocuries per liter" (pCi/l).

How can I get a radon detector?

Homeowners in some areas are being provided with detectors by their state or local government. In many areas, private firms offer radon testing. Your state radiation protection office may be able to provide you with information on the availability of detection devices or services.

The U.S. Environmental Protection Agency conducts a Radon Measurement Proficiency Program. This voluntary program allows laboratories and businesses to demonstrate their capabilities in measuring indoor radon. The names of firms participating in this program can be obtained from your state radiation protection office or from your EPA regional office.

How should radon detectors be used?

Obtaining a useful estimate of the radon level in your home may require that several detectors be used to make measurements in different areas. Following the steps below should provide the information needed as you decide whether or not further action is advisable. (In making radon measurements, you should be sure to follow the instructions of the manufacturer as to the proper exposure period for the particular device you are using.)

Step One: The screening measurement

The first step you should take is to have a short-term "screening" measurement made to give you an idea of the highest radon level in your home. Thus, you can find out quickly and inexpensively whether or not you have potential radon problems.

The screening measurement should be made in the lowest livable area of your home (the basement, if you have one). All windows and doors should be closed for at least 12 hours prior to the start of the test, and kept closed as much as possible throughout the testing period. This is necessary to keep the radon level relatively constant throughout the testing period. Because of the need to keep the windows closed as much as possible, we recommend that you make short-term radon measurements during the cool months of the year.

Step Two:
Determining the need for further measurements

In most cases, the screening measurement is not a reliable measure of the average radon level to which you and your family are exposed. Since radon levels can vary greatly from season to season as well as from room to room, the screening measurement only serves to indicate the potential for a radon problem. Depending upon the result of your screening measurement, you may need to have follow-up measurements made to give you a better idea of the average radon level in your home.

The following guidance may be useful to you in determining the urgency of your need for follow-up measurements.

If your screening measurement result is greater than about 1.0 WL or greater than about 200 pCi/l, you should perform follow-up measurements as soon as possible. Expose the detectors for no more than one week. Doors and windows should be closed as much as possible during testing. You should also consider taking actions (see page 13) to immediately reduce the radon levels in your home.

If your screening measurement result is about 0.1 WL to about 1.0 WL or about 20 pCi/l to about 200 pCi/l, perform follow-up measurements. Expose detectors for no more than three months. Doors and windows should be closed as much as possible during testing.

If your screening measurement result is about 0.02 WL to about 0.2 WL or about 4 pci/l to about 20 pCi/l, perform follow-up measurements. Expose detectors for one year, or make measurements of no more than one week duration during each of the four seasons.

If your screening measurement result is less than about 0.02 WL or less than about 4 pCi/l, follow-up measurements are probably not required. If the screening measurement was made with the house closed up prior to and during the testing period, there is relatively little chance that the radon concentration in your home will be greater than 0.02 WL or 4 pCi/l as an annual average.

Step Three: The follow-up measurement

Follow-up measurement will provide you with a relatively good estimate of the average radon concentration to which you and your family are exposed. We strongly recommend that you make follow-up measurements before you make any final decision about whether to undertake major efforts to permanently correct the problem.

Follow-up measurements should be made in at least two lived-in areas of your home. If your home has lived-in areas on more than one floor, you should make measurements in a room on each of the floors. An example is to take a measurement in the living room on the first floor and another in a second-floor bedroom. The results of the follow-up measurements should be averaged together.

What do my test results mean?

The results of your follow-up measurements provide you with an idea of the average concentration throughout your home. The actual risk you face depends upon the amount of time your are exposed to this concentration....

How quickly should I take action?

In considering whether and how quickly to take action based on your test results, you may find the following guidelines useful. EPA believes that you should try to permanently reduce your radon levels as much as possible. Based on currently available information, EPA believes that levels in most homes can be reduced to about 0.02WL (4 pCi/l).

If your results are about 10.0 WL or higher, or about 200 pCi/l or higher:

Exposures in this range are among the highest observed in homes. Residents should undertake action to reduce levels as far below 1.0 WL (200 pCi/l) as possible. We recommend that you take action within several weeks. If this is not possible, you should determine, in consultation with appropriate state or local health or radiation protection officials, if temporary relocation is appropriate until the levels can be reduced.

If your results are about 0.1 to about 1.0 WL, or about 20 to about 200 pCi/l:

Exposures in this range are considered greatly above average for residential structures. You should undertake action to reduce levels as far below 0.1 WL (20 pCi/l) as possible. We recommend that you take action within several months.

If your results are about 0.02 to about 0.1 WL, or about 4 pCi/l to about 20 pCi/l:

Exposures in this range are considered above average for residential structures. You should undertake action to lower levels to about 0.02 WL (4 pCi/l) or below. We recommend that you take action within a few years, sooner if levels are at the upper end of this range.

If your results are about 0.02 WL or lower, or about 4 pci/l or lower:

Exposures in this range are considered average or slightly above average for residential structures. Although exposures in this range do present some risk of lung cancer, reductions of levels this low may be difficult, and sometimes impossible, to achieve.

Remember: There is increasing urgency for action at higher concentrations of radon. The higher the radon level in your home, the faster you should take action to reduce your exposure....

Are there other factors I should consider?

Most of the risk information given in this pamphlet, as well as the recommendations for taking corrective action, are based on the general case. Your individual living patterns could influence your assessment of your risk and your decisions about the need for further action. Your answers to the following questions may help you evaluate your personal risk.

- Does anyone smoke in your home? Scientific evidence indicates that smoking may increase the risk of exposure to radon. In addition, smoking significantly increases your overall risk of lung cancer.

- Do you have children living at home? Although there are no studies of children exposed to radon to determine whether they are more sensitive than adults, some scientific studies of other types of radiation exposure indicate that children may be more sensitive. Consequently, children could be more at risk than adults from exposure to radon.

- How much time does any family member spend at home? The risk estimates given in this pamphlet assume that 75 percent of a person's time is spent at home. If you or your family spend more or less time at home, you should take this into consideration.

- Does anyone sleep in your basement? Since radon concentrations tend to be greater on the lower levels of a home, a person who sleeps in the basement is likely to face a greater risk than a person who sleeps in a second-floor bedroom.

• How long will you live in your home? The risk estimates in this booklet are based on the assumption that you will be exposed to the radon level found in your home for roughly 70 years. As you evaluate your potential risk, therefore, you might consider the total amount of time you expect to live in your home. But remember: other houses you have lived in—or will live in— may have the same or higher radon levels.

How can I reduce my risk from radon?

Your risk of lung cancer from exposure to radon depends upon the amount of radon entering your home and the length of time it remains in your living areas. Listed below are some actions you might take to immediately reduce your risk from radon. These actions can be done quickly and with minimum expense in most cases.

• Stop smoking and discourage smoking in your home. By doing so, you should reduce your family's overall chance of developing lung cancer, as well as reducing your family's risk from radon exposure.

• Spend less time in areas with higher concentrations of radon, such as the basement.

• Whenever practical, open all windows and turn on fans to increase the air flow into and through the house. This is especially important in the basement.

• If your home has a crawl space beneath, keep the crawl-space vents on all sides of the house fully open all year.

While the above actions will help reduce your risk from radon, they generally do not offer a long-term solution. You can find more information about permanent, cost-effective solutions to a radon problem in the EPA publication, *Radon Reduction Methods: A Homeowner's Guide.*...[This publication is free, and may be obtained from your state radiation protection office or from your EPA regional office.]

Before undertaking major modifications to your home, we recommend that you consult with your state radiation protection office to obtain whatever specific advise or assistance they may be able to provide for your particular situation. ❖

How to Check Your House Without Getting Ripped Off

WASHINGTON POST, SEPTEMBER 27, 1988

NINE ALERT INDIANA residents last year helped put a stop to what government officials said was a radon scam.

A company called Retrotec USA Inc. offered to pay the $20 to attend a seminar on radon, according to a complaint filed by the Indiana State Attorney General's Office. Then the company agreed to test their homes for the gas at no cost.

But then, according to the complaint, Retrotec employees "intentionally elevated the radon levels found in the homes" by placing test canisters down sump pumps and in other locations that would inflate the readings.

The company employees also conducted follow-up tests that they "knew could neither confirm nor deny the presence of radon" gas, according to court papers. The company allegedly told one of the homeowners that exposure to their supposedly high levels of radon gas would cause them "to glow."

The solution, Retrotec employees advised, was to make repairs of $1,000 to $8,500—repairs offered by the company itself.

The attorney general's office sued Retrotec, alleging that the firm committed "deceptive acts" and attempted to defraud or mislead the consumers.

The case was settled with a consent decree, in which the company denied all wrongdoing and liability.

In the decree, Retrotec agreed that it would not incite "unjustified fear" in consumers' minds about radon and would not sell repair work unless a different firm had performed the radon test.

The firm paid $1,500 to the attorney general's office for investigating the matter. Since then, Retrotec has stopped doing business in Indiana but continues to operate in Canada.

In an interview yesterday, Richard Jordan, former vice president of Retrotec, said the firm signed the consent decree only because legal defense was too expensive and that the state had unfairly solicited complaints against Retrotec. State officials denied that allegation.

Whether more will come of the Indiana case remains to be seen. But in the wake of the Environmental Protection Agency's new recommendation that most Americans screen their homes for radon, there is concern that citizens across the country could fall prey to unscrupulous companies ready to take advantage of radon hysteria.

Radon is an invisible, odorless gas that forms when natural uranium in rocks and in the soil decays. Outdoors, radon poses no risk. But when the gas accumulates indoors, it poses significant risk to consumers.

Radon is measured in picocuries per liter of air. Levels are highest in winter, when doors and windows are closed, so an annual average is necessary to judge exposure levels.

If the average radon level in a house over a year's time is four picocuries per liter of air—the EPA's acceptable threshold—people in the house have an increased cancer risk equivalent to that caused by smoking half a pack of cigarettes a day.

Radon is thought to be responsible for an estimated 15 percent of lung cancer deaths—about 20,000 deaths—in the United States each year. Cigarette smoking is still, however, the leading cause of lung cancer, and the combined effects of radon and cigarette smoke are especially damaging.

In the wake of the new recommendations to screen most American homes for radon, EPA officials warned consumers to be careful of the companies they turn to for testing.

"Be on guard for someone who comes in with a mayonnaise jar or a light meter," says Steve Page, chief for policy and public information at EPA's radon program. Also be wary of firms that promise results after a five-minute sample; a real radon test takes at least a few days and usually longer.

Consumers who have doubts about a company or its method of testing are advised to call the EPA's regional office or check with the state health department. Both agencies are keeping lists of some 700 companies nationwide that have passed EPA proficiency exams for testing radon.

State health departments—and state attorneys general—keep lists as well of fraudulent radon-testing companies and of firms that conduct unsatisfactory home repairs for radon....

Fixing Your Home

The EPA lists six techniques that will reduce radon levels in a home. Over the past several years, most contractors have gravitated toward a procedure called a subslab suction for houses with severe radon problems. "It has a very high success rate; it's idiot-proof and doesn't require maintenance," says David Saum, president of Infiletech, a company that does research for EPA and also offers home repairs.

In the subslab process, pipes are run underneath a house and attached to a fan, which draws gases from beneath the house and into the outside air. It takes a two-member crew about a day to install the equipment. Average cost is about $1,200.

But there also are less expensive do-it-yourself ways that homeowners can use to lower radon levels, depending on the radon levels. "It's really not that complicated to fix your house," says NYU's Harley. Some can be as simple as enclosing an open sump pump or adding fans to help ventilation.

Prevention is the best bet for new homes. "It's really inexpensive and easy to lay down a network of plastic pipe (in the subslab) that will allow the radon gas to be removed before it gets into the home," she says. In a home under construction, the costs of this preventive radon measure is a few hundred dollars, compared with $1,000 or more for repair of older homes.

It's never too late to lower radon levels, say health experts. "Some people say, 'Gosh, I've been living in my house for 20 years with high radon levels. Why should I do anything about it now that the damage has already been done?" says Guimond of the EPA's Office of Radiation. "But that's not true. Our data suggest that if you reduce your exposure to radon, in time you will reduce your risk of lung cancer."

And that, says Guimond, "should be incentive for people to learn what their home radon levels are, and if they are elevated, to make the changes to reduce them."❖

Three of Seven Radon Kits Fail Blink Tests

PRESS RELEASE, PUBLIC CITIZEN, JANUARY 5, 1989

THREE OUT OF SEVEN of the nation's largest radon home detection kit companies all of which passed the Environmental Protection Agency's tests failed blind tests conducted by Public Citizen, the consumer advocacy organization founded by Ralph Nader, which today issued a comprehensive guide rating the home testing devices of 34 companies.

"While million of Americans are testing their homes for radon gas, some may be using do-it-yourself kits that provide dangerously misleading results," said Joan Claybrook, president of Public Citizen.

Following a year-long study, Buyers Up, the group-buying division of Public Citizen, ranked EPA-approved test kit companies according to laboratory quality measures and found that over half of the companies rated "fair" or below.

Based on the results of the study, Public Citizen today released a letter to the EPA appealing for more stringent study and testing procedures for makers of radon test kits.

"The EPA estimates that up to 20,000 people a year could die from radon, and they're on the right track when they urge residents to test their homes for the gas," said Christopher Dyson, research director for Buyers Up and director of the radon research program.

"But their methods of regulating the accuracy of the home test kit results leaves much to be desired," he said. "When the EPA runs its tests on the companies, the companies are told that they are being tested, and so they take special care in measuring the radon levels accurately."

Buyer's Up tests, Dyson said, were done with strict anonymity.

"If test results fail to detect the presence of high levels of the gas, homeowners could be exposing their families needlessly to dangerous levels of radon, thinking they are in the clear," charged Dyson.

On the other hand, people can be misled into spending thousands of dollars to minimize the level of radon in their home by false positive results, he said.

To help consumers deal intelligently with the problem of radon, Public Citizen today released the "Citizen's Guide to Radon Home Test Kits," which includes the ratings of those companies tested and survey by the group. The brochure is available to the public for $2.00 by writing Buyer's Up, P.O. Box 33487, Washington, D.C. 20033-0487. ❖

EXCERPT FROM

Safer Termite Control

THE HAZARDS OF CHLORDANE CAN BE AVOIDED

BY DON BEST

RODALE'S *PRACTICAL HOMEOWNER*, JULY/AUGUST 1987

MARK TWAIN ONCE remarked that the towns-people of Hannibal, Missouri, didn't insure their homes against fire—they insured them against the volunteer fire department. For modern-day homeowners trying to defend against termites, Twain's quip contains an important truth: Be careful that the solution you choose doesn't make things as bad as the problem.

Termites are a growing nuisance in the United States, particularly in the Southeast. Dr. George Rambo, director of research at the National Pest Control Association (NPCA), estimates that these subterranean devils caused $800 million in damages last year. While no one downplays the problem, there's mounting evidence that some of the chemicals used to battle termites—particularly a family of chemicals called cyclodienes—are more dangerous to human health and the environment than previously suspected.

Diane Baxter, a toxicologist with the National Coalition Against the Misuse of Pesticides (NCAMP), says hundreds of pending lawsuits involve chlordane and its three cousins in the cyclodiene family: heptachlor, aldrin, and dieldrin.

Besides the health issues, the spillage or misuse of termiticides can cost a homeowner. A Pennsylvania woman saw her property value plunge after her chlordane-tainted soil had to be scraped up and hauled to a toxic waste dump. All total, she suffered $150,000 in property loss and out-of-pocket fees.

Since chlordane was first registered for use against termites in 1948, it has become the nation's best-selling termiticide because it's effective, inexpensive, and long lasting. By impregnating the soil underneath and around the foundation of a home, termites can be kept at bay for decades. Unfortunately its high toxicity and longevity, qualities that make chlordane so effective, also make it a threat to humans. "It's a known carcinogen. It ends up in human fat and stays there for years," says Baxter.

The Environmental Protection Agency (EPA), which is studying air quality in homes treated with cyclodienes, wants chlordane and its cousins off-limits to homeowners and other untrained individuals. "We've traced a lot of misuse of this stuff to homeowners," says EPA's Jim Roelofs. "Some don't read the labels, and most don't have the proper equipment or training to apply it safely and effectively." [On April 8, 1988, the EPA banned the sale and commercial use of chlordane, heptachlor, aldrin and dieldrin, for all purposes.]

The NPCA agrees that cyclodienes should be restricted to trained professionals, but opposes a ban. "We think chlordane still has a valuable role to play in protecting homes from termites," says Dr. Rambo, "but the quality of training for applicators needs to improve. And homeowners are entitled to full disclosure."

"Full disclosure" means you have a legal right to know what your options are when choosing a termiticide and what the implications are likely to be. In other words, you can veto chlordane or any other chemical you consider hazardous if a professional exterminator says that's what he intends to use....

The controversy over cyclodienes poses a dilemma for homeowners, who want a safe and healthy home free of toxic materials, carcinogens, AND termites. The pests are so prevalent in the South that some building codes mandate preventive chemical treatment. Similarly, FHA and VA home loans are often contingent on proper termite protection.

With so many regulatory and health questions still unanswered, homeowners should concentrate on preventive measures, such as:

• Make an annual inspection, probing wood near the foundation with an ice pick or screwdriver. Holes in the wood, soft spots, or missing chunks can be signs of termites at work. Termites sometimes build earth tubes between soil and wood that can be easily spotted. Periodic inspections also ensure you'll catch the termites in the early stages when localized treatments will do the job. The longer you wait, the greater your chances of an infestation and the need for a whole-house treatment.

• Make sure the soil around and under your home is well drained and that crawlspaces are dry and well-ventilated.

• Get rid of potential termite habitats by removing scrap wood, stumps, cardboard, firewood, and other sources of cellulose close to the house.

• Treat wooden piers, posts, and trellises with a careful application of wood preservative before placing them in the ground. Another option is to use pressure-treated lumber.

• Fill voids, cracks, and expansion joints in concrete or masonry with cement grout, coal-tar, or rubberoid sealers.

• Wherever possible, remove soil within 18 inches of floor joists and 12 inches of girders.

• Replace any heavily damaged or rotted sills, joists, or flooring.

In New Construction:

• Invest in a metallic termite shield between the foundation and sill. It's not absolute protection, but it'll force termites to build earth tubes you can see.

• Don't let wood touch soil. For instance, wooden steps and porches should rest on a poured concrete base or be constructed with pressure-treated lumber.

• Hollow brick or a brick foundation should be capped with at least four inches of poured concrete or solid concrete blocks.

If the need to battle termites arises:

1. Avoid chlordane and the other cyclodienes by having your house treated with one of the new termiticide on the market. NCAMP's Baxter points out that Dursban isn't a carcinogen and breaks down in the environment faster than cyclodienes. She stresses, however, that it should be used only for sub-surface treatments by professionals.

You can also consider one of the permethrins, known by the trade names Torpedo and Dragnet. These synthetic termiticides are manufactured from plant derivatives.

2. Don't do it yourself. Find a well-trained, state-certified professional who's sensitive to your health and environmental concerns.

3. Take your time. A well-established termite colony of 60,000 workers eats only one-fifth of an ounce of wood a day so don't rush your decision.

4. Get rid of old chlordane, but don't toss it in the garbage can. Contact your local EPA office or the state agency that deals with toxic-waste disposal. Moreover, don't follow label instructions that say chlordane is safe if diluted, because the label may have been printed before the revelations about the potential dangers, says Baxter. ❖

The Environmental Protection Agency and Termiticides: An Update

ON APRIL 16, 1988, the Environmental Protection Agency (EPA) banned the sale and commercial use of the termiticides chlordane, heptachlor, aldrin and dieldrin. But the agency has a special agreement with Velsicol, the chemicals' manufacturer: These pesticides may go back on the market "only after Velsicol has conducted air-monitoring studies for each application method being considered, and only if such studies demonstrate that no detectable levels of chlordane/heptachlor are found in houses experimentally treated by a specific application method," according to the EPA pamphlet "Termiticides." Velsicol has yet to prove that these chemicals can be applied safely.

As of October, 1987, five alternative termiticides were registered with EPA: chlorpyrifos (e.g., Dursban), permethrin (i.e., Torpedo and Dragnet), cypermethrin (i.e., Demon), fenvalerate, and isofenphos (i.e., Pryfon 6, formerly Oftanol 6). The EPA has safety files on all these chemicals, and claims that, when used according to label directions, they are all safe to use. ❖

EXCERPT FROM

Statement by Christine G. Carpenter

AT HEARING ON H.R. 2622, AMENDMENT TO THE CLEAN AIR ACT BEFORE THE SUBCOMMITTEE ON HEALTH AND THE ENVIRONMENT, COMMITTEE ON ENERGY AND COMMERCE

JUNE 24, 1987

...AFTER TREATING THE interior of my home, the exterminators assured me that treatment had been completed and that I was free to lock up and leave my home to run errands, shop, etc. When I returned that evening between 6:30 to 7:30 p.m., I was immediately aware of a strong chemical odor as I approached my front door. I also noticed that the exterminators had further treated my home from the exterior. Holes had been drilled into the exterior brick wall and chlordane injected through these holes directly into the house itself. The chlordane entered a bulkhead on the interior side of the brick wall, ran down the interior cinder-block wall, and emptied onto the basement cement slab floor in the utility room. A mini-lake had formed; rugs were saturated; carton boxes of storage items were also saturated, along with the stored items within the boxes.

Not knowing that the substance was toxic, I proceeded the next day to clean up the "mess", disposing of the saturated newspapers which I had used the day before to absorb the milky fluid, and also cutting up the saturated rugs so as to dispose of them in plastic trash bags. I did not realize that I was absorbing a toxic chemical through by bare skin.

I also took advantage of this opportunity to implement plans to redecorate my home and began work in the basement area, sealing and painting the cement floor, discarding unneeded storage items, etc. I worked in the utility room for the next three weeks or so, further endangering my health by inhaling the toxic pesticide. It never occurred to me that the pesticide might pose a health problem, my reasoning being that the exterminators would never have been so careless, otherwise.

I had never heard the word "chlordane" until a few weeks later when I visited Management on another matter and related the "mess" the exterminators had left in my basement and that I "had practically bathed in it." I was then told that it was chlordane and nothing more was said.

Within a few days or so, I viewed a TV program about chlordane, its toxicity, associated health hazards, and a case history of a family's nightmare due to chlordane contamination of their home. It was then that my own nightmare began.

I realized that my two granddaughters (aged 10 months and four years) had visited me for three days just two days after my home was contaminated. I remembered, too, that I had been worried because, for no apparent reason, they were coughing and sneezing. I became distraught....❖

EXCERPT FROM
Under Siege
ORGANIC GARDENING, APRIL 1988

Warning Signs

Pesticides can damage and tax your immune system at the same time. The damage can be both acute and cumulative. Since many toxic chemicals are stored in your fat cells and lymph glands, they can remain in the body for decades. Thus, health problems can build up over a long period in ways that science doesn't yet fully understand.

One of the most dangerous effects of pesticides is that they weaken your immune system so you are less able to combat even ordinary infections.

Symptoms of a weakened immune system might include: skin rashes, nausea, fatigue, depression, leukemia, frequent infections, and fever.

How do you protect your immune system from pesticides? The best way, of course, is not to use them. But that may not be realistic in all circumstances. "We don't need to abolish the use of toxic chemicals," San Francisco immunologist Alan Levin, M.D. says. "The solution is common sense." That means:

- Wear gloves and a respirator.
- "Ventilate, ventilate, ventilate," Levin says.
- Dispose of the waste properly.
- Keep your immune system in top shape. Almost every nutrient is important for proper immune function but a few are key—vitamin C, vitamin A, and zinc. Good sources of C are peppers, broccoli, cantaloupe, cabbage, spinach, tomatoes, and strawberries. Sources for A include sweet potatoes, carrots, spinach, cantaloupe, kale, broccoli, asparagus, green beans, corn, parsley. You can get zinc from soybeans, lentils, pinto beans and sunflower seeds.
- Reduce stress. Research shows that people who have more anxiety and depression in reaction to change can weaken their immune systems. Start gardening. Not only is it relaxing and enjoyable but it gives you some control over your food supply. ❖

Organic Gardening *Magazine is available for $12.97 a year. Published monthly. Address: 35 E. Minor Street, Emmaus, PA 18049.*

"Someone's Been Poisoned. Help!"
What To Do in a Pesticide Emergency
A CONSUMER'S GUIDE TO SAFER PESTICIDE USE
U.S. ENVIRONMENTAL PROTECTION AGENCY, SEPTEMBER 1987

IN RECENT YEARS, control of pesticides has been one of EPA's top priorities.

While pesticides can provide substantial benefits, they can also pose significant risks. The potential for a pesticide to produce injury depends upon several factors:

• Toxicity of the active ingredient

Toxicity is a measure of the inherent ability of a chemical to produce injury. Some pesticides, such as pyrethrins, have low human toxicity while others, such as sodium fluoroacetate, are extremely toxic.

• Dose

The greater the dose of pesticide, i.e. the amount absorbed, the greater the risk of injury. Dose is dependent upon the absolute amount of the pesticide absorbed relative to the weight of the person. Therefore, small amounts of pesticide might produce illness in a small child while the same dose in an adult might be relatively harmless.

• Route of absorption

Swallowing a pesticide usually creates the most serious problem. In practice, however, the most common route of absorption of pesticides is through the skin, and the more toxic pesticides have caused fatalities through this route.

• Duration of exposure

The longer a person is exposed to pesticides, the higher the level in the body may occur. However, there is a point at which an equilibrium will develop between the intake and the output. Then, the level will no longer continue to increase. This point may be either above or below the known toxic level.

• Physical and chemical properties

The distribution and the rates of breakdown of pesticides in the environment significantly alter the likelihood that injury might occur.

• Population at risk

Those who run the greatest danger of poisoning are those whose exposure is highest such as workers who mix, load, or apply pesticides. Those who pick or consume pesticide treated foods have much lower exposures. But... the general public also faces the possibility of exposure. Pesticides may be encountered in an office or home as the result of a treatment for ant, roach, or termite control. Pesticides may also be encountered outdoors from area-wide pest control application such as mosquito abatement programs. One of the points of highest exposure to some pesticides occurs right in your own backyard as you mix and apply pesticides to your garden or lawn.

Recognizing Pesticide Poisoning

As with any other chemical, pesticides may produce injury externally or internally.

External irritants may cause a contact-associated skin disease which is primarily of an irritant nature-producing redness, itching, or pimples. It may be an allergic skin reaction, producing redness, swelling, or blistering. The mucous membranes of the eyes, nose, mouth, and throat are also quite sensitive to chemicals. Stinging and swelling can occur.

Internal injuries from any chemical may occur depending upon where a chemical is transported in the body. Thus, symptoms are dependent upon the organ involved. Shortness of breath, clear sputum production, or rapid breathing occurs as the result of injury to the lung. Nausea, vomiting, abdominal cramps, or diarrhea may occur as the result of direct injury to the gastrointestinal tract. Excessive fatigue, sleepiness, headache, muscle twitching, and loss of sensation occur as the result of injury to the nervous system. In general, each class of pesticide has a set of symptoms which are unique to that particular class.

For example, organophosphate pesticides may produce symptoms of pesticide poisoning which affect several different organs, and may progress very rapidly form very mild to severe. Symptoms may progress in a matter of minutes from slight difficulty with vision to paralysis of the diaphragm muscle, causing inability to breathe.

Therefore, if someone develops symptoms after working with pesticides, seek medical help promptly to determine if the symptoms are pesticide-related. In certain cases, blood or urine can be collected for analysis or specific exposure tests can be made. It is better to be too cautious than too late.

It is always important to avoid these symptoms by minimizing your exposure (and dose) when mixing and applying pesticides by wearing gloves and other protective clothing.

The appropriate first aid treatment depends upon which pesticide was used. Here are some tips for first aid that may precede, but should not substitute for, medical treatment:

• Poison on skin

Drench skin with water, and remove contaminated clothing. Wash skin and hair thoroughly with soap and water. Dry victim and wrap in blanket. Later, discard contaminated clothing or thoroughly wash it separately from other laundry.

• Chemical burn on skin

Drench skin with water and remove contaminated clothing. Cover burned area immediately with loose, clean, soft cloth. Do not apply ointments, greases, powders or other drugs. Later, discard or thoroughly wash contaminated clothing separately from other laundry.

• Poison in eye

Eye membranes absorb pesticides faster than any other external part of the body; eye damage can occur in a few minutes with some types of pesticides. Hold eyelid open and wash eye quickly and gently with clean, running water from the tap or a hose for 15 minutes or more. Do not use eye drops or chemicals or drugs in the wash water.

• Inhaled poison

Carry or drag victim to fresh air immediately. (If proper protection for yourself is unavailable, call for emergency equipment from the fire department.) Open doors and windows so no one else will be poisoned by fumes. Loosen victim's tight clothing. If the victim's skin is blue or the victim has stopped breathing, give artificial respiration, and call a rescue service for help.

• Swallowed poison

A conscious victim should rinse his mouth with plenty of water and drink up to one quart of milk or water to dilute the pesticide. Induce vomiting only if instructions to do so are on the label. If there is no label available to guide you, do not induce vomiting if the victim has swallowed a corrosive poison or an emulsifiable concentrate or oil solution, or if the victim is unconscious or is having convulsions.

In dealing with any poisoning, act fast; speed is crucial.

First Aid for Pesticide Poisoning

First aid is the first step in treating a pesticide poisoning. Study the product label before you use a pesticide , especially the statement of treatment on the pesticide label. When you realize a pesticide poisoning is occurring, be sure the victim is not being further exposed to the poison before calling for emergency help. An unconscious victim will have to be dragged into fresh air. Caution: Do not become poisoned yourself while trying to help. You may have to put on breathing equipment or protective clothing to avoid becoming the second victim.

When initial first aid has been performed, get medical help immediately. This advice cannot be repeated too often. Bring the product container with its label to the doctor's office or emergency room where the victim will be treated; if you bring the container, keep it out of the passenger space of your vehicle. The doctor needs to know what chemical is in the pesticide before prescribing treatment (information that is also on the label). Sometimes the label even includes a telephone number to call for additional treatment information.

A good resource in a pesticide emergency is NPTN, the National Pesticide Telecommunications Network.

Funded primarily by EPA and operating out of the Texas Tech University School of Medicine, NPTN is a toll-free telephone service. Operators are on call 24 hours a day, 365 days a year, to provide information on pesticides and on recognizing and responding to pesticide poisonings. If necessary, they can transfer inquiries directly to affiliated poison control centers.

National Pesticide Telecommunications Network

Call Toll-Free 1-800-858-7378

NPTN operators can answer questions about animal as well as human poisonings. To keep your pets from being poisoned, follow label directions on flea and tick products carefully, and keep pets off lawns that have been newly treated with weed killers and insecticides.

EPA is interested in receiving information on any adverse effects associated with pesticide exposure. If you have such information, contact Frank Davido, Pesticide Incident Response Officer, Hazard Evaluation Division (TS-769C), Office of Pesticide Programs, EPA, 401 M Street, SW Washington, D.C. 20460 (telephone 703-557-0576). You should provide as complete information as possible, including any official investigation report of the incident an medical records concerning adverse health effects. Medical records will be held in confidence. ❖

Is EPA Registration a Guarantee of Pesticide Safety?

BY ANN TATTERSALL
THE JOURNAL OF PESTICIDE REFORM, SPRING 1986

MANY PEOPLE, including some commercial and public agency users of pesticides, believe that Environmental Protection Agency (EPA) registration guarantees the safety of pesticides. In fact, this is far from the truth, for a number of reasons.

First, it is essentially impossible to prove a product safe, though tests can be and are done to try to discover the risks of its use. At any rate, chemicals that are intended to be used as poisons pose risks.

Secondly, the law does not say that EPA registration guarantees the safety of pesticides, but merely indicates the benefits of the pesticide are expected to exceed costs (i.e. damage).

Lastly, as has come to light in Congressional inves-

tigations and various published reports, EPA has in many respects failed to carry out its mandate to serve the environment and public through regulation of pesticides.

Money Has The Final Say

Even with the best of intentions, sound procedures, and adequate staff, registration would not mean that a pesticide is safe. There is a strong economic component in the decisionmaking process, indeed in the law, which guarantees that the registration process is a matter of weighing health and environmental hazards against "social" and economic gains. In practice, the economic gain component is based on projections by chemical companies and users who do not subscribe to or investigate integrated pest management or non-chemical alternatives. As John Bonine, University of Oregon environmental law professor, describes the registration process, "If the costs of using the pesticide are considered to be 90 cents worth of cancer and the benefits are estimated at a dollar's worth of profits, the pesticide is registered."

To reduce the pesticide risk will take more than tinkering with the regulatory process, although a great deal of harm could be prevented if the EPA were to do the job laid out for it in the law. Strengthening the pesticide law would help matters, and an administration sympathetic to public concerns about safety would encourage EPA to follow the law. Ultimately, however, the adverse health and environmental effects of pesticides can be avoided only by not using pesticides. Pesticides are, as California law describes them, "economic poisons." Whether they are in reality economic to use is debatable; that they are poisonous is not. ❖

The Journal of Pesticide Reform is published quarterly by the Northwest Coalition for Alternatives to Pesticides (NCAP), P.O. Box 1393, Eugene, OR 97440. $25 a year for charter members and institutions, $15 for members of limited income and individuals within institutions.

Ecological Illnesses
BY EARON S. DAVIS
TRIAL MAGAZINE, 1986

Chemically induced diseases are emerging as major public health problems. But there is little definitive medical information on the causes and mechanisms of the illnesses.

The symptoms are often disabling, affecting multiple organ systems with disorders like impaired mental functioning, fatigue, muscle and joint problems, or respiratory and skin ailments. Insufficient recognition of ecological illnesses by the government and the medical community, as well as the unusual nature of this apparent immune system disregulation, pose major but not insurmountable obstacles to just compensation for chemical victims and their lawyers.

ECOLOGICAL ILLNESSES (EI) is a term used to describe some of the more subtle but devastating health effects of chemical exposures in the workplace, at home, and outdoors. These illnesses, according to San Francisco immunologist Alan S. Levin, appear to stem from damage to the immune system, from either acute poisoning by toxic chemicals or from chronic, low-level exposures to many substances that ultimately overwhelm the system.

The exact symptoms of EI (also known as environmental hypersensitivity disorder, chemically induced immune system disregulation, total allergy syndrome, maladaptation syndrome, and the twentieth century disease) may vary from person to person, but they generally involve an increasing intolerance to a wide range of chemicals, including ubiquitous substances like formaldehyde, pesticides (either as indoor or outdoor pollutants or as food and water residues), natural gas fumes, perfumes and scents, and solvents. The EI victim may experience a wide range of disabling conditions, from a generalized weakness and joint or muscle pain to mental confusion, depression, and even hypertension, lung disease, heart disease, and neurological disorders.

As the 1979 U.S. Surgeon General Report on Health Promotion and Disease Prevention says, "There is virtually no major chronic disease to which environmental factors do not contribute, directly or indirectly."

A special commission of the Ontario Ministry of Health (Canada) calls ecological illness "environmental hypersensitivity" and describes it as follows:

Environmental hypersensitivity is a chronic (i.e., continuing for more than three months) multisystem disorder, usually involving symptoms of the central nervous system and at least one other system. Affected persons are frequently intolerant to some foods and they react adversely to some chemicals and to environmental agents, singly or in combination, at levels generally tolerated by the majority. Affected persons have varying degrees of morbidity, from mild discomfort to total disability. Upon physical examination, the patient is normally free from any abnormal objective findings. Although abnormalities of complement and lymphocytes have been recorded, no singly laboratory test, including serum IgE, is consistently altered. Improvement is associated with avoidance of suspected agents and symptoms recur with re-exposure.

Try explaining that to a jury, while deftly countering defense arguments about peculiar susceptibility, multiple causation, lack of "objective" evidence of the illness, and foreseeability. Clearly, EI presents major problems for the trial lawyer. For all the excellent work done on behalf of victims of formaldehyde and other substances, many of whom suffer from EI, it is difficult to find evidence of compensation for EI itself in the reported verdicts and settlements. ...

Much of the difficulty surrounding EI revolves around its lack of similarity with traditional occupational and environmental illnesses. First, EI has no threshold (the exposure level below which there is no risk of developing the illness). In fact, it may be multifactorial, including multiple chemical exposures and host factors. Liability would often be based on indirect proof of causation. Second, EI does not have the unique symptoms found in the readily compensable occupational diseases like asbestosis. Since the symptoms are nonspecific to the disease (headaches, fatigue), it is more difficult for victims to even be properly diagnosed, let alone compensated.

The scope of this unusual cluster of illnesses is broad. EI may befall a student moving into a new apartment that has formaldehyde emissions from carpeting and furnishings, a high-tech industry worker exposed to hazardous solvents, or a schoolteacher working near a spirit duplicator. A major cause of EI appears to be the pollutants in modern, air-tight office buildings.

Indoor pollutants like pesticides, fumes from gas ranges or poorly vented attached garages, detergents, disinfectants, glues and solvents, paints and coatings, defective furnaces, unvented kerosene space heaters, and tobacco smoke play a major role in the development of EI. For these indoor pollution cases, choices must be made about proceeding against potential defendants like product manufacturers, employers, building owners and managers, and architects and engineers. In many cases, it will be impossible to isolate even one defendant....

Treatment

The best treatment for EI, it appears, is for the sufferer to avoid all offending substances. This advice may be far more difficult to follow than one might believe. For example, formaldehyde is involved in 8 percent of the U.S. gross national product. Formaldehyde is present in pressed-wood products in building materials and furnishings; in a wide range of products and byproducts like tobacco smoke, perfumes, toilet paper, permanent-press clothing, carpeting, drapes, and shampoos; in scientific and medical laboratories, many industrial processes, and mortuaries; and in outdoor pollution.

Avoiding formaldehyde means avoiding the modern office building and factory. Such a limitation on a person's possible work environment could result in total disability. Avoiding formaldehyde means no restaurants, theaters, shopping malls, and courthouses. Also, the victim must find or create a place to live that excludes all sources of the substance. That takes money.

Avoiding pesticides is also difficult, as many workplaces use chemical pest controls periodically. Also, exposures come from chemicals used on lawns or by exterminators in apartment building, residues on food, mosquito and other pest sprays, etc. Heavy pesticide use may make agricultural regions uninhabitable for those with EI.

Natural gas is also difficult to avoid. Finding an all-electric building may be difficult. It may be impossible to find a workplace that does not have natural-gas emissions and other offending agents as well.

Besides the difficulty and cost of avoiding exposure to substances like formaldehyde, EI victims must face the social isolation that results from their illness. Most people simply cannot understand that some people must, for the sake of their lives, avoid twentieth-century conveniences. The emotional cost to the victim, who is often ridiculed and abandoned by friends and family, is high. And these costs are insidious in that they cause the victim to withdraw even further from a normal life.

As EI becomes better understood, the stigma will diminish, and government research and assistance will be available. Until then, victims are in a vulnerable position. The same disabilities that interfere with their employability also interfere with their ability to find and secure medical treatment, government entitlements, and legal representation for personal injury and product liability actions....❖

Trial *Magazine is available for $24 a year. Published monthly. Address: Association of Trial Lawyers of America, 1050 31st Street NW, Washington, D.C. 20007.*

Alternatives for Common Household Hazardous Products

RESOURCES NEWSMAGAZINE, VOLUME 7, NUMBER 2

Drain Openers/Cleaners

The primary component of drain cleaners is lye, an extremely corrosive material that can eat right through skin. Lye itself poses no danger by inhalation, but in liquid drain cleaners lye is mixed with volatile chemicals that can release harmful vapors.

Alternative: Try to prevent clogging: 1) use a drain strainer to trap food particles and hair; 2) do not pour grease down the drain; 3) pour boiling water down your drain twice a week as a preventative measure. When the drain gets sluggish: 1) Pour 1 handful baking soda and 1/2 cup white vinegar down the drainpipe and cover tightly for one minute. The chemical reaction between the two will build up pressure in the drain and dislodge any obstructive matter. Rinse with hot water. 2) Pour 1/2 cup salt plus 1/2 baking soda or 2 tablespoons trisodiumphosphate (TSP—available in hardware stores) down the drain, followed by lots of hot water. If your drain remains clogged after all, unclog with a metal snake or plunger.

Ammonia and other all purpose cleaners, such as toilet bowl, window, and surface cleaners

Ammonia is great for attacking household grease and grime, but it also attacks the skin—rashes, redness, and chemical burns during exposure are common. It is a very volatile chemical and its fumes are extremely irritating to eyes and lungs. Ammonia fumes can be especially harmful to anyone with respiratory problems. Any ammonia contact with the eyes can cause severe damage.

Alternative: Clean often. You can make your own all purpose cleaner by mixing one teaspoon of TSP (for heavy duty cleaning), liquid soap or borax in 1 quart of warm or hot water. Add some lemon juice or vinegar to cut grease. For mirrors and windows use vinegar and water (1:1). Vinegar with salt and water is a good general surface cleaner. For cleaning coffee pots, chrome, copper and tile, use dissolved baking soda.

Oven Cleaners

The greatest dangers in oven cleaners comes from lye (see above) and ammonia (see above). Oven cleaners in aerosol spray form are especially hazardous, because the spray sends tiny droplets of lye and ammonia into the air, where they can easily be inhaled, or land in eyes or on skin.

Alternative: Keep oven clean as you use it. Dirty ovens can be cleaned with baking or washing soda: 3 tbsp. soda in 1 cup warm water. Sprinkle salt on spills when they are warm, then scrub. For baked on, put 1/4 cup ammonia in oven overnight to loosen, then scrub with baking soda.

Abrasive Scouring Powders

Almost all scouring powders contain chlorine bleach which acts as a whitener and stain remover. When the powder comes in contact with water it produces chlorine fumes, which can be irritating to eyes, nose, throat, and lungs. Some people react with headaches, fatigue, and difficulty in breathing. Never mix any products that contain chlorine with products that contain ammonia—the resulting chloramine fumes can be deadly.

Alternative: Dry baking soda, borax, or table salt sprinkled on a wet sponge act as effective abrasives for scouring.

Laundry Detergent

Detergents cause more poisoning incidents than any other household product. A lesser hazard comes from the residues left on clothing and bed sheets that can cause severe skin rashes (especially on sensitive baby skins), or from "springtime fresh" fragrances that linger long after articles are laundered. There have also been reports of flu and asthma symptoms associated with breathing air that contains detergent dust.

Alternative: Try products made from natural soap. If your clothes are not really dirty but just need some "freshening up," use about 1 cup of plain baking soda, white vinegar, or borax, or 1 tablespoon of trisodiumphosphate per washload of clothes. All these natural substances are excellent for removing smells, and they don't add any odors of their own.

Chlorine Bleach

While the greatest danger of chlorine bleach is accidental ingestion, the fumes inhaled during use also pose a hazard. Even though the amount of fumes released is well within recognized safety limits, many people report adverse reactions to chlorine fumes at these low levels, and even to chlorine residues left in fabics after laundering.

Alternative: Use baking soda or borax to whiten.

Spot Removers

Spot removers usually contain the solvent perchloroethylene.

Perchloroethylene fumes are carcinogenic, highly toxic, and can cause light-headedness, dizziness, sleepiness, nausea, loss of appetite, and disorientation.
Alternative: Club soda, or immediate application of cold water. 1/4 cup of borax dissolved in 2 cups of cold water makes a good all-purpose spot remover. Grass or milk spots are softened by glycerine or glycerine soap. Other spot removers are vinegar, lemon juice and cornmeal-and-water paste.

Rug and Upholstery Cleaners

The active ingredient in most rug, carpet, and upholstery shampoos is perchloroethylene, which is a known human carcinogen (Immediate effects: see above). Long term exposure can damage the liver or central nervous system. Another ingredient in rug and upholstery cleaners may be napthalene, which is toxic by inhalation, and can cause headaches, confusion, nausea and vomiting, excessive sweating and urinary irritation. Ethanol, ammonia, and detergents are also sometimes present.
Alternative: Sprinkle cornstarch on rug and vacuum. To brighten the color of your carpet, vacuum to remove dust, then apply a mixture of 1 quart white vinegar and 3 quarts boiling water with a wet rag. When necessary, use soap-based, non-aerosol rug shampoos.

Furniture and Floor Polish

A common ingredient is phenol, a suspected human carcinogen. Skin contact can cause swelling, peeling, burning or breaking out in hives and pimples. Ingestion can cause circulatory collapse, convulsions, cold sweats, coma, and death. Furniture and floor polishes also often contain nitrobenzene which can cause skin discoloration, shallow breathing, vomiting, and death—from skin contact. Repeated exposure can cause cancer, genetic changes, birth defects, and heart, liver, kidney, and central nervous system damage.
Alternative: Light, soapy water to clean and a soft cloth to shine. Melt 1 tbsp. of Carnauba Wax into 2 cups of mineral oil, or dissolve 1 tsp. lemon oil into 1 pint of mineral oil. You can also rub crushed, raw nuts on the wood for an oily polish or use plain mayonnaise. Rub toothpaste on wood furniture to remove water marks.

Air Fresheners

The only thing air fresheners do is mask unpleasant smell with a more pleasant one. Ingredients often found in air fresheners are: napthalene, phenol, cresol, ethanol, xylene and formaldehyde. Many people with allergies and respiratory problems are bothered by the smell of air fresheners.
Alternative: Ventilate. This will also help reduce any toxic fumes that are building up indoors. Set vinegar out in an open dish. Use an opened box of baking soda in enclosed areas such as refrigerators or closets. To scent the air use fresh flowers or pine boughs, or make sachets of fragrant herbs and flowers.

Insecticides

One of the most frequently used pesticides in home sprays is pyrethrin, which is just the crushed, dried flowers of Crysanthemum cinerarifolium. It's harmless for humans or pets to swallow, but kills bugs on contact. Unfortunately, commercial pyrethrin formulations are often mixed with other, not so harmless, pesticides.
Alternative: To combat ants pour a line of cream of tartar, red chili powder, paprika or dried peppermint at point of entry. Roaches can be enticed into non-chemical traps by placing a banana in a jar which contains grease or Vaseline as an adhesive. A tongue depressor can be used as a ramp to the jar. Pets can be protected from insects by feeding them brewers yeast or vitamin B as a preventative. Also, it can help to regularly give herbal baths to dogs. ❖

Resources is available for $16 a year. Published quarterly. Address: The Environmental Task Force, 1012 14th Street NW, 15th Floor, Washington, D.C. 20077-1816.

Penta Present in Common Items

BY ROBERT STERLING

MEDFORD MAIL TRIBUNE, MEDFORD, OREGON, AUGUST 10, 1986

IT'S ON TELEPHONE POLES, fence posts, picnic tables, patio furniture, decks, paints and stains. It's used by lumber and paper mills and makers of pesticides and glues. We can breathe it, absorb it and ingest it, and because of that we sometimes get sick and sometimes die.

The toxic wood preservative pentaclorophenol, also known as penta and PCP, has been used widely mainly by the wood products industry for at least the past 30 years.

Light brown in its solid form and readily identified by its pungent odor when hot, the chemical is an effective and inexpensive insecticide and a potent herbicide, fungicide bactericide and anti-mildew agent.

But it is also a health hazard, and its use has caused problems throughout the U.S., both in the home and workplace.

As more about it has become known in recent years, many log home builders and others have switched to other wood preservative solutions that don't contain penta.

All log home builders contacted in Medford and Ashland said they use only natural wood, and recommend stains and preservatives that don't contain penta.

Many lumber mills have switched to a related chemical, tetrachlorophenol, but that has been found to have similar properties as penta.

The mills, including many in the Medford area, mix the chemicals with water and spray it on some lumber to control unsightly mold and bacteria.

Wood preserving companies combine penta with oils or creosote and apply it in a pressure-treatment process to products such as utility poles, window frames and fence posts.

Sometimes, as is being alleged by the Joneses in Ashland, it's mixed with a stain and painted directly on wood in log homes.

Exposure is know to irritate the eyes, nose and throat and cause coughing, weakness, weight loss, sweating, headaches, dizziness, nausea, chest pains, fever and skin disease.

It can kill by causing extremely high fevers, by poisoning the liver and kidneys and by apparently suppressing the immune system.

In some, symptoms never appear, or show only after years of exposure; others seem to react quickly even to brief exposure in low concentrations.

"For the susceptible individual, it can be extremely dangerous," says Dr. Phillip Leveque, a Mollala-based forensic toxicologist who investigated the Jones' case.

"The problem is, you don't know how susceptible you are until you're exposed to it," he says. "It's a bad way to die."

Penta is known to cause birth defects in laboratory animals and in experiments at Oregon State University, to suppress the immune system in mice.

Its harmful effects can be compounded because the chemical is frequently tainted with cancer-causing dioxins, which are formed as impurities during the manufacturing process.

The Environmental Protection Agency, which classifies penta as a hazardous substance and toxic pollutant, will impose new regulations on its use beginning Nov. 10.

The rules, which were to take effect in 1984 but were delayed because of legal challenges from chemical manufacturers, would limit sales to certified applicators and require protective clothing such as gloves and coveralls and respirators in certain situations.

The makers of penta will be required to limit the amount of hexachlorodioxin contamination to 15 parts per million and, after 18 months to reduce that level to one ppm.

Already, the labels of penta products warn against indoor application. The new EPA regulations will ban indoor use and the application of penta to logs used to make log homes.

Use of pressure-treated wood indoors will be prohibited, except for laminated beams or window molding, and then only when two coats of a sealer such as urethane, shellac, latex epoxy enamel or varnish are used.

Penta won't be allowed where there may be contamination of feed, food, drinking or irrigation water.

The wood products industry has already begun a voluntary consumer awareness program, which includes details on application and handling techniques.

An information sheet recommends that consumers avoid frequent and prolonged skin contact with penta-treated wood, such as lawn chairs and other outdoor furniture, unless two coats of an effective sealer have been applied.

The labels of all penta products will include a warning that penta should be avoided during pregnancy.

Although the new regulations will help, many believe they don't go far enough.

"It's a damn disgrace," Leveque says. "Knowing what the EPA knows about this stuff, they're doing nothing."

At the time the rules were to take effect in 1984, a top EPA official said the regulations would protect the public by eliminating potentially hazardous uses and by providing information on proper handling.

The EPA had wanted to make the consumer awareness program mandatory, but later agreed to allow a voluntary information program.

John Heller, an EPA pesticides official in Seattle, called the voluntary program a "sloppy" way of disseminating information, because, he said, without regulations, information sheets will easily be separated from penta products or otherwise hidden from view.

Dennis Lindsay, product manager of Vulcan Chemical Co. in Wichita, Kan., the only domestic maker of penta, says "there's no such thing as a non-toxic wood preserver."

"Too much of anything will kill you," he says. "Pentachlorophenol is a toxic chemical, and if people don't treat it with respect, it can cause problems."

He refused comment on the EPA regulations, except to say "we intend to continue to produce penta and intend to be legal with our production and sale."

Lindsay says Vulcan produces about 24 million pounds of penta per year, most of which is used by the wood products industry.

Medical studies have found traces of penta in the blood and urine of the general population; scientists say the most likely exposure is from food and direct skin contact with penta-treated products.

Penta residues have been found in powdered milk, soft drinks, bread, candy bars, cereal, noodles, rice, sugar and wheat.

Scientists say food probably becomes tainted from storage in penta-treated wooden containers.

Workers in wood products plants are frequently exposed through direct contact of penta solutions on skin and clothing, and by breathing fumes.

Those who live near such factories have also claimed health problems. Earlier this summer, a Molalla couple's $4.5 million lawsuit against a wood products maker and sawdust supplier was settled out of court.

Although none of the defendants admitted liability, the couple alleged that water, dust, smoke and sawdust containing penta had made them severely ill and killed several of their horses.

Log Home Builders Say They Avoid Use of Penta

Log home builders in Medford and Ashland say log homes are great places to live, but they agree penta, as one builder put it, is "bad stuff."

"We wouldn't use it on anything," says Len Sherbourne, owner of Log Cabin Shop & Supply in White City. He and others say they make sure their log suppliers haven't pretreated the wood with penta, and they recommend wood preservatives that don't contain penta.

Scott Kline, co-owner of Forrest Log Homes in Ashland, says he recommends varnishes, Varathane, log oils or water-based latex products.

Tom Salade, owner of Homestead Log Homes in Central Point, says he recommends Penofin, which despite the similar-sounding name, contains no penta.

"The wood should never be pretreated," says Ned Barraclough, owner of Circle B Builders in Ashland. He says he recommends a clear, odorless solution called Woodguard be used for house exteriors.

An article on preservatives in the winter 1985 *Log Home Guide for Builders & Buyers* noted that some forest products experts recommend a five percent penta solution on log home exteriors.

"But it's nasty stuff to be around and has been labeled a dangerous substance by the EPA and the Centers for Disease Control. All agree, penta should never be used on the interior of a log home, and if used, extreme caution to avoid body contact, or breathing vapors, must be exercised," the article said. ❖

Letter to Ralph Nader

FEBRUARY 22, 1986

I am interested in learning if any one is starting a class action suit against the perfume industry.

There are so many outcries about smoking, yet the perfume industry invades my home in magazines, catalogues, monthly bills, even on toilet tissue.

I have Emphysema and was in a respiratory crisis for three days in December because of a catalogue that contained a perfumed ad.

I'm only one of many who can no longer go grocery shopping or replenishing my clothes because everything is super saturated with scent. I can't do anything about this but get damn mad when they take over my home. ❖

Letter to Ralph Nader

DECEMBER 12, 1988

A few notes to accompany the enclosed material. This is the bare minimum and I can send lots more.

The wood test taken by Cleveland Investigations and processed by Columbia Laboratories was an eye opener. The test was conducted two years after the wood was treated and a lot of penta was still present.

The blood test from Enviro Health was done nine months after my first contact and six months after my hospitalization. The chemical(s) were still present.

The most important point is about our attorney. We've located a chemically aware attorney who has had other pentachlorophenol cases...

If I can provide you with anything else—please call. I am attempting to contact other victims of contaminated homes so they too may send you their story. ❖

Passive Smoke
Children suffer toll of illness that lasts a lifetime
THE BOSTON GLOBE, MONDAY, OCTOBER 31, 1988

MASSACHUSETTS HEALTH OFFICIALS were worried about the effects of breathing second-hand cigarette smoke in stuffy railway cars, so they asked Massachusetts Institute of Technology to investigate. MIT's conclusions, outlined in a letter from Professor William Ripley Nichols, were unambiguous:

"The products of the tobacco consumed mix with the air and render it oppressive to most nonsmokers...A very little tobacco smoke does indeed affect the eyes and throat of a person unaccustomed to its use, but our senses are often affected by quantities too small to weigh, too small even to detect by chemical means."

That report was prepared 114 years ago. The only change since then has been a dramatic improvement in the means of measuring the chemical constituents of tobacco smoke and of weighing their deadly effects.

Using techniques that measure down to parts per billion, scientists now know that so-called passive smoke contains carbon monoxide, nitrogen dioxide, polycyclic-aromatic hydrocarbons, nicotine, inhalable particles and hundreds of other dangerous compounds. It also contains about 50 chemicals, such as benzene, which are known or suspected to cause cancer.

And researchers suspect carbon monoxide, ammonia, benzene and other toxins may be present in higher concentrations in passive smoke than in what a smoker inhales, which has been burned at higher temperatures that destroy some of the pollutants. In a 1986 report, Surgeon General C. Everett Koop said there is evidence "sidestream smoke may be more carcinogenic."

Recent reviews suggest that passive smoking causes up to 5,000 deaths a year from lung cancer, said James Repace, a scientist at the Environmental Protection Agency. "Our program is putting out a consumer booklet advising people not to smoke in the home, to smoke outdoors," he said.

Passive smoking takes a particularly harsh toll on children, Koop said. Those exposed to it are more likely to be hospitalized for bronchitis and pneumonia during the first year of life, have a higher rate of tracheitis, bronchitis, laryngitis and other acute respiratory illness before age 2, and are more vulnerable to middle ear problems and coughs in early childhood.

Studies conducted in Watertown and East Boston by the Harvard School of Public Health and Brigham and Women's Hospital suggest children exposed to passive smoke also suffer lung damage that makes them more susceptible to serious disease later in life.

"It shows up as very small differences at this point in life, when the children have lots of excess lung capacity, and they won't sense it through middle age," said Douglas Dockery, who helped run the study on 1,841 first graders in Watertown, half of whom were followed through high school. "But when they get into their 60s or 70s, those small changes can put them at very significant risk of chronic obstructive pulmonary disease."

Some scientists believe passive smoking also increases the risk of heart disease the way smoking does, and recent studies in Japan and Scotland tend to support that position. Koop, however, said further study is needed to make that link. He also said "the simple separation of smokers and nonsmokers within the same space may reduce, but does not eliminate, the exposure of nonsmokers to environmental tobacco smoke."

Massachusetts has made major progress controlling passive smoking since Professor Nichols wrote his report in 1874, most recently by restricting smoking in government buildings, nursing homes, day care centers, restaurants with 75 seats or more and other public places. But Gregory Connolly, director of the Office of Nonsmoking and Health, is worried that "we are still behind the rest of the nation by not restricting smoking in the workplace."

Dispersing smoke
How to test
- Laboratory tests, costing under $50, can tell such things as whether children are being exposed to passive smoke at school or other settings.

How to eliminate
- Confine smoking to certain rooms.
- Disperse smoke with fans or air purifiers, and open windows. ❖

Humidifiers
Unsolved Problems Study finds ultrasonic humidifiers can fill air with particles that can cause allergies or illness.
BY JANE E. BRODY
NEW YORK TIMES, 12/22/88

MILLIONS OF BUYERS of ultrasonic humidifiers who thought they had finally found a safe and effective way to add moisture to the home in the winter heating season have something new to worry about.

Scientists at the Environmental Protection Agency have discovered that the ultrasonic machines can fill household air with tiny particles of minerals and pieces of microorganisms that can be inhaled deep into the lungs, where they may cause allergies or illness.

The potential hazard of ultrasonic humidifiers may come as a bit of a shock to those who bought the machines in the last five years because they are whisper quiet, energy-efficient, effective moisturizers that, unlike cool-mist humidifiers, did not breed harmful microorganisms and spew them into the air.

The new finding explains a number of complaints from consumers who have reported that the use of ultrasonic humidifier produced a chronic cough or allergic symptoms in one or more household members.

The problem is especially severe when consumers use ordinary mineral-laden tap water to fill their humidifiers and when the machines are not cleaned each day to keep bacteria and molds from accumulating. Particle levels in a closed bedroom could exceed the federal standard for particles in outdoor air by nearly 50 times, the study showed.

"Since humidifier use occurs primarily during periods when the occupants are present, long-term exposure to these increased levels may potentially result in either acute or chronic human health hazards," the researchers concluded in their report published in the September issue of *Environmental Science & Technology*, a journal of the American Chemical Society.

"Although the high-frequency sound waves of the ultrasonic units apparently kill microorganisms, the scientists said fragments of bacteria and molds can be spewed into the air; these may cause allergic symptoms in some people. In addition, if the indoor air is too humid, molds and other microorganisms may grow on household surfaces.

The scientists also warned that "users should be aware of the potential respiratory irritations and health hazards that may result from the use or improper treatment of tap water" in humidifiers.

The Association of Home Appliance Manufacturers said the E.P.A. findings were "preliminary and raised questions that call for additional research."

Many people had assumed that ultrasonic machines solved the health risks associated with earlier types of humidifiers, which were linked to many cases of "humidifier fever"—shortness of breath, cough, fever and malaise resulting from a reaction to microorganisms that can grow in the lukewarm or room-temperature water in the humidifier reservoir. But the newly discovered threat illustrates two problems.

One is a lack of standards and an enforcement agency to assure that consumer goods intended to prevent or correct health problems actually work as advertised. The other is the failure of many consumers to follow manufacturers' directions for safe and effective use of over-the-counter devices for health care.

While makers of ultrasonic humidifiers advise daily cleaning and most also recommend the use of filtered, demineralized or distilled water, the expense and inconvenience often prompts users to ignore these directions. But even when the devices are filled with distilled water, the E.P.A. researchers found that a large number of fine particles can fill the air, twice the standard for a single day.

In addition to calcium, the main mineral in hard water, particles sprayed into the air by ultrasonic humidifiers can include any impurities found in water, such as lead, asbestos, aluminum and dissolved organic gases. There is also a possibility that hazardous gases like radon may find their way deep into the lungs by hitchhiking onto the fine particles.

These findings prompt a re-evaluation of the need for humidifiers and, if they are considered desirable, their safe and effective operation.

Humidifiers and Health

While there is no question that adding moisture to heated indoor air can increase comfort, experts debate its direct health value, with most saying that evidence for its benefits to health are slim or nonexistent. They point out that people live healthfully in deserts without humidifying their air.

Makers of humidifiers tend to cite the same two studies suggesting a health benefit. One showed a 20 percent reduction in absenteeism among Canadian schoolchildren when the average relative humidity in school hours was increased to 35 percent from 22 percent. The other demonstrated a decrease in upper respiratory infections among soldiers when their Army barracks were humidified.

But the Association of Home Appliance Manufacturers makes no medical claims for the devices, saying only that adding moisture to indoor air in winter can protect furniture, plants and painting from the effects of excessive dryness, as well as reduce static electricity.

Respiratory specialists point out that nasal and oral passages readily moisturize inhaled air before it reaches the lungs, even when the air is very dry. You may wake up on cold winter mornings with a dry, raspy feeling in your nose and throat, but this is not a sign of ill health

or even an overly stressed respiratory system. The discomfort tends to disappear within minutes.

On the other hand, health problems can arise from using a humidifier, especially if you are not fastidious about keeping it clean. Those devices that hold pools of water at room temperature can be breeding grounds for infectious or allergy-promoting microorganisms. The organisms are then carried by water droplets into the air you breathe.

Particularly troublesome are the large, old evaporative devices with rotating drums and, to a lesser extent, the newer table-top size cool-mist humidifiers. Units that attach centrally to forced-air heating systems may also cause problems if they hold a reservoir of stagnant water.

Steam vaporizers, which are often medically recommended for patients with croup and other lower respiratory infections, are usually free of contamination because the water boils before it is released into the air, and the heat kills most troublesome organisms. Still, to minimize growth of microorganisms, these devices as well as cool-mist and ultrasonic units that hold cool water should be emptied daily and thoroughly washed before they are refilled.

But even when the water in humidifiers is itself not contaminated, an overly humid room can grow allergy-provoking molds on furnishings and fabrics.

Coping With Winter Dryness

Several measures may obviate the need for a humidifier. One is not to overheat your home or to seal it too tightly against outdoor air. When you wake up in the morning, hold a hot wet washcloth over your face for a minute to relieve nasal dryness.

If you use a wood stove for heating, place a rust-protected cast iron kettle on the stove and replace the water in it every day. Pans of water on the radiator do not add much moisture to the air, but every little bit helps.

If you choose to use a humidifier, two options stand out as least hazardous. The newer models of steam vaporizers, those manufactured since the early 1970's, meet industry safety standards that all but eliminate the risk of accidental scalding and electric shock. They have also been designed with a low center of gravity that reduces the possibility that they will tip over.

The ultrasonic units, despite their potential problems, are still better than other cool-water units if properly used. They are least likely to create a hazard if cleaning instructions are followed closely and the units are filled with water that has been filtered or distilled. Some come with filtration cartridges that should be replaced periodically.

If you ignore this advice and use tap water in an ultrasonic humidifier, you should expect that about 98 percent of the substances dissolved in the water will be emitted into the air you breathe in particle sizes that can easily penetrate deep into your lungs. Adding bleach or disinfectants to the water in the humidifier is no help; in fact, it may precipitate allergic reactions in some people.

Those concerned about the health of house plants could spray them with a plant mister every few days.

As for dry itchy skin in the winter, several simple measures can bring relief. One is to avoid overly hot, prolonged showers and baths and alkaline or "natural"

soaps, which ultimately dry the skin by removing protective oils. Take quick warm showers and use a superfatted soap. If you bathe with bath oil, soak in the tub for five minutes before adding the oil to assure that your skin is first moisturized.

To protect the skin's natural oils, pat yourself dry instead of rubbing. After washing, apply a moisturizing lotion while your skin is still damp. You may prefer a lighter moisturizer on your face, but for hands and limbs look for products that also contain a humectant (it attracts water from the air) like urea, lactic acid and phospholipids. ❖

Section Three
Repairs and Remodeling

REPAIRS AND REMODELING conjure up memories of weekend home improvement warriors (see an article by that name in this section) and hassles trying to get the repairman to do it right the first, then the second time, without charging you twice. Some of these repair firms have much nerve—one in Washington, D.C. sent a letter of "dismissal" to a *Time* magazine editor who had the gall to question its repair billing practices for his home. The materials in this section invite you to learn how best to choose and hold contractors to the expected standards they advertise.

Given the marvelous proliferation of handy home improvement tools and simple designs, more Americans are trying to do repairs, additions and enlargements of their homes by themselves. The late peoples' architect, Richard Ridley of Washington, D.C., pioneered a weekly column called "Making Space" (see back cover) in the *Washington Post* in which he clearly and simply encouraged residents to savor the many ways to use available space in the home for useful and aesthetic purposes.❖

1988 Remodeling Survey
RODALE'S *PRACTICAL HOMEOWNER*, MAY/JUNE 1988

IT'S THAT TIME of year again. The land is green, the sap is flowing, warm temperatures are here, and the Sunday newspapers are plump with sale supplement from the local hardware stores and building supply centers. Spring fever has given way to remodeling fever.

And in the midst of all this come the remodeling surveys—those seasonal attempts by well-meaning people to tell you, the homeowner, which remodeling projects are the best bets when it's time to sell your house and recoup your investment.

It's all fine and good. The problem is that most of those surveys are based on the opinions of professionals who automatically assume a contractor will be doing the work. They don't take into account the do-it-yourself angle, which can mean hefty immediate savings on the cost of the job, plus an even greater payback when you sell your house.

Here then, is a better mousetrap: a remodeling survey that not only considers contractor vs. DIY costs, but also the type of house you live in, which can make a big difference. We also surveyed two different groups of professionals—appraisers and Realtors—for their opinions ont the value of certain renovations.

Finally, to bring it all home, we surveyed homeowners like you, to find out what the majority of homeowners are actually doing to their homes and why. Surprisingly, enjoyment is an even more impor-

tant factor than profit for most homeowners.

Before you climb into this, our third annual remodeling survey, keep a few points in mind. In general, any improvements that suit your needs and lifestyle are worth the investment—just don't expect the person who eventually buys your home to pay for the cost of those projects. Also, before undertaking any improvement, be sure to bring routine maintenance up to date. It's throwing good money after bad to add air conditioning or a deck if you've got peeling paint inside and out.

A home's value is also a consideration. Our survey shows a significant difference between improvements to a 25-year-old ranch and a 10-year-old contemporary. In general, the more expensive the home, the more likely it is that a buyer will pay for extra improvements.

One final point. When you look at the cost-recovery figures for each project, keep in mind that they are national averages and should be adjusted for your neighborhood. A project with a low national return—an in-ground swimming pool, for instance—could return a lot more of its cost in your neighborhood.

Central Air

One of the best guides in deciding what improvements to make is to understand which are most valued in your market. For instance, regional weather conditions are of primary importance in rating air conditioning the number-one improvement in our survey with an average 115 percent return on the cost of putting it in. Realtors and appraisers alike give it high marks—but only in those places where it's more than an amenity.

On a sweltering hot day in Atlanta, central air is no luxury—it's a necessity. Says local appraiser Arnold Schwartz: "A house without central air isn't as marketable as one with it. The lack of airconditioning definitely hurts."

It's the same in other hot climates like Dallas and Phoenix, and in any area that has sweaty, humid summers. Appraiser William Watkinson of Philadelphia says, "In today's market, it's kind of like the first-floor family room: People have come to expect it."

The only panelists giving low marks to airconditioning were those in Seattle and Minnesota, where there are few truly hot days.

Interior Face-Lift

Some home improvements are a good investment regardless of climate, such as an interior facelift, the second-highest-rated remodeling project in our survey. Virtually all of our experts say it's a good idea to keep the inside of your home spruced up with paint, wallpaper, and carpeting, since the effort can net you a hefty 109 percent return if you pay someone to do it, and a whopping 210 percent if you buy the materials and do it yourself.

Besides increasing the value of your home, an interior face-lift can decrease the time it takes to sell it. But many of our panelists caution that this is the Catch-22, of home improvements. "It's just considered upkeep, until you don't do it, and then it's going to bring the price down," warns Dallas Realtor B.J. Smith.

With that in mind, many of our experts say, don't be surprised if some buyers aren't willing to pay the full cost of the redecorating job. According to Realtor Johnny Isakson of Atlanta, "People always think they can do things for less than it's going to cost."

Bathroom

When it comes to bathrooms, buyers are always happy to see one that has been updated, our experts say. Whether you pay to have it done or do it yourself, you can expect a good return on your investment.

In general, baths, like kitchens are important items at resale time. (The kitchen renovation ranked seventh in our survey.) "People are looking for eye appeal in bathrooms and kitchens," says Philadelphia appraiser Watkinson.

Our panel suggests that if you own a house similar to our 25-year-old ranch, renovate the bathroom if you already haven't. "The fixtures in older houses are usually colored and out of style," said realtor Isakson of Atlanta.

The realtors and appraisers all agree that it might be an unnecessary improvement for the newer contemporary. "A 10-year-old bathroom should still be in pretty good condition," says San Francisco realtor Helen Campos.

Our experts criticized the materials used in our bath project. The less expensive items, such as a fiberglass tub surround and the vinyl flooring, might be passable in the less expensive ranch house. But they could detract in the more expensive contemporary.

I don't think you could sell vinyl flooring and the fiberglass tub surround as a renovation," says appraiser William Warner of Wayzata, Minnesota. "It's ceramic tile that people are looking for in baths." Realtor William Bain of Seattle says a good bathroom renovation in the 10-year-old contemporary should include more then merely replacing fixtures. "You've spent $3,500 and it's still cramped and tight. An expansion might be in order."

Fireplace

While there's no denying the importance of a room like the bath, our experts were almost equally enthusiastic about one of the amenities on our survey: adding a fireplace. It ranked fourth among our Top 10 improvements, finishing closely behind the bathroom renovation.

Our experts agree that fireplaces have come to be valued in homes of all price ranges. In many areas, they're almost a standard feature in all but the most basic starter homes. In our contemporary, for instance, most panelists say it's a must. "A house without one is competitively at an extreme disadvantage," said realtor Isakson of Atlantaa.

While a prefab fireplace is considered a good investment by most of our panelists, a few concede that a masonry model would be better. Also important is where in the house you add it. "Location means a lot," says appraiser Watkinson of Philadelphia. "Most people prefer it in the family room or the rec room because of the dust and dirt."

Panel members warn that fireplace popularity will vary from state to state, and will also hinge on the availability of firewood.

Garage

Local preferences were also on our panelists' minds when they considered a two-car garage addition, which ranks fifth on our Top-10 list. Most say it's because garages have become a standard item. Texas appraiser Don Stovall sums up the feelings of most panel members when he says, "You almost can't buy a home down here without one."

Weather is a big factor in determining the importance of a garage. Panelists in warm climates say garages protect a car's paint job form the damaging rays of the sun. In colder regions, our experts say the effects of ice and snow also make a garage desirable. In a few mild climates, such as in San Francisco, however, garages are not important. "It wouldn't pay to build a garage to sell a house here," realtor Helen Campos says of San Francisco.

But climate can make a detached garage a poor choice. Realtor Carl Nardone of Norwood, Massachusetts, says, "With the cold weather we have here, people want an attached garage because they can go right into the house."

Some appraisers and Realtors say a lower-priced home like our 25-year-old ranch might be able to do without one.

Basement Conversion

Getting to the bottom of things among our panel experts isn't as easy when it comes to a basement conversion. Most of them give it high marks for the amount of space it adds to both homes in our survey. But they don't agree on the desirability of this improvement. Many share Massachusetts appraiser John Cena's assessment that using basements for living space is passe. "People don't like to live in basements anymore. In the old days, you could throw the kids down there and never hear the noise. All the new developers are putting the family room on the upper level."

The exception seems to be in regions where daylight or walk-out basements are the norm. These basements, which have windows and a door opening outside, are brighter and better suited for use as a recreation room or other living space, our panelists say.

Appraiser Schwartz of Atlanta says converting a daylight basement is a wise choice for homeowners in his area. He endorses it for both homes in our survey, adding that it's a fairly inexpensive way to increase livable space substantially. "If I were in a 10-year-old house, I would not finish the attic or do a room addition," Schwartz says. "The first thing I would do is finish the basement."

Kitchen

There's little dissent among our experts when it comes to kitchens, our seventh-ranked improvement. "More time is spent in the kitchen than in any other room," says appraiser Rex Dungan of Van Nuys, California. "It's a room with a great emotional factor for the buyer, so wise homeowners spend more on the kitchen than on any other room."

Some panelists criticize our kitchen renovation, saying the inexpensive cabinets and mid-priced appliances are too cheap for a 10-year-old contemporary. They also point out that a contemporary won't be as likely to need a new kitchen as an older ranch house. Therefore, any renovations should be carefully thought out before work begins.

Philadelphia appraiser Watkinson echoes several of our other experts when he offers these factors to consider before remodeling your kitchen. "It depends on the age and condition of the kitchen. You also have to take into consideration what other homeowners in your area are doing. You have to be careful your ideas aren't too upscale. Buying kitchen cabinets is like buying furniture. Everyone has different tastes."

Exterior Paint

You don't have much choice when it comes to the exterior of your home: keep it painted, our experts emphatically say. There's no magic formula needed to calculate its importance.

"You won't get a second chance at a first impression," said realtor Isakson of Atlanta. "It's a maintenance and an upkeep item that puts a house in a better light and makes it more marketable."

Like its interior counterpart, an exterior paint job may not impress buyers enough to get them to pay for the full cost of the work, our panelists say, but present them with a peeling exterior, and they'll be quick to deduct a couple of thousand dollars from their offer.

When painting the outside of your home, again it's a good idea to check out your market for the latest trends before choosing colors. Sticking with neutrals and avoiding garish tones is always your best bet, our experts agree.

Deck

Not all the improvements in our top 10 can be described as practical. Adding a deck, an item that can only be termed an amenity, ranks high with our experts and closes out the top 10 in this year's survey. Decks gain in popularity each year, our experts say. Homeowners just plain like them. Add to this the relatively low cost per square foot—especially if you do it yourself—and you've got a fairly good investment.

But several panel members say a deck like the one in our survey is too elaborate for a 25-year-old ranch house. Appraiser Steve Strickland of Cincinnati, Ohio says, "It's a bit of an overimprovement."

A deck is considered almost a standard feature on a house like the 10-year-old contemporary, though. "Contemporaries and decks go hand in hand," said appraiser Thomas Strauss of Walnut Creek, CA.

Furnace Replacement

Another maintenance item that earned a place on our Top 10 is replacing an old, worn-out furnace with a new energy-efficient model. But because most homes are expected to have a furnace in good repair, our experts stress that it's hard to get a buyer excited about this improvement.

"I don't think this is a big selling item," says appraiser Watkinson of Philadelphia. "It may shorten the marketing time on a property, but people don't want to pay in advance for something they'll get back over time, such as energy savings."

Those savings may be enough inducement for you to invest in a new furnace, however. Do it while you plan to live in the house for a few years, our panelists say, and you'll enjoy the financial benefits. ❖

Confessions Of A Weekend Warrior
BY JOHN VIEHMAN
RODALE'S *PRACTICAL HOMEOWNER*, DECEMBER 1987

NAILING DOWN A hardwood floor is hardly what you'd call a high-risk job. Likewise, there doesn't seem to be a lot at stake cutting a piece of drywall, or jacking up a basement ceiling joist, or even belt-sanding a piece of wood. Yet within the past few years, those activities have put me in a neck brace, cut open four inches of my forearm, enlarged my big toe to the size of a grapefruit, and scratched my right eye.

Don't get me wrong, I'm not clumsy. And I'm no more fond of the hospital emergency room than the next guy. But during my last visit—as the pain in my right eye at last subsided—I realized that my string of injuries followed a pattern.

The incident that put me in a neck brace could have been predicted, if not avoided. Installing 1,000 square feet of cherry floor requires hundreds of nails to be driven home manually with a 15-pound mallet and a "power nailer." The jarring can inflame the shoulder tendons of even a seasoned carpenter, for me pushing to finish that much flooring in a weekend was like taking an express lane to the hospital.

Another weekend found me hanging drywall. It was the last cut on the last sheet to be hung at eleven o'clock Saturday night. Pulling the razor knife toward me, I sensed something was wrong but was tired to the point where my actions were a few seconds behind my thoughts—that is, until the knife unexpectedly broke free of the drywall and sliced through my forearm.

My house-jacking and belt-sanding injuries were more of the same. After moving the jack dozens of times around the basement to level the first floor, I stopped double-checking its footing; when it slipped, my toe absorbed 20 tons of thrust. Finally, another injury came while I was sanding an edge of particle-board. A simple job, it didn't seem to require safety glasses...until a wood chip blew into my eye.

The moral: Had I set realistic expectations of the time required and acknowledged the potential for injury, I wouldn't have fatigued myself or rushed past safety precautions. And four weekends wouldn't have been interrupted by trips to the hospital.

I'd like to think I'm alone in these experiences. But according to government figures, that's not the case. Last year 87,000 people were treated for injuries caused by power tools. Hand tools are no less injurious: 10 years ago, when they still were counting them, 30,000 people were treated for hammer-related injuries alone. Other kinds of DIY mishaps undoubtedly are a big part of the 3.1 million at-home accidents reported each year. (That translates into one incident every 10 seconds. Ouch!)

Studies have found that injuries are just as likely for the rank novice as they are for the expert. One suffers from lack of skill and experience with the equipment; the other from too much experience, which leads to risk-taking and a casual attitude toward power tools.

However, for those of us pounding away at it weekend and week out, there are simple, common-sense ways to avoid all the statistics. If you're rushed, force yourself to slow down. If you're tired, take time out or quit for the day. If a situation feels dangerous, it probably is. In the end, the right attitude and 100 percent concentration on the task in front of you are the only things between you and the hospital emergency room.

Take it from a Weekend Warrior. ❖

Dealing With a Damp Basement

Controlling the Temperature and Humidity is the First Step

BY MIKE MCCLINTOCK

WASHINGTON POST, JULY 18, 1985

ONE OF THE MOST common complaints about houses, new or old, is downstairs dampness—wet walls in cellars, basements and finished rooms that are partially or completely below ground level. Even if foundation walls keep out ground water and periodic deluges from gutters and downspouts, condensation inside the house can produce as much water as serious, widespread leaking.

The wetness is certainly unpleasant. But the mildew, bad odors, possible allergic reactions, and the deterioration of building materials and furnishings are the real problems. And in many cases mildew and bad odors linger despite stringent preventive measures.

The amount and frequency of condensation depends on things such as wall mass, depth below grade, room temperature and the dew point at different percentages of relative humidity. When it's hot and humid your walls are likely to sweat.

One of the best ways to prevent sweating is to minimize, if not eliminate, the temperature difference between the cool foundation wall and the warm, humid air inside the house. The other, complementary approach, is to reduce the inside air temperature (air conditioning) or the inside air humidity level, or both. Air conditioning does both jobs. A dehumidifier only removes moisture from the air (and actually produces some heat from the compressor motor). Vent fans at key locations where moisture is produced (above stoves, in bathrooms and laundry areas, for example) can reduce the load on both appliances.

The first step in altering existing basement walls to prevent sweating is to clean away the mildew patches thriving in the dark, damp corners. In most cases a cup of bleach to a gallon of hot water, applied vigorously with a stiff scrub brush, then rinsed, will kill the fungus and odors. Any leaks must be stopped before adding materials and closing in the wall. If there are small, thin cracks that let in some water during heavy rains, patch them with hydraulic cement after scraping out and thoroughly drying the crevices.

In most cases there are two components of the anti-sweat project: first, some form of insulation to minimize temperature differences at the wall surface; second, some form of frame to support wallboard or paneling to cover the insulating material.

The prototypical, do-it-yourself cellar renovation (unchanged for decades) calls for 1-by-2 foot furring strips (usually an inferior grade of spruce with a lot of knots and twists and bows) secured with cut or concrete nails directly to the concrete or block walls every 16 inches, in rows parallel to the floor. The next step is to add insulation between the furring strips. A good choice is 3/4 inch (same as the strips) foam board. It's light, easily cut, shaped, and set in place with a spot or two of construction adhesive.

That part of the job takes care of temperature variation against the wall. Adding a vapor barrier before installing wallboard or paneling prevents moisture at any temperature from reaching the masonry surface. Without a barrier, moisture would work its way through wallboard, through insulation, then condense on the masonry and rot the furring strips. The most effective barrier is foil. It is impervious, but more expensive and more difficult to use without tearing than the very inexpensive alternative, plastic sheeting.

After the frame and insulation (thin batts of fiberglass work well, too) are in place, a continuous sheet of 4-mil plastic (as an alternative barrier to foil) is draped over the wall. Attach it temporarily with only a few staples, since even small punctures will let moisture into the insulated space. The sheets will be punctured as you nail the finished wall panels in place. But those punctures will be sealed by pressure between the panel and furring strip beneath.

This simple renovation project does have a few drawbacks. Even nails designed for masonry don't always work. They snap (which can be dangerous) or make the hammer rebound out of your hand, or put a crack in the furring strip. If this happens, try putting the nail in a few inches away. Maybe that one goes in; maybe not.

Sometimes this sequence can split the furring strip in two, which means you have a row of nails firmly embedded in concrete that must be removed so you can install a new strip. It's a frustrating task. Also, it can create a fault line in the masonry wall. If you had a dry wall, and, for some reason, wanted to make it leak, what better way than to drive a line of nails into it.

Substituting 2-by-2s for 1-by-2s solves these problems. They cost more, but not a lot more. And it's worth it. First, the extra depth lets you add more insulation, which better separates the cool masonry wall from the warm and humid interior air. Second, the larger framing is strong enough to be built like a house wall—studs every 16 inches on center are held between 2-by-2s top and bottom parallel to the floor—which can be tipped up into position.

After careful measuring (the frame must clear the lowest ceiling joist) the wall frame can be nailed together on the floor. Set the bottom against the masonry wall in a bed of construction adhesive. Nail

through the top horizontal 2-by-2 into the ceiling joists.

If you have measured for a snug fit this will be more than adequate. Remember, these are not bearing walls carrying structural loads from the roof. They support some wallboard, but that's all. This method eliminates the need to nail the structure to the masonry, increases insulation protection, and makes the work easier since there is simply more wood to work with, and less chance of splits and bent nails. ❖

Home Improvements

EXCERPT FROM *GETTING WHAT YOU DESERVE*
BY STEPHEN A. NEWMAN & NANCY KRAMER

HI! WE JUST FINISHED blacktopping a driveway in the neighborhood, and we've got some extra materials left over. If you like, we can do your driveway too, for half price. Our boss will think we used up all the materials on the first job, and you'll do us a favor by not making us drive back to the office with this load.

So begins one of the time-honored frauds in the home improvement field. Some blacktoppers collect their bargain fees, go back to the truck—and just drive away. Others stay to put down a black, oily concoction which washes away with the next rain, leaving a mucky residue on the front lawn.

A variation on this scheme has the seller offering a remarkable bargain "if you will merely allow our company to use your home as a model to show your neighbors and to display in our advertising." The offer may be to install a new roof, to remodel a kitchen, to sell aluminum siding, or to waterproof a basement. The job either is never begun or is abandoned as soon as a substantial payment is received. In some cases, the work is performed, but with such cheap materials and shoddy workmanship that even the "bargain" price is a rip-off.

Some "home improvers" can more accurately be termed "house wreckers." Consumers dealing with one New York contractor were left with gaping holes in their walls, plaster falling from the ceilings, and debris coating their floors. Others found themselves cooking their meals on portable stoves for months, because the home improver had disconnected the gas lines. One woman, who wanted a bathroom renovated for her elderly sick mother, was reassured by a promise to complete the job "immediately." Five weeks later nothing had been done and the woman called to complain. "That same day a worker arrived and took

the bathroom apart," she said. "Then everyone disappeared again."

Purchasing a home improvement job from an itinerant worker is very risky. While reputable businesses usually maintain offices in the community, shady characters frequently operate solely out of a truck, and can never be located when the victimized homeowner realizes what has happened. Government officials have become particularly familiar with the handiwork of one notorious band of gypsy con artists who travel in caravans throughout the country, cheating homeowners with an endless variety of home repair rackets. After going through a community, the clan picks up and moves on, before homeowner complaints bring out the authorities.

Scare tactics are common in these rackets. Sales agents for one furnace company posing as government safety inspectors, told furnace owners that "old Betsy" was about to blow and probably destroy the entire house. The "inspector" made this ominous diagnosis after totally disassembling the homeowner's furnace. With the furnace on the floor in a thousand pieces, even the most reluctant homeowners agreed to buy the new model recommended by the phony inspector.

Choosing a Contractor

These outright frauds are just the most flagrant examples of abuse in the home repair field. Millions of people are disappointed with the quality of work performed by hired contractors who do incompetent work, who fail to give reliable cost estimates, or who choose low-grade, inadequate materials. Because of this, it is important to choose a home improvement contractor with care.

First, think carefully about what you want done. An

outside contractor may not be needed at all. Many jobs can be done with the help of do-it-yourself manuals, some of which are provided free or at low cost by the federal government (write to the U.S. Department of Agriculture Extension Service, Washington, D.C., 20251 and to the U.S. Department of Housing and Urban Development, Washington, D.C. 20410). At a minimum they will give you an idea of how much work is involved and what is a reasonable fee for doing it. Local utility companies, also issue advice on home insulation and other energy-saving tips (an excellent booklet is "How to Save Money by Insulating Your Home," available in New York from Consolidated Edison, Consumer Affairs Department, 4 Irving Place, New York, N.Y. 10003).

For complicated tasks, it is best to seek out a local contractor with a proven reputation. A good way to begin is to ask for recommendations from people who have lived in the community and from friends who have had work done in the past. Do not rely on the local Yellow Pages or on newspaper ads.

Ask several contractors for price estimates. Beware of markedly low estimates and unbelievable bargains—these may indicate general incompetence, the intended use of cheap materials, or fraud. Visit the contractor's place of business. Is it a real office, preferably one that's been there for a while, or is it the back of a truck? Ask prospective contractors for a bank reference and for one or two customer references (good contractors will be happy to have you examine their prior work). Check with the Better Business Bureau or local consumer affairs office to make sure there's no backlog of complaints about the contractor, particularly if it's a major job. For very substantial projects, such as adding to an existing structure, consider hiring an architect, who will choose the contractor for you, design the addition, and supervise the work. As a source of professional advice and planning, an architect may well be worth the additional cost.

In many cities and counties, home improvement contractors must be licensed in order to operate. Contact the local consumer office or the state attorney general's office to see if this is the case in your area. If so, ask to see the contractor's license number. A license is no guarantee of honesty or competence, but it guarantees a minimal compliance with the law and will provide you with a place (the licensing agency) to go with complaints. Unlicensed dealers may be "fly-by-nighters" with no ties to the community. Avoid them at all costs. Before hiring the licensed contractor, see if the licensing agency has any negative information about it in its files.

Paying the Contractor

Always get a written agreement before giving someone money to begin work. That contract should provide for payment in installments which are scheduled to coincide roughly with the amount of work performed. The larger the final payments are, the more incentive the contractor has to finish the job on schedule. The completion date and the amount of each payment should be specified in the written contract. The contract should also specify the exact job to be done and the materials to be used (listing them by brand name and model numbers wherever possible). You may want to consult with local building supply dealers or home improvement experts in a local consumer agency to ensure that the materials suggested are of reasonable quality. Never make final payment until the job is done to your satisfaction: it's your only leverage.

Many state laws create "materialmen's liens" on a homeowner's house or property. This is a legal right which gives suppliers of materials (such as siding, roofing, and lumber) the right to seize your property if their bills are not paid. While the general contractor will hire and pay subcontractors to supply materials, a dishonest general contractor may abandon the job and leave you stuck with the subcontractors' bills. The existence of liens is an important reason to make sure the contractor is financially responsible and of good reputation. It is wise to consult a lawyer before undertaking an expensive transaction involving your home, to ensure that you are not placing what is probably your most valuable asset in jeopardy. This can be remedied by putting a clause in the contract requiring the contractor to provide you with an affidavit that all materials suppliers and laborers have been paid before final payment is due the contractor.

Seven Danger Signs

Beware of any home improver who:
1. Has no license (where law requires one).
2. Asks you to sign a Certificate of Completion before the work described in the certificate is performed.
3. Maintains no permanent business location.
4. Claims to be working "in the neighborhood" and has extra materials left over.
5. Offers to make yours a "model home" in the neighborhood.
6. Will not supply names of previous customers whom you can call for references.
7. Pressures you to decide quickly or lose the chance to get the work done.

Your Legal Rights

Many cities, counties, and states require home improvers to meet minimal standards of honesty and fairness in performing evene where no laws specifically regulate this field, consumer agencies can act under the general anti-fraud statutes which exist in all states. It is important to note, however, that, as a practical matter, most agencies have a difficult time proving improper behavior by a home improver. Most cases require the testimony of an expert who can evaluate the quality of the work done and determine if the job contracted for was adequately performed. Few consumers and few consumer agencies have access to this kind of expertise. As a consequence, many legitimate complaints go unresolved because of lack of legally sufficient evidence. Small claims court lawsuits by consumers are often unsuccessful for this very reason. Nevertheless, the court or a consumer agency may be able to mediate some mutually acceptable compromise, so they should not be ignored by dissatisfied consumers. But here, as elsewhere, avoiding trouble in the first place is the only sure remedy.

Before you sign any contract, take two important measures. First check the contract for the fourteen points listed below. Second, take your time—don't sign until you've had a chance to think about it, to comparison-shop, and to show it to someone whose judgement you trust. ❖

Getting What You Deserve *was published in 1979 by Doubleday & Company, Inc., 666 Fifth Avenue, New*

Small Claims Court

EXCERPT FROM *GETTING WHAT YOU DESERVE*

IN THE EARLY 1900s court reformers dreamed and schemed to set up "people's courts" where ordinary citizens could sue without suffering the crushing expense and delay of the regular court system. The speedy, low-cost justice which they envisioned is available today in most parts of the country, in "small claims courts" (also known as "justice of the peace" or "magistrate" courts).

Small claims courts vary a great deal from state to state. What they have in common is an informal, simplified court procedure set up to enable people to collect money in small cases without hiring an attorney.

When you sue in small claims court, you've got several things going for you before you begin. The first is that the vast majority of plaintiffs win—often receiving less than they sued for, but recovering something. Second, the remedy is usually cheap; one 1973 nationwide study found that the majority of small claims court plaintiffs and defendants spent less than $25 for the filing fee and for all costs. Finally,as two recent studies of small claims court observed, the people suing derive a great deal of satisfaction from the very experience; they repeatedly say that the psychological benefits were at least as important as the money they recovered....

You can use small claims court in an almost limitless number of situations. Basically, you can take your problem to small claims court if you have a complaint which you've tried to resolve in other ways; if you think you know who (individual, business, or both) is responsible; and if a dollar value, actual or estimated, can be put on your loss. Generally, small claims courts do not have the power to order someone to finish a job, to perform a service or to stop acting unlawfully. All they can do is order your adversary to pay you money, so you must be prepared to translate your gripe into a dollars-and-cents figure. ❖

You may obtain a useful pamphlet on how to take your case to small claims court without a lawyer by contacting your state attorney general's office or consumer affairs department.

Buying, Selling and Inspecting the Home

FOR THOSE PEOPLE who are moving out or moving in, this chapter has one basic message: it pays to take a few hours and study how to be a sagacious buyer or seller and what your rights and remedies are in your state. The first article's title puts it aptly: "The Rewards of Doing Your Housing Homework."

For the homeless and other Americans who cannot find affordable housing, the article on a low-cost housing program in Boston affords lessons that can be learned elsewhere.

If you are contemplating buying a condominium, the advisory by the Department of Housing and Urban Development takes you step by step. Imagine how many buyers take those steps without this information only to find themselves unpleasantly surprised.

Finally, some pointers on getting the best homeowner's insurance coverage. ❖

Housing

BUYER'S MARKET, VOLUME I, NUMBER 7, JULY 1985

Buying a Home

For many people, buying a home is the American Dream. But the process of homebuying can have many pitfalls. Homebuying is complicated, and usually comes at a time of changes in your family size, in your job, or in your city. To buy the right house at the right price, you need to worry about the quality of the house, the fine print on numerous legal documents, and the increasingly complicated choice of mortgages. You also need to keep closing costs down.

Your problems are compounded by the many people you meet in the home-buying process: the home seller, the real estate broker, the mortgage lender, the title company representative, and the closing attorney. Each of them can help you, but each has interests different from yours. Many would like to close the deal whether or not the home and mortgage are the most suitable for you.

We suggest two basic rules for buying a home:

Rule #1

Don't rush into the process. You will be living with your house and mortgage for years; it is worth the extra time to be sure you make a good choice. Your chances of making a mistake go up significantly if you are under personal pressure, such as if you must move quickly to a job in a new city. To avoid mistakes, Ellen

Eatough, a California housing consultant, advises clients never to take their checkbooks when looking at homes, and to always look at homes twice, with another person and at different times of day, before making an offer....

Even though you must pay directly for your lawyer or real estate agent (it is usually excessive to hire both), you will reap many benefits. Most people buy only one or two houses in their lives, and an experienced professional can help you with the brokers and lenders and lawyers who deal with houses and mortgages on a daily basis. There are dozens of technical details and potential gauges; your experienced representative will help raise issues and negotiate them on your behalf. A good advocate can also keep down closing costs by helping you shop for title insurance, an inspector, and other needed services. When it's all over, your representative will probably have saved you much more money than you spent on his or her fee.

With these two rules in mind, we can turn to some specific tips.

- Shop around a lot. Some experts say to look at least a dozen houses. Why not? Buying your home is the biggest purchase you will ever make. Take notes. If you write things down, you'll be better able to make comparisons at your leisure when you get home. Bring a tape measure along,

to compare hallway widths, closets, and the like.
• Be sure of the quality of the house. Especially in the first years after you've bought a house, you don't want to get hit by unexpected repair bills. In newly-built homes, the most frequent problems involve the roof, yard drainage, operability of windows and doors, the plumbing, and the foundation or basement.

If the house is newly constructed, be sure to get a good warranty (see "Home Warranties"). For a previously owned home, a professional inspection is essential warranties on used homes simply do not provide adequate protection (an inspection in a new house is a good idea, too). Go along with your inspector; you'll learn a lot about your possible new home and will be better able to bargain about the price. Some of the things an inspector should look for include: termite infestation and wood rot, sagging structure, poor electrical wiring, run-down heating system or plumbing, leaky roofs, wet basements, inoperative doors and windows, asbestos and urea formaldehyde insulation.

Insist that your agreement to buy the house include a clause letting you drop the deal if you don't like the results of the professional inspection (the seller may insist that you complete the inspection and decide within five or 10 days—this is fair). If the seller or the broker objects to an inspection, don't buy the house. They may be hiding something serious.

Experts advise reviewing your homeowner's policy every two years to avoid underprotection.
• Check out the energy efficiency of your home. Ask to see the owner's utility bills for the previous 12 months. They will give you an idea of how much you would be paying. A home without adequate insulation or with inefficient appliances can cost thousands of dollars more over its life than an energy efficient home. Likewise, if you invest in energy efficient home improvements when you first move in, the initial investment may pay for itself in energy savings.
• Understand the closing costs. Taking care of closing costs can be the most confusing part of buying a home. These costs usually include "points," an origination fee, credit report, survey, title insurance, and attorneys fees, as well as prepaid items such as taxes and insurance escrow payments. There are also charges made for service performed by local government bodies relating to real estate transfer taxes and fees for recording the deed and mortgage. Most of the burden of closing costs normally falls on the borrower (home buyer).

"Points," or percentage points of the mortgage value, are a one-time charge asssessed at closing by the lender to increase the yield on a mortgage loan. If you plan to stay in the home only a short time, try to bargain for lower points in return for a proportionately higher interest rate (to reduce up-front costs); the opposite holds true if you plan to stay in your home for a longer period.

The origination fee is typically charged for the work involved in evaluating, preparing, and submitting a proposed mortgage loan. The mortgage lender charges this nonrefundable fee to reduce your incentive to shop elsewhere for a lower-priced mortgage. If rates are dropping, wait and shop before paying an origination fee.

The Truth-In-Lending Act requires your lender to compute the effective loan cost or annual percentage rate (APR) with closing costs for you. A number of different costs, such as required mortgage and property insurance, and prepaid finance charges, such as loan application fees and discount points, are included when calculating the APR.
• Know what is in the sales contract. Before you sign the sales contract, make sure it correctly expresses your agreement with the seller on such important details as the sales price of the home, method of payment, the time for your taking possession, your right to have a satisfactory inspection, and what fixtures, appliances, and personal property are to be sold with the home. The sales contract should provide for the following:
• A refund of your deposit (sometimes referred to as "earnest money") by the seller or escrow agent at cancellation of the sale if you are unable to secure a mortgage loan within a stated period of time for an amount, interest rate, or length of term set forth in the contract.
• The title, free and clear of all liens and encumbrances.
• A certificate, provided at the time of settlement, stating that the house is free from termites or termite damage; that the plumbing, heating, electrical systems and appliances are in working order; and that the house is structurally sound.

Mortgages

Shop for your mortgage. Over the 30-year life of the mortgage, financing costs will be two to three times the cost of the house itself. The mortgage market is changing rapidly, and most homebuyers can use help shopping for a mortgage. The following rules are intended to be general guidelines, and are similar in part to advice from *Consumer Reports* (July 1981, pages 403-406).
• Shop several lenders. Mortgage rates can vary

from lender to lender. Be sure to include some mortgage bankers in your search; they have lower overheads and may give better rates than savings and loan institutions. In some areas, a real estate broker may be able to show you a weekly listing offered by local lenders.

Know what you can afford. It is difficult to predict your future mortgage payments, especially with the new adjustable-rate mortgages. Keep a savings cushion to meet unexpected payment problems. Have the lender calculate the worst-case scenario on your mortgage—for instance, if it's adjustable and interest rates jump eight or 10 percent and stay there—and be sure you know what to do if that worst case comes about. Also, if you can make a larger down payment you can save yourself the monthly fees for mortgage insurance (lenders will usually insist on mortgage insurance unless the down payment is at least 20 percent of the appraised property value).

- Is the seller's existing mortgage assumable? If the seller's mortgage is large enough and at a low enough rate, assumption of the existing mortgage may save money in interest payments and settlement costs.
- Consider the fixed-rate mortgage. The choice between a fixed-rate and an adjustable-rate mortgage depends on your tolerance for risk and on price. You may want to pay a premium for the 30-year fixed rate mortgage just to be able to predict your monthly budget; use this mortgage as the basis for comparing your alternatives. If the fixed-rate is priced close to the adjustable-rate mortgage, take the fixed rate. On the other hand, if you plan to move soon, the lower adjustable-rate mortgage may be more attractive. ❖

High Marks For Low-Cost Housing in Boston
PAUL GOLDBERGER
THE NEW YORK TIMES, NOVEMBER 6, 1988

CAN THERE BE such a thing as "affordable housing" that is decent, even wonderful, as a work of design? That manages to make sense both economically and aesthetically? The answer, at least in Boston, is yes. Two complexes of apartments have recently been completed in this city that achieve what is often thought to be no longer possible in our age—they are desirable places to live for working-class families and at the same time they add to the city's body of good architecture. In other words, they do something both for the people who live in them and for everyone else.

The very phrase "affordable housing" is a nicety of the 1980's. It began as a euphemism, an attempt to break away from the stigma of publicly assisted housing; that the phrase exists at all points up a tragic reality of this moment, which is that most housing is not affordable. Less than a generation ago there was housing; no adjectives were needed, for it was taken for granted that the average person could afford average housing. If there was any special category, it was luxury housing. But now conventional housing is luxury housing, affordable only by the rich or the near-rich, and it has become necessary to invent this new category, a constant reminder of the absurdity of the economics of housing today.

The two complexes are Tent City, at the edge of Boston's South End, designed by Goody, Clancy & Associates, and the Charlestown Navy Yard Row houses, designed by William Rawn Associates. Together with a third complex in the Mission Hill section of Boston, known as Back of the Hill Rowhouses, also designed by Mr. Rawn and still under construction, these projects give Boston a remarkable inventory of first-class buildings that happen to contain reasonably priced apartments.

How is it possible here, where it is so difficult everywhere else? In truth, it is not all that easy in Boston; the relationship of planning and architecture to politics is as intense here as anywhere—the Tent City project, in fact, takes its name from a demonstration in 1968 mounted by community activists who camped out on the site in tents to protest the gentrification of the South End neighborhood. But what makes Boston notable is that ultimately subsidized housing, rather than a complex of purely luxury condominiums or commercial buildings, did get erected there, and it is characteristic of Boston's benign attitude toward such matters that the protest, instead of being purged from the history books, was memorialized in the name of the complex.

The Massachusetts Housing Finance Agency's enlightened programs for subsidizing mixed-income housing were critical to this project; at the Charlestown Navy Yard and Mission Hill, the lucky break was the vision of Thomas McIntyre, head of the local Bricklayers and Laborers Union, who became, in effect, the developer. Through his union Mr. McIntyre started a nonprofit corporation to build affordable housing and show off the union's brickworking skills at the same time, and the corporation now has more than 300 units of affordable housing under way in Boston, making it a real-estate developer to be reckoned with. But unlike conventional developers, who build only for short-term profit, this kind of nonprofit corporation—which is becoming an increasingly common vehicle for constructing affordable housing all across the country—can afford to invest in the long-term benefits of design quality.

Now for the architecture. Tent City manages a particularly remarkable trick of urban design: it fills a long-empty site between the townhouse-filled neighborhood of the South End and Copley Place, an immense development that consists of two high-rise hotels and an upscale shopping mall. Tent City is a bridge between two worlds that are as different architecturally as they are sociologically, and it ties them together deftly.

Tent City's largest element, a 12-story wing, is, logically, at the end closest to the Copley Place megaproject. The rest of Tent City, which is constructed of reddish-orange brick with narrow bands of colored brick trim, steps down gradually to the scale of the town houses of the old neighborhood on the other side. The design of the complex never imitates the 19th-century town houses of the South End directly, but it echoes many critical elements: double-hung bay windows, mansard roofs, front stoops.

And the various sections of this 271-apartment complex are arranged in a conventional street pattern rather than on some huge and bland superblock. The fundamental philosophy here, as at Battery Park City in New York (where Joan Goody, one of the partners in charge of this design, has done studies for affordable housing), is the notion that there is wisdom in accepting the traditional and common elements of the existing city—that it is not timid but enlightened to use what is familiar as the starting point for new architecture. The Tent City apartments, which are as thoughtfully designed within as without, are conventional in

the best sense of that word: they seek to serve the demands of reasonable, comfortable, normal life.

William Rawn has been slightly more assertive in his design for 50 units of housing at the former site of the Charlestown Navy Yard, which is now being redeveloped. But the values here are the same: Mr. Rawn, too, celebrates the conventional, and has struggled hard to design housing units that are both functional and uplifting to their occupants. To this end he has oriented most units toward views of Boston Harbor, given them large family room-dining areas adjacent to kitchens, and made bedrooms easily divided. And many of the apartment units here have private outdoor decks just outside the kitchens that are safe for children and easily supervised from within.

But here, as at Tent City, it is the overall architecture, the public presence of this complex, that is the truly special thing. Mr. Rawn has come up with a design for this narrow site that is at once monumental and gentle, a building of brick that recalls the old industrial buildings of the Navy Yard (some of which still remain as its neighbors) and also evokes the brooding, primal forms of the architect Aldo Rossi.

The Navy Yard building is shaped something like a long wharf structure. It has three distinct sections: a high, gabled frontal section, set along the street and echoing in shape the front gables of the older buildings; a long wing behind this front section, set perpendicular to the street, and then, at the far end, a cylindrical wing with a conical top. The buildings are constructed entirely of brick, with tiny decorative insets of granite, and there are handsome arches at the base, intended both to evoke the spirit of the older buildings and also to show off the virtuoso talents of the bricklayers' union.

The building is sumptuous, yet spare, and it stands beside Boston Harbor with an eloquent but quiet presence. There is nothing coyly imitative of 19th-century architecture here, but there is something highly respectful of the spirit of older buildings, and determined to express that spirit in a way that is the architect's own. This is a building that manages to speak to the needs of its occupants and to the needs of the city, with equal attention to both. Tent City and the Charlestown project will house more than 300 families, but they improve the quality of urban life for everyone in Boston. ❖

Having Your Next Home Inspected

BY KENNETH T. AUSTIN
RODALE'S *NEW SHELTER,* APRIL 1986

HORSETRADERS HAVE A habit of examining livestock in the mouth, just as used-car customers are known for kicking tires. But what can homebuyers do to test the soundness of their potential purchases? They can get the house inspected.

Professional home inspectors can provide an unbiased evaluation of the condition of the mechanical, electrical, and structural elements of any house you may be considering. By taking advantage of such a service, you'll find out about the house's problems before they become your problems.

Home inspections are becoming more and more popular, but as a decision-making tool and as a source of bargaining power. One national home inspection organization estimated that American home buyers paid for 750,000 inspections in 1985. That represents about 25 percent of all home buyers—up from about 20 percent in 1983. The upward trend will probably continue as more buyers become convinced of the psychological and financial benefits of a professional home inspection. Also, a growing number of banks and mortgage companies now require that an inspection be done before they'll make a mortgage commitment.

If a real estate agent is involved in your house hunting, ask the agent if an inspection clause is written into the agency's standard contract. Many agencies use contracts that include inspection-option clauses, and other offices routinely insert inspection contingency clauses into their contracts or supply special contract addenda for this purpose.

These clauses or addenda usually provide the buyer with the option, at the buyer's expense, to have a professional home inspection performed on the house. Should the inspection report make note of any major defect (one that would cost $100, $250, or more to fix), the seller would have the option of either correcting the deficiency or negotiating the cost of correcting the deficiency with the buyer. Should the seller not correct the problem or negotiate it, the buyer would have the option of withdrawing from the contract without penalty.

A professional home inspection should require about two hours to complete and should include a thorough evaluation of the major elements of the house. These elements include the major systems (heating, cooling, plumbing, electrical), the roof, siding, and structure (foundation, framing, walls, ceilings, and floors).

Following inspection, the buyer is presented with either a handwritten report, or, in some cases, a formal typed report. The cost for this service should range between $200 and $250.

In addition, some home inspection services offer homebuyers a post-purchase inspection warranty for added peace-of-mind during the important first year of ownership. These warranties usually cover the systems of the house, as well as the roof, structure, and kitchen appliances.

To be assured that an inspection service is unbiased and capable, prospective clients should inquire about:

- *Affiliation:* Is the home inspection service totally independent? Contractors, exterminators, real estate agents, and others may be using the home inspection for their purposes, not for those of the home buyer. A truly independent home inspection service has no affiliation with another service or organization.
- *Experience:* How long has the inspection service been in the business? An inexperienced or untrained inspection could overlook expensive defects and prepare a misleading report for the home buyer. Ask if the service offers a warranty to back up its inspection.
- *Insurance:* Are you protected if the inspector damages the house or its contents? And what happens if the inspector is injured during the inspection? An uninsured inspector might very well seek damages from the home buyer.

Once you have an inspection report, resist the temptation to negotiate every minor defect found in the house. Buyers should be ready to accept certain normal, age-related deficiencies found in all homes of a particular age. Focus on the big-ticket items like the roof, wiring, furnace and septic system. And don't forget to accompany the inspector on his or her tour: It's a good way to get acquainted with what may be your new house. ❖

Rodale's New Shelter *is now* Practical Homeowner.

FACT SHEET

Home Owners Warranty Corporation

OCTOBER 1988

... Registered HOW builders carry insurance on their two-year warranties as well as eight additional years of insurance against major structural defects on every home they build. They are screened carefully and then agree to abide by the HOW Approved Standards which govern the acceptable levels of quality in construction. Also, they agree to use the HOW informal dispute settlement procedure.

The program has the following benefits:

Warranty

First Year: The builder warrants the home to be free from defects in workmanship and materials in compliance with the program's Approved Standards. The builder warrants the home against major structural defects and against defects in the wiring, piping and ductwork in the electrical, plumbing, cooling, ventilating and mechanical systems according to the HOW Approved Standards.

Second Year: The builder continues to warrant against major structural defects and against defects in the wiring, piping and ductwork in the electrical, plumbing, heating, cooling, ventilating and mechanical systems.

During this two-year period, builders insure their liability for performance under this warrant. If the builder fails to make repairs in compliance with the Approved Standards, HOW will make those repairs in his or her stead over the initial $250 aggregate cost.

Third Through Tenth Years: The builder insures against major structural defects in each home he or she builds subject to limitations.

Dispute Settlement

This is a neutral, third-party procedure to determine responsibility for repairs on warranted items. Decisions made by the dispute settler in favor of the homeowner are binding on the builder when accepted by the owner. The procedure is free to the homeowner.

The 5-Year Remodelers Plan

This unique plan is patterned on the new home plan and is available through registered, screened remodelers.

Protection in Transfers on Resale

The benefits of the builder's HOW warranty/insurance plan remain in force for the full ten years regardless of how often ownership may change. The protec-

tion adds to the resale value.

Builder Screening

Prior to acceptance in the program, builders are screened on their record of customer service, their technical ability and their financial stability. They must enroll every eligible home they build. HOW builders agree to adhere to the HOW Approved Standards which determine the acceptable quality levels of construction performance.

Remodelers are also screened and are required to enroll all jobs over $10,000. The Approved Standards for remodelers are similar to those for new housing.

Government Recognition

New Housing HOW Builders are eligible for special programs under VA, FHA, and FmHA.

1. The Veterans Administration (VA) recognizes HOW's insured warranty and has set up two special programs waiving some of its regulations for HOW builders.

On proposed construction, builders must submit plans for approval. The VA waives its first and intermediate inspections for HOW builders.

On existing construction, the VA will accept homes built by a HOW builder at the trim (customer preference) stage that were not processed by VA when construction began.

2. Federal Housing Administration (FHA) has also set up two special programs for HOW builders.

On proposed construction, homes built by a HOW builder may be exempt from HUD first and intermediate inspections.

FHA has initiated a second program which makes HOW builders' homes eligible for high-ration loans.

In this program, single-family dwellings which were not approved by FHA prior to construction and which have never been previously occupied and are less than one year old may be qualified. Builders may self-certify or use architects or engineers to certify that all plans and specifications of the house meet HUD's Minimum Property Standards. This is done through the local FHA office.

3. Farmers Home Administration (FmHA) waives its first and second inspections on homes built by a HOW builder provided builder plans and specifications meet FmHA guidelines. Loans may be obtained

for 100% of the appraised value or the cost of the house (whichever is the lesser).

State Warranties and HOW

New Jersey, Minnesota and Louisiana have passed state warranty laws patterned after the HOW 10-year new home program. In New Jersey, builders registered with HOW are exempt from the state warranty program which requires builders to provide a 10-year plan with coverage similar to HOW's. The Minnesota and Louisiana warranty laws also require builders to provide an express warranty similar to HOW coverage and terms. Indiana allows builders to disclaim implied warranties if they provide an express warranty similar to that provided by HOW builders.

History

HOW got its start when the National Association of Home Builders (NAHB) discovered that England's builders were offering a 10-year warranty/insurance plan on all new homes built in England. In August 1974, HOW enrolled its first home.

In May 1981, HOW became an independent program. It is a wholly-owned subsidiary of the Home Warranty Corporation which also owns HOWIC.

Statistics

- HOW has more than 12,000 builder-members who have enrolled more than 2 million homes.
- HOW is the industry leader, writing 85 percent of business under new home insured warranty programs.
- Approximately 47,000 builder/owner disputes have been processed through HOW's unique informal dispute settlement procedure.
- HOW, established in 1974, was the first 10-year home builder/home buyer protection plan.
- HOW Insurance Company, a Risk Retention Group, (HOWIC) operates in 49 states and the District of Columbia.
- HOWIC is incorporated in and regulated by the state of Virginia.
- 25 major reinsurers in the United States and Europe provide reinsurance to HOWIC.
- HOW is the only program of its type exclusively endorsed by the national Association of Home Builders and by several hundred local and state builders associations. ❖

EXCERPTS FROM

Questions About Condominiums

U.S. DEPARTMENT OF HOUSING AND URBAN DEVELOPMENT, MARCH 1980

IF YOU ARE thinking of purchasing a condominium dwelling unit, don't be afraid to ask questions. This booklet will supply you with some answers and stimulate more questions to ask as you learn about this relatively new form of homeownership.

Condominium living is rapidly gaining in popularity and, as land costs increase, it is destined to become even more popular in the future.

Condominiums come in many forms, from towering inner-city structures to suburban townhouses with beautiful, environmentally designed surroundings. Some are conversions of luxurious old rental structures which have been rehabilitated and modernized into highly desirable dwellings. Some, however, are merely old, exhausted rental properties which have been painted, carpeted wall to wall, given new kitchen equipment and cast into the condominium market. Condominium laws can be applied to either kind.

Also, there are many kinds of developers of condominiums. The majority are highly reputable and have no desire to limit their careers by marketing shoddy products. They know that there is no substitute for integrity in their relationship with consumers, whether or not they are operating in a State which has consumer protection laws or under a federally regulated program. There are, however, many opportunists who thrive on popular trends.

Contrary to the belief of many, condominiums are not created under Federal laws. There is, however, a law covering mortgages insured by HUD under the National Housing Act. This will be discussed in a later section of the booklet.

Condominiums are actually created under a special real estate law in the State where they are located.

Each of the 50 States, U.S. Territories, (i.e., Guam Virgin Islands) and Puerto Rico has its own condominium law. The laws provide a legal framework within which conditions, covenants, and restrictions (C,C,R's) can be imposed on a property. The laws differ as to detail and the condominium documents used in each State will differ accordingly. Condominium documents also differ from one development to another because they must describe the characteristics of the development they represent.

In the basic explanation only the fundamental condominium concept will be discussed. The conditions, covenants, and restrictions will be discussed as each document is explained.

Don't hesitate to ask anything—even questions that may seem silly to you. It's better to feel silly now than sorry later.

Request any and all available informational material. Don't be reluctant or apologetic. You have a right to insist upon receiving copies of not only the basic documents but anything else that would make a full disclosure of the sale terms to you.

Don't sign a Subscription and Purchase Agreement or any other form of sales contract until you have received and read a copy of the Declaration Bylaws, Operating Budget, Management Agreement, and other important information. Sales contracts or Subscription Agreements normally contain a clause which states, over your signature, that you have received the organizational documents.

Don't accept the answer that the Condominium Declaration can only be seen at the local land records office.

Don't make a downpayment until you are sure of your mortgage loan—unless the purchase agreement states that the downpayment will be refunded if you are unable to get mortgage credit on terms acceptable to you.

Ask about settlement costs. They will require cash over and above your downpayment.

Ask for a budget. Each prospective owner must be aware that the extent of obligation assumed is not limited to the cost of the unit. Besides the mortgage debt (principal, interest, taxes, and insurance) which will run over an extended period, there will be monthly assessments to cover your proportionate share of maintenance and related expenses of the common area. Find out how much that will be beforehand, not after you sign a binding contract.

If you don't understand the documents—and even if you think you do—seek legal aid. It is necessary that you understand what is in them, since they will control not only your future rights as a condominium owner but also your obligations.

Ask about an information Bulletin, Offering Statement, or its equivalent to give you a clear overall picture of the condominium development in which you're purchasing a unit. Remember, however, these do not substitute for the documents which legally create the condominium.

Find out on what basis your ownership, assessments and voting rights are being determined. If there is a lease involved be sure you understand that you are not the owner of the property it covers. You should find out how much it will cost you to rent and maintain the leased property over and above your condominium charges.

A Declaration normally provides for a master hazard insurance policy, insuring against loss by fire and other perils. Such policy should contain a condominium property endorsement which recognizes that condominiums have a multiple number of beneficiaries. Each prospective condominium purchaser should be certain that such an endorsement is part of the insurance package. Ask about it.

The prospective purchaser should be sure that there is sufficient liability coverage for the entire condominium development and that the liability insurance policy names, as insured, the board of directors and each unit owner individually as co-owner. Find out for sure.

Does the developer have sufficient capital to complete the entire condominium without using your downpayment?

The entire condominium development includes the common facilities. (The selling price as well as the cost per square foot allocated to each unit includes a proportionate amount of the common area and its facilities.) Failure to complete the common facilities will result in an overpayment for the value you actually receive. HUD and some States require that down payments be deposited in escrow until the dwelling units and associated common area are substantially completed.

Ask whether the condominium you see is the entire development or if the developer plans to enlarge the condominium or rental units. Has the developer's right to do so been predefined in the Declaration? You need this information to make an intelligent decision whether or not to purchase a unit in a condominium which does not have a firm percentage of interest at the time you purchase. The developer must predefine his intention in order to add any kind of additional units whether compatible or not, i.e., commercial units, or expensive amenities not anticipated by you at the outset.

Determine the extent of any other control by the developer, both before and after the condominium is legally constituted, and the effect, if any, on your future rights and obligations.

Ask what your individual dwelling unit estate encompasses. What are its boundaries? What are the boundaries of the common estate? Are there any restricted common areas and how do they apply to you?

If this is to be your permanent home find out to what degree transient occupancy is allowed. For developments with federally-insured mortgages, HUD requirements specify that a family unit cannot be rented by the owners for transient or hotel purposes. This is defined in part as; (1) a rental for any period less than 30 days or; (2) any rental if the occupants of the family unit are provided customary hotel services. The owners of the respective units, however, should have the right to lease for residential purposes, subject to the covenants and restrictions contained in the Declaration and Bylaws.

Inquire about any "Liquidated Damage Clause" in the Sales Agreement i.e., conditions under which you could lose your downpayment.

How many days are allowed for you to review the sales contract and basic condominium documents? Is it a long enough period for you to understand the documents and to seek legal assistance, if necessary?

In order to be assured of a good title, free and clear of any liens, you should consider purchasing an "Owner's Title Policy."

Are there any restrictions on your right to re-sell?

Do you have the right to sell your condominium unit on the open market or must you first offer it to the condominium association for a stipulated period of time? In HUD-regulated condominiums restrictions such as the "right of first refusal" are not permitted.

A condominium regime cannot be established within a given area without meeting State requirements. Remember—not all condominiums are subject to HUD requirements—only those which have mortgages insured by HUD.

Have all State requirements been met? (Verification can be obtained through your State Real Estate Commission or other appropriate State agency with authority to regulate condominiums.) Have all municipal building code requirements been satisfied?

Can you afford it? Weigh your present income, expenses, and living style against what they will be as a condominium owner.

Ask the seller to explain the condominium concept and how it applies to the particular development that interests you. The explanation will supply you with useful information and help you determine the capability of those with whom you are dealing.

Most States require licensed salesmen to be bonded. If you are negotiating with a salesman, determine that he is licensed before making any cash outlays.

Is it really a condominium or something else you're buying?

Not all townhouses, which surround a community area, are condominiums. The so-called planned unit development (PAD) or planned subdivision comprises a number of traditional estates (see Sketch No. 2 in Chapter 4) each of which has a membership interest in a separate property owned by a homeowners' association. There is no undivided interest in such an arrangement.

A number of separate condominiums may surround another separate and independent area which contains streets and recreation facilities. The independent area will not normally be a part of the common estate of any condominium. The area is normally on a separate traditional estate and owned by a non-profit organization (usually a corporation). All condominium unit owners automatically become members of the organization with ownership of their unit and will be responsible for maintenance and operation of the independent area.

Note: The term "air space estate" is often misunderstood and has been interpreted as being applicable only to units in a high rise structure. Such is not the case. The dwelling units may also be in a low rise, garden type, row structure or in semidetached or detached townhouse structures. A large condominium may have a combination of different types of structures. The term air space is more fully explained in Chapter 4.

Are the expenses underestimated? Look at the operating budget so you can determine whether or not the items listed for maintenance realistically compare with the kinds of maintenance costs you can anticipate as you tour the development: grounds; swimming pool, clubhouse maintenance; building exterior and common interior area maintenance; and street maintenance, if streets are part of the common area of the condominium and not maintained by the municipality. If the initial budget is underestimated it could mean an increase in assessments soon after you move in. Be

Ruling Ties Realty Broker to Seller

Buyers Said They Thought Maryland Agent Represented Them

BY SAM HANKIN

THE WASHINGTON POST, APRIL 30, 1988

A MARYLAND APPEALS court has tossed out a jury verdict awarding $10,000 to a couple who sued a Talbot County real estate company for failing to represent their interests during an unsuccessful attempt to buy a house, upholding the often misunderstood principle that a broker typically works for the seller, not the buyer....❖

sure the seller isn't understating operating expenses to expedite sales.

Look at the justification or explanation for the budget items to see if a reasonable basis was used in calculations.

Compare the proposed monthly assessment with the actual assessments being charged in other nearby condominiums which have been in operation for a few years.

Be sure the expenses include a reasonable reserve—funds to be set aside for eventual major repairs and replacements.

Are there any hidden leasehold costs? Some condominium developers retain ownership of parts of a project, usually the recreational facilities and sometimes the land, and lease them back to the buyers for 99 years. It is important to be aware of the difference between full ownership (fee simple title) which gives the owners control of the common area and a leasehold which gives the lessee full control over the property under the lease.

A developer or salesman may claim that more amenities can be provided by a leasehold arrangement and the condominium can be offered at lower prices. However, what can and does sometimes happen to the consumer is that he may be subjected to exorbitant rental charges initially and still higher rates over an extended period of time, in addition to the monthly assessment on the condominium. Failure to pay the monthly obligations could result in complete loss of your investment through foreclosure....

The Condominium Concept

Traditional Real Estate—To understand how an estate in real property is established under condominium law, consider first how an estate in real property is established under the traditional real estate law, using single home properties as an example.

It is not necessary to know the geometry and other mathematical details of surveying to get a general picture of how properties are established. By use of surveying techniques a parcel of property (lot) can be located on the surface of the earth by relating the boundaries of the parcel to previously established bench marks or other reference points. Once established (staked out) it can be recorded in a land records office for future identification....

Remember, even though the vertical planes of the unit spaces no longer extend from the earth's core to infinity, the property lines of the condominium do. In large, complex condominiums you must know the boundaries of your condominium to know where your undivided interest stops.

The common space in a condominium is referred to by different names—common area, common elements, common property, and common estate. It will be referred to in this booklet as common estate. The cube of dwelling space will be referred to as an individual unit estate or unit estate.

The plat of this property must show the exact location of the structure within the common estate and the architectural plans must show the exact location of each unit within the structure. The enabling declaration must contain not only a legal description of the boundary lines of the total property but also of the internal boundary walls of the dwelling space, in other words the unexposed surfaces of the four walls, floor and ceiling. The condominium comes into existence when the declaration, together with the plat and plans, are recorded on the property. The effect is to convert a previous single deed (traditional) estate into a multiple number of deeded dwelling unit estates within a common estate, the deed of which is shared by all the individual estate owners.

Ownership Characteristics— As can be seen from the foregoing discussion, condominium ownership from traditional ownership. Condominium ownership is actually created by a special real estate law which

A Word On Mobile Homes

IN 1975, MOBILE homes composed fully one-third of new single-family housing, and 95 percent of single-family homes selling for less than $15,000. Competitors in the industry numbered over four hundred producers and one thousand suppliers. A sense of pride and self-reliance exists among the industry's many entrepreneurs. Nevertheless, consumers have been complaining about the poor quality of construction; the prevailance of often fatal electrical fires caused by faulty wiring, and the difficulty of having the company agree to make repairs. The Center for Auto Safety in Washington, D.C. received so many letters of complaint that they published a book entitled *Mobile Homes: The Low Cost Housing Hoax* (Grossman Publishers, 1975), which explores the industry's dismal safety and service records. ❖

permits individual dwelling unit estates to be established within a total and larger property estate. After all of the individual unit estates have been described within the total property estate, all of the property not so described, such as the land and structural parts of the buildings, becomes a common estate, to be owned jointly by the owners of the individual estates. Departures from this basic concept will be discussed under the section on function of legal documents which follows. Remember this: A condominium individual unit estate is not complete without its undivided interest in a larger common estate.

Operating Characteristics—A condominium is usually operated on a nonprofit basis but does not necessarily have to be. The common areas could contain commercial units. Each month an owner makes a mortgage payment (if any) to a lender. The payment usually will include a payment into a tax escrow account. In addition a share of the cost to maintain and operate the common areas is paid to the Association. This payment normally includes a share of the hazard insurance which is paid in lump sum payments by the Association. In most condominiums the owner is also required to share the cost to fund reserve accounts.

Tax Characteristics—In a condominium all taxes and special assessments must be levied against the individual units separately and not against the whole condominium. Also, each unit must be capable of bearing its own mortgage. Therefore, an owner's title is not endangered by default on the part of other owners in meeting mortgage and real estate tax payments, nor is the owner required to meet deficiencies in such payments.

A condominium owner has the same income tax advantages as a conventional homeowner. The owner may deduct from his/her income, for Federal tax purposes, the real estate taxes and mortgage interest paid during the year. ❖

Condo Owners Have Duty

BY BENNY L. KASS
WASHINGTON POST, OCTOBER 15, 1988

Q: We have been exploring the idea of hiring a board of directors for our condominium association. There are about 150 units in our complex, and we have encountered serious difficulty getting unit owners to show up at the annual meetings and to volunteer to serve on the board. Many people have suggested that we hire a professional board of directors to govern our association. What do you think about this idea?

A: I don't like it.

First, most condominium bylaws state that a member of the board of directors will not be paid for service on the board. Thus, from a practical point of view, you probably will have to amend the bylaws. And if you are having difficulty getting people to show up at meetings, how do you think you will muster enough votes to get the amendments to your bylaws adopted?

But more important, the concept of a condominium involves—indeed, requires, in my opinion—that unit owners serve on the board of directors. Your association needs guidance from within its ranks. If you are having difficulty getting members to serve on the board, I suspect that a hired board of directors also would suffer a lack of guidance and leadership.

Let's look at the practical problems involved with a hired board. First, who will elect (or select) the members? If you can get a quorum at an annual meeting for the purpose of hiring a board of directors, it seems to me that you should be able to find a few unit owners who are willing to serve on the board.

All too often, condominium unit owners do not understand the function of a board of directors. The board is the governing body, and it makes the rules to guide the unit owners. If the majority of unit owners do not like certain rules, they can throw the old board out and elect directors more sympathetic to their views. As with any other election, the voters are the ultimate watchdog over the elected officials. What mechanism would you adopt if you were dissatisfied with the plans and policies of your hired board?

Serving on a condominium board has been described as a thankless task. All too often, directors have to serve long hours and take the heat from the other unit owners.

But a properly run board can correct this situation somewhat. The hired staff should be your management company, who can handle most of the day-to-day operating details. Let the project manager take the heat for enforcing the rules or for taking a hard line on collection of delinquent accounts.

A well-run board does not meet often. If the relationship between the board and the management company is working, the board needs to meet perhaps only once every three months. Of course, in emergencies, the board will have to respond. ❖

Strategies for Sellers in a Buyers' Market

BY KENNETH R. HARNEY
WASHINGTON POST, OCTOBER 29, 1988

IF YOU'RE TRYING to sell your home and are frustrated at how slowly the market is moving, don't pull your hair out. ... Just change your strategy, which may include even taking your property off the market temporarily, at least until next spring.

That's the heads-up sane advice from top brokers in New York, the heart of what may be one of the most challenging markets in the country this season. Injured by post-Black Monday layoffs in the financial community, the huge suburban New York-northern New Jersey-Connecticut housing market is now loaded with excess homes for sale. Properties that had been jumping in value by 20 percent to 30 percent a year 18 months ago now sit flat in the water.

Similar situations exist in the once high-flying New England markets and even suburban Washington. For seasonal reasons, buyers' markets also exist in large numbers of other metropolitan areas across the country.

So what do you do if you happen to be a seller in any of these? One thing you can do is listen to the counsel of Matt Broderick of New Jersey-based Schlott Realtors, the third-largest independent real-estate brokerage firm in the country. Broderick's firm sells $6.5 billion worth of homes a year through 175 offices in five states.

Broderick's all-weather advice for selling in cyclical softness includes, for starters, words you thought you'd never hear from a real-estate sales broker: "you may want to postpone [putting your place on the market] or pull it off the market" until you see signs of a turnaround.

But there's no compelling reason to do so, he adds quickly, if you follow a sound strategy for selling in a buyers' market. The essential rules boil down to four:

- First, restrain your own natural inclinations on pricing. Discount to your market up front, and you'll come out ahead, sooner.

"A buyer's market doesn't mean you take less than what your house is worth, or that you've got to take a loss on the sale," counsels Broderick. "But it may mean that your own mental picture of what your house is worth isn't in touch with current realities in the marketplace."

To make certain that properties move rapidly in suburban New York's 1988 buyers' market, Broderick's firm uses what it calls a "power-house" contract. Sellers who want to list with Schlott under this contract have to agree in writing not to ask for more than 10 percent above what Schlott appraisers define as the current market price.

That requirement may lose some listings, Broderick concedes, but it tends to impose a discipline on both seller and buyer that otherwise would be missing. Schlott has found that it saves agents and sellers time, brings serious buyers to the table sooner, and keeps low-ballers and bottom-fishers away.

- The second rule after realistic pricing, according to Broderick, involves financing flexibility. In a tough market climate, sellers need to be willing to "put some of their paper profits (from prior years' appreciation) into the buyer's mortgage-financing equation." That means offering to pay loan discount points or closing costs from the very start of the transaction. (Loan discount points are the up-front cash fees charged by lenders for originating, processing and closing a mortgage.)

"If you can tell a buyer on the first visit that this house not only is fairly priced but comes with some or all of your (mortgage) points paid," says Broderick, "we find this to be a tremendously attractive way to motivate serious offers." Rather than cutting the listed price, some "power-house" sellers agree in advance to buy down the purchaser's mortgage by one or more percentage points.

A buy-down is a rate subsidy. If the purchaser can qualify for a 10 percent loan, for example, the seller might offer to pay a stated fee at closing to the lender. That fee—taken out of the sales proceeds of the house—would be used to lower the purchaser's effective rate to, say, eight or nine percent. Each month's mortgage-payment differential would be subsidized by the seller for an agreed-on period—typically two to three years. After that, the buyer's effective rate would return to the original 10 percent.

- The third essential for selling in a buyers' market involves getting an extra edge through physical appearance. Although fresh paint, repairs and tidying up are important in any market climate, they are "absolutely critical right now," Broderick said. Now, you've got to look better than the place down the street or you'll get nobody but bargain-hunters.
- Finally, he urged, stay cool. Be patient and let the market cycle work its way out. The buyers who are staying home this fall watching the World Series and election results are likely to be out in force early in 1989. ❖

Your Housing Rights
U.S. DEPARTMENT OF HOUSING AND URBAN DEVELOPMENT, NOVEMBER 1981

Title VIII of the Civil Rights Act of 1968

Under Title VIII of the Civil Rights Act of 1968, it is illegal to discriminate against any person because of race, color, religion, sex, or national origin:

- In the sale of rental housing or residential lots.
- In advertising the sale or rental of housing.
- In the financing of housing.
- In the provision of real estate brokerage services.

Blockbusting is also illegal.

If you are discriminated against:

You may call on the Federal Government for help. You may file a complaint with the Department of Housing and Urban Development (HUD) within 180 days of the incident. You can:

- Send a complaint to the Department of Housing and Urban Development:

Address:

Fair Housing
Washington, D.C. 20410

- Call (toll free) 800-424-8590, if you live outside the Washington, D.C. Metropolitan Area or 426-3500 if you live in the Washington, D.C. Metropolitan Area to file a complaint with HUD. OR
- Go directly to Court.

HUD may:

- Investigate if the law has been broken.
- Attempt to resolve the discriminatory housing practice by informal methods of conference, conciliation and persuasion.
- Refer your complaint to a state or local Human Rights Commission, if there is one where you live, for investigation and possible resolution.
- Recommend you go to court.

The nearest local HUD office will be glad to assist you in preparing your complaint. There are offices throughout the nation. Try your telephone book, if you live in a large city, under: U.S. Government, Housing and Urban Development.

1866 Civil Rights Act

Under a Supreme Court decision upholding an 1866 Act of Congress,[1] racial discrimination in the sale or rental of all housing is illegal. Under this law, an attorney can help you if, because of race, any of these things happened:

- You were denied the opportunity to buy or rent a house or apartment.
- You were told a house or an apartment wasn't available when it really was.
- You were offered different terms or conditions of sale or rental than someone else.

Under the 1866 Civil Rights Act:

- You can immediately file a suit in a Federal court. You may wish to consult an attorney or local Legal Aid Society for assistance.
- The court could stop the sale of the house or the rental of an apartment to someone else. It could help make it possible to buy or rent the housing you want. It could award you damages and court costs or take other actions that could help you.

[1] 42 USC Sec. 1982 Civil Rights Act of 1866. ❖

Are You Paying Too Much to Protect Your Home?

CONSUMER REPORTS, JULY 1988

IF YOU BOUGHT a home during the past few years in an area where real-estate prices have risen rapidly, chances are your house is overinsured. You probably had to buy the excess insurance as a condition of getting a mortgage.

For years, mortgage companies in most states have forced some homeowners to insure their homes for the full amount of their mortgage—the loan for the house plus the land, not just the replacement cost of the building.

The practice made sense only from the lender's point of view. Mortgage companies devised the full-insurance guideline when the cost of a typical house represented about 80 percent of the selling price of a piece of property. Most buyers made a 20 percent down payment, so mortgage companies figured they could protect the rest of their investment by requiring insurance for the full amount of the mortgage.

That old formula doesn't hold true any more, however. Over the past five years or so, land values have risen faster than building costs.

According to the Natonal Association of Home Builders, the average house now accounts for about 75 percent of the total cost of the average piece of property. In many areas, such as the east coast, in California, and near metropolitan centers, the house often accounts for only 65 percent of the purchase price.

A closer inspection of your insurance policy could save you a lot of money. If you bought a $250,000 house in metropolitan New York, where land values are exceedingly high, you might have made a $50,000 down payment and financed the balance. The replacement cost of the house might be only $165,500, but under the old formula, you'd have needed $200,000 worth of insurance to get the mortgage. Paying for the extra $37,500 of coverage could cost as much a $161 annually.

To rectify this inequity, several states have passed laws prohibiting lenders from requiring that homeowners over-insure their homes. California, Connecticut, Massachusetts, and Rhode Island specify that you need only insure your house for the actual cost of rebuilding it.

Recent home buyers should check to see if their insurance covers only the full replacement cost of the house. More is waste, less means you're underinsured. If you suspect you might be protecting the dirt that your house sits on, ask you mortgage lender what procedure you should follow to have your insurance requirements revised. You'll probably need to have your home appraised and to provide documentation to the lender. (An independent appraiser usually charges about $150 to $300.) In most cases, the mortgage lender will permit you to carry less insurance if the house is covered for its full replacement cost. ❖

Consumer Reports *is available for $18 a year. Published monthly. Address: P.O. Box 53029, Boulder, CO 80322-3029.*

The Best Policies

Sensible Options For Getting Good Homeowner's Insurance With Premiums You Can Afford

BY WALTER L. UPDEGRAVE
HOMEOWNER, APRIL 1988

WHEN IT COMES to protecting your home and your family's future, how much security is really enough? It's a question that can unnerve even the most rational head of household, but when you're buying homeowner's insurance, you have to make decisions that balance your need for protection against premium payments you can realistically afford. The best way to begin sorting things out is to learn how a basic homeowner's policy works. From there you can tailor it to meet your specific needs and budget.

Most standard homeowners' policies cover three things: your house, your possessions and any liability you might have if someone is injured on your property. Insurers refer to their standard homeowner's policies as "broad coverage" or "all-risk insurance," but the truth is, no insurance policy covers everything. Scan the fine print and you'll find that most policies don't cover losses that result from war, nuclear accidents, civil disturbances, earthquakes and—to the surprise of many—floods. You can, however, buy "named-peril" policies to supplement broad coverage, and that's a smart thing to do in areas that are subject to risks that aren't ordinarily covered.

How Much Do You Need?

When you sit down with an agent to discuss coverage start by figuring out how much you need for the house itself. "Often, people don't understand the difference between a home's 'replacement cost' and its 'market value,'" says David Hurst, a spokesman for State Farm Mutual, the largest home insurer in the country. "And the confusion can result in either over- or underinsuring your home. The amount of coverage should be based on the replacement cost, which is what you'd pay to reproduce your house exactly."

Setting A Home's Value

That figure may be higher or lower than your home's market value. For example, if you live in an exquisitely refurbished Victorian mansion with original woodwork in pristine condition, chances are its replacement cost far exceeds its market value. Most insurers gauge the replacement value of a house by calculating factors such as the number of rooms, the square footage, the type of materials and the overall condition. This method is fine for most homes, but if you own a period-style house or have added expensive custom details, you'd do well to have a certified real estate appraiser figure the replacement cost.

It's important to know that most insurers will only agree to rebuild with "commonly available" materials. That means hand-carved moldings will be replaced with standard millwork, and plaster walls will be restored with drywall. A few companies will insure unique houses. They'll itemize special details and in the event of a loss, reproduce them as faithfully as possible, but you'll have to seek out those companies.

Once an insurer determines the replacement cost of your house, the agent will generally suggest insuring for 100 percent of that amount. If you do, many major insurance companies add a guaranteed replacement cost endorsement, which assures that they'll rebuild your house even if it costs more than the face amount of the policy. While that can offer you peace of mind, it's probably more insurance than you need. Complete wipeouts are rare. State Farm's Hurst points out, for example, that less than one percent of house fires, the most common insurance claim, cause a total loss. You can play on these odds and insure your home for 90 or even 80 percent of its replacement value and save roughly 10 to 20 percent on your annual premium.

This makes good financial sense for most people, but it's not a good strategy for everyone. Don't do it if, for example, you live near the San Andreas fault or if you don't have enough money tucked away to make up the difference between the policy's reimbursement and your rebuilding costs.

And no matter how tantalizing the savings, don't ever insure for less than 80 percent of replacement costs. Once you sink below the 80-percent threshold, the insurer can invoke the little-known Did-Should Rule and only partially reimburse you for small losses. Here's how the rule could work against you: Say your home's replacement cost is $100,000. You insure it for 60 percent, or $60,000, and you suffer a $40,000 loss in a fire. Even though you've got a $20,000 cushion, the insurer may reimburse you for only $30,000, leaving you $10,000 in the hole. Why? The insurance company divides what you did insure for by what it says you should have insured for, and pays you that percentage, in this case, 75 percent, of your loss. This may not sound fair, but it's a fairly common practice among insurers.

Besides insuring the structure, homeowner's coverage also protects virtually all your personal property. But there are several important limitations. Most policies limit the coverage of items like furniture, appliances, clothing and other personal possessions to 50 percent of the amount of insurance on the house itself. So if you've insured your house for $130,000, you can't collect more than $65,000 for personal items, no matter what your actual loss. And though the coverage on the house structure is based on replacement cost, most policies come with actual cash value (ACV) coverage on personal property.

"Actual cash value" sounds like pretty solid coverage, but what it really means is that you'll be reimbursed for an item's replacement minus depreciation. So if your sofa burns up, and the current price tag is $1,200, ACV coverage might get you $600—the $1,200 replacement cost minus 50 percent.

You're better off upgrading your policy with a replacement cost endorsement for your home's "personal contents." This adds about 10 percent to your yearly premium, but you can easily make up the difference in a single claim. For example, you'd get the full $1,200 for that sofa instead of $600.

When you upgrade from ACV to replacement cost, most policies raise the overall personal contents limit from 50 to 70 percent of the face amount of the policy. That's important because the higher reimbursement for each item lost can easily take you over the standard 50 percent limit if you have a large claim involving many household items.

In addition to overall ceilings on personal possessions, there are lower limits for certain items. For example, most policies restrict claims for silverware to $2,500 and jewelry, furs and watches to $1,000. You can raise those limits two ways: One is to add what's usually called "blanket coverage," or an endorsement raising the limit in a specific area. You can, for instance, raise the overall limit on jewelry from $1,000 to as high as $5,000 by paying an extra $18 to $20 for each $1,000 of additional coverage. But some blanket coverage endorsements may apply limits on specific items. For example, even though you'd be entitled to collect $5,000 if all your jewelry were stolen, you might only collect $1,000 for a single piece, even if its value is $2,500. When you insure special items, ask your agent about the actual extent of special coverages so you won't be surprised in the event of a loss.

For especially valuable items, you're better off with a personal articles floater, which is, in effect, a separate policy for the particular item. Premiums on floaters vary depending on where you live, but generally you'll pay about $2 per $100 of art and $1 per $100 for furs.

To insure a valuable painting under a floater policy, for example, you'd have it appraised, and the insurer would issue a stated value policy, which covers the painting for the amount of the appraisal.

Floaters have some advantages over blanket coverage. The policy's deductible—the amount of the loss you have to pay before the insurance kicks in—doesn't apply to floaters as it does to blanket endorsements. The coverage is also more comprehensive. If your $3,000 Ming vase were shattered, a floater would cover the loss; a standard policy would only cover theft or destruction by fire.

You should beware, though, of one limitation insurers impose on floaters: although you pay a premium based on the stated value, you may not get that amount if you opt for cash reimbursement instead of item replacement. Example: you report as lost the $7,500 bracelet you bought at Tiffany's, and your insurance agent assures you the company will replace it immediately, with one from a wholesaler but not from Tiffany's. When you ask for the money instead, the agent tells you the company will pay only its replacement cost—say $6,500—not the bracelet's price at Tiffany's. This is another case where you should ask in advance how the coverage really works so you'll avoid costly and disappointing misunderstandings.

Liability Coverage

One of the least known but most important parts of a homeowner's insurance package is the liability coverage. It protects you from damages you might incur if, say, an acquaintance has an accident at your Fourth of July barbecue and then sues you for gross negligence. The coverage in a basic policy may be as low as $25,000, although most policies today provide a minimum of $100,000 of coverage.

For most people, even $100,000 liability protection isn't enough. "If you get into a legal battle, settlements can easily reach $500,000," says Richard Simpson, an agent for the Hartford Insurance Group.

The cost of increasing liability coverage is so low, it's foolish to scrimp on it. Virtually all middle-income families should spend the extra $15 a year it takes to increase coverage to $300,000 or even spring for an additional $30 a year to go up to $500,000. If you have a net worth in excess of $500,000—or an income high enough to get an ambulance chaser thinking about attaching future wages—you should consider an umbrella liability policy. Such policies raise the liability coverage of both your home and auto policies to $1 million or more. Premiums for million-dollar liability usually run between $100 and $140 a year.

If all we've said here about homeowner's insurance seems complex, jargon-riddled and technical, that's because it is. It's important to take time to assess your needs and know your options. Along with getting the best coverage, a little insurance savvy will get you the best value for your premium dollars. ❖

UTILITIES: BEATING THE BILLING BLUES

AHA, THE PITFALLS and pratfalls of getting just the right heat, air conditioning and electricity for your home at the best savings. This section starts right off with the bills you receive and the way these can be erroneous and unfathomable. Computerized billing provides more opportunities for trickery and an all purpose alibi when you catch them cold: "Sorry, it was a computer error." But when you catch them, do they correct this "computer error" for all the rest of their customers? "Beating the Billing Blues" is a tour de force that gives you the detective-like intensity that these bills and their companies so deserve. No more nice patsies! Other readings cover efficiently heated homes, mistaken meters, the future of energy applications (even old-fashioned ceiling fans are coming back). Note in particular the energy life cycle costing example which all homemakers should calculate when buying a new appliance, furnace or other energy guzzler. ❖

Beating The Billing Blues

BUYER'S MARKET, VOLUME II, NUMBER 5, MAY 1986

IF YOU HAVE A hard time figuring out your bills, or happen to find an occasional error on one, you are not alone. Indecipherable or erroneous computerized bills are becoming commonplace. And they're costing consumers billions of dollars in needless and unjust charges.

Billing errors can be big, stealing thousands of dollars from their victims, or small, amounting to just a few cents. Some bills are so confusing or inscrutable that it is impossible to determine whether the bill is accurate at all.

Either way, billing problems are bad news. Many consumers simply ignore them, thinking it is not worth the bother making phone calls and writing letters because they won't get anywhere. That's a self-defeating idea. Honest and reputable companies want to know about billing problems—they want to keep their customers satisfied. The unscrupulous companies rely on the inconvenience of complaining to deter customers from doing so—and will continue the abuse as long as they can get away with it.

Becoming a smart and savvy bill-payer is not difficult. The following pages contain the tips and information you need to detect and resolve billing problems. Major areas of billing abuse—credit card, medical and utility bills—are explained in detail. You will also learn where to go for more help.

Six Major Types of Billing Problems and How to Detect Them

Here is what to watch out for when you sit down to pay your bills:

1. Unitemized bills. These are one-page bills which contain nothing more than a few totals; they are essentially useless because they make it impossible to verify the accuracy of the charges. When you get a bill, ask yourself: Is the price of each product or service ordered listed individually, so that I can identify it, or have I been given only a total amount due? Examples:

- A California woman received a one-line bill for $36,000 for a hospital visit. When she demanded an itemized bill, she discovered two erroneous charges—for $15,000 each. The hospital removed the charges from her bill.
- An entertainment lawyer billed his client $775 for "meetings...telecons and correspondence... additional conferences, telephone conferences, correspondence and memoranda..." without noting the number of hours spent or the fee per hour.
- A woman hospitalized for a hip replacement

received a bill for $21,655; dozens of the charges on the bill were listed simply as "Miscellaneous—$999.99" or "Supply Charges." When she added the "Supply Charges" up, they did not amount to the subtotal on the bill.

2. Indecipherable bills. Many bills are so complicated and obscure that they could be a foreign language or a secret code. Most indecipherable bills contain terms which are undefined or have no intrinsic meaning, making it impossible to determine whether the charge was calculated correctly. Like unitemized bills, they shield themselves from adequate scrutiny and prevent consumers from comparing products or services with competitors. Ask yourself insistently when reading the bill: do I understand how they calculated the charge in question? Here are some typical stories:

- Monthly telephone bills from GTE list local call charges by multiplying the length of the call in minutes by a meaningless numerical unit that equals the cost of the call.
- One five-page hospital bill contained so many indecipherable items that it was incomprehensible even to a medical doctor also trained as a lawyer.
- An AT&T bill for telephone equipment used by a small business coded all the items in unidentifiable serial numbers rather than product names.

3. Overcharges. Numerous bills contain grossly-inflated charges for legitimate products and services. Many consumers forget to look at the amount in question, particularly on bills containing many charges. When paying a bill, make a mental check to be sure the charge on the bill is the price you agreed to. And compare the charge to any receipts you received at the time of purchase.

- A waiter in a New York restaurant added $10 to the tip on a dinner charged on an American Express Card by changing a digit on the receipt; when the cardholder caught the mistake by comparing it to the original, the restaurant quickly corrected the error.
- The GTE Sprint long-distance company charged some of its customers who used the service during Thanksgiving and Christmas of 1984 the regular business rate, rather than the holiday rate. Though they were aware of the problem—the company readily corrected bills of those customers who were able to calculate that a mistake had been made and called the company to complain—GTE Sprint did not notify its customers of the mistake, or offer to make automatic refunds until it was sued by a consumer group.

4. Phony charges. Some bills contain imaginary or "phantom" charges for items never ordered by the consumer. And some companies send out materials which look and read like bills, but are only solicitations. Do not be fooled by letters asking you to pay for items you have not ordered yet, or suggesting that your "account will lapse" if you do not pay right away. Always ask yourself: did I ask for and receive the item charged for? Beware: Many mail-order scams involve billing for products or services not ordered.

- A Roanoke, Virginia couple answered an ad for a $100 round-trip airplane flight to Hawaii—and ended up being billed on their VISA card for an additional $325 for ten pen and pencil sets.
- A Columbus, Ohio woman received outpatient surgery but was charged for a semi-private room for two days; she was also billed for an oral thermometer, use of a prep room and anaesthetic services she never received. Since her husband happened to be a doctor at the same hospital, the administrator of the hospital agreed to review the bill. She received a refund of $581.60—about 25 percent of the total bill.
- A vacationing consumer rented a car from General Rent-A-Car in Orlando, Florida and paid for it by credit card. The agency added an extra day's rental to the charges; when the consumer complained to the credit card company and the rental agency, he was told, "this happens often." While the credit card company reversed the second charge, it still charged him interest on the amount.

5. Interest on billing mistakes. As in the last example, many billing errors are often only partly rectified, leaving the consumer to incur the interest costs, late fees or other penalties for the company's mistake. Whenever you catch a billing mistake, always check on subsequent bills to make sure you are not being charged interest on the erroneous item, or other penalties for non-payment of a mistaken charge.

- A Minneapolis bank erroneously debited a customer's checking account $500 two months in a row. The bank reversed the charges, but failed to reverse the overdraft and penalty fees which occured when the balance fell below the minimum as a result of its mistake.
- Shortly after moving into a new office space,

a Utah business received an erroneous state fuel tax bill for $15,000 in interest charges accrued since 1906.

6. Bill processing charges. The latest wrinkle in billing abuse, the "processing charge," is appearing on computerized bills with increasing frequency. Processing charges are nothing more than an effort to bill you for the cost of billing you—a cost which used to be calculated into the price of a product or service. And bill processing charges usually bear little or no relation to the actual cost of preparing and mailing the bill.

Processing charges are a way to charge you a higher price than you agreed to for a product or service you have purchased. Like "postal and handling charge" abuses, they can substantially increase your costs (note: these are not the same as small processing charges added to installment payments, which are a form of interest on the loan). If the total on a bill is slightly higher than it should be, check to see whether a "billing fee" or "processing charge" has been added.

- A Los Angeles woman rented a TV while in the hospital; the television leasing company, a subcontractor of the hospital, charged her a $2 "billing fee" in addition to the $36 rental. She refused to pay the billing fee and the company backed down.
- A car buyer in Irwin, Pennsylvania negotiated a price of $16,000 for a new Oldsmobile; when he looked at the sales contract, the dealership had added a $50 paperwork fee.

Fixing Those Billing Mistakes

Catching mistakes on bills is half the battle; the other half is getting them fixed. Resolving billing disputes is a step-by-step process that usually begins with a phone call. Often, that is all it will require; sometimes, however, you will have to go further. Below are the proven techniques we've used to resolve billing mistakes.

Computer vs. Human Error

Companies caught making mistakes on their bills frequently blame them on "computer error"—as if the company was not responsible for the problem. But, as nationally-syndicated computer columnist Lawrence Magid points out, "computer generated errors can always be traced to people, be they programmers, engineers, or those who enter the data into the computer. The saying in the computer industry is: 'garbage in, garbage out.'"

Step 1. Read what the bill says you should do in case of error. Once you have found a billing problem—or if you simply do not understand the bill—you should contact the company. Some bills include a statement explaining how to do this. Examine the bill to see whether it contains a telephone number or address where you can complain.

Some state and federal statutes provide consumers with specific rights when it comes to billing errors—particularly in the credit, banking and utility areas. Such laws usually require companies to print a statement on each bill telling you how to protect your rights. Always follow the procedures listed, particularly concerning deadlines for filing a written complaint, if required.

Step 2. Call the company. It is always best to contact the company by phone first, because when you speak to a company employee by his or her name, you are in effect investing him or her with personal responsibility for resolving your problem. This psychological factor helps get immediate individual attention.

If the company is located in a distant city, check the bill or "800" information to see if they operate a toll-free number. If not, you can always try to call collect. When you call, explain that you have a billing problem and ask to speak to the person who can resolve it.

Step 3. Explain your problem, and how you want it fixed. Once you are talking to the right person, give the date of the bill and explain the problem in detail. Make sure the person you are talking with has retrieved a copy of the bill—so he or she can see the problem and make the correction right away.

One Texas couple received a bill for $368 for work they had paid for over five months earlier; when they called the company to ask about it, the company immediately cancelled the charge. As the company told them, whenever it "comes across an unexplained slip that relates to an order, they mail it on to the customer and let him explain or pay." It pays to speak up!

If your bill contains overcharges or phony charges—including undisclosed bogus charges for "bill processing"—demand that they be removed. Make sure the company also removes any interest charges or penalty fees at the same time. Ascertain from the person the correct amount you owe, and agree you will pay that amount. Make sure you write down the names of each person you speak with, and what they say.

Step 4. If you have a problem, ask for a supervisor. Never accept poor performance or rude behavior from the person you are speaking with. All too frequently corporate employees forget that without you, the consumer, they are out of business. If the employees you speak to appear uninterested in your problem or do not know how to help, ask politely to speak with their supervisor. Use their names when you do so. Many times, just making the request to speak with a superior will get you the attention you deserve from the person with whom you are speaking. Employees do not want to appear incompetent to their bosses, and will work harder to help you to avoid bothering their superiors.

Be polite but very firm when you speak to supervisors. Make sure you explain why you asked to speak with them, and indicate your displeasure at the poor performance of the person you spoke with before. Let them know you intend to do everything necessary to resolve the problem—and expect the same from them.

Finally, note that supervisors have superiors too. If you have to, work your way right to the top. Many corporate executives are insulated from those in their company who deal directly with the public, and they should want to know if employees are doing a poor job. When a White Plains, New York man complained to the Rocky Mountain Bankcard System about an erroneous charge, Rocky Mountain President Dale Browning personally wrote him and corrected the mistake. Sometimes, corporate leaders have Administrative Assistants or Executive Secretaries who are used to handling crisis situations when they arrive at the top. They can be very helpful, and will usually do everything they can to avoid having to badger the chief executive.

Step 5. Write a note and pay the bill. Once you have rectified the problem, pay the bill. Even if you are convinced you have taken care of the mistake, it is always advisable to note in writing—either on the bill or in a separate letter—the mistake and whom you have talked with at the company. If you are sure the problem has been taken care of, a few lines scribbled on the bill will suffice (for example, "per conversation with John Doe, 11/4/85, I am enclosing $21 instead of $25, because of mistaken billing").

However, if the mistake is complicated, sizeable, or if you think the person you spoke with might not adjust the bill correctly, then write a letter to the person directly. Refresh the employee's memory about your phone conversation....state the agreement reached, and enclose the bill and check. Letters are a particularly good way of following up, since they can serve as proof of your efforts should problems arise later. Always keep a copy of your letter and the bill in question. Whenever federal or state law stipulates that you need to put a complaint in writing, do so, even if it is just to acknowledge a phone conversation resolving the matter.

Step 6. What to do if the company will not fix your problem. Some companies—dishonest firms, or those which are simply insensitive to consumers—will refuse to help you out. You have several choices:

You can give up and pay. You lose, and so do other consumers who will continue to be abused by the deterred company.

You can refuse to pay. If the company believes it is correct, it may take you to court. Companies which dishonestly take advantage of consumers will rarely go to court, though, for obvious reasons. Be aware, however, that even if the company declines to come after you, it might still be able to impair your credit rating. State and federal laws govern reports to credit bureaus and prohibit false reports to credit rating bureaus.

You can sue. If you want to avoid affecting your credit rating no matter what, you can pay the bill and sue the company (this also applies if you have already paid the bill). All states have small claims courts where citizens can sue without lawyers and without any technical knowledge of law—all you need is your bill and accompanying letters to the company (the more detailed the records are, the better). Small claims courts are usually limited to cases involving a thousand dollars or less; if the dispute involves a large amount of money, you may wish to hire an attorney. If the billing abuse is a widespread pattern, be alert for the possibility of a class-action suit against the company.

You can seek other help. Government agencies can assist you in many disputes. Many states and large cities have consumer protection departments; some non-profit public interest organizations will assist consumers.

Finally, where fraud or other criminal activity is involved, contact the local police, district attorney, state attorney general's office, and the U.S. Postal Service, if the mails are involved. Note: When you

The Network Project

The Network Project is a non-profit research organization which studies the impact of technology upon consumers. If you have found an example of one of the many billing scams mentioned in this newsletter, send us a copy at the address listed below; we do not at present resolve individual disputes, but copies of your bills help us spot patterns of abuse and come up with solutions. You can obtain more information about the Network Project by sending a stamped, self-addressed, business-size envelope to Network Project, P.O. Box 1736, Santa Monica, CA 90406.

seek government agency assistance, it can be a time-consuming process, and you may have to be as persistent as you were with the company involved...

Telephone and Other Utility Bills

Telephone bills are increasingly difficult to understand. Monthly service fees are rarely broken down into equipment rental and line charges; companies do not itemize usage of services like information and extended local calling, which used to be free but are increasingly charged to customers; and many phone bills contain unexplained items or additional charges. According to a recent Gallup Poll, 28 percent of the people surveyed did not understand their telephone bills.

The problems have been compounded by the AT&T divestiture and the deregulation of many telephone services by the federal government. Few state utilities agencies take more than a passing interest in the format of utility bills (one exception is New York, which has established rules which mandate readable bills) and many regulatory bodies are too poorly staffed to protect consumers or are captives of the utilities themselves. As a result, consumers must be especially vigilant in checking telephone bills. Among the recent problems reported to us are these:

- AT&T and other telephone companies have been found charging customers rental fees for telephone equipment which has been purchased or else returned.
- Several long distance companies have been signing up residential and small business customers for long distance calling service without obtaining the customers' authorization.
- Charging for local and long distance calls dialed but not completed has been a widespread practice. Some companies "start the meter running" after five or six rings, even if no one answers the phone. Check your phone bills carefully for calls never completed. Look for one-minute telephone calls on your bill—

one customer of Pacific Bell found over 100 one-minute calls on his bill. This practice will diminish as all long distance companies get "equal access" to long distance lines.

- Poor quality long distance service is commonplace; if you experience trouble hearing the other party, or are suddenly disconnected, contact the long distance company immediately or mark the call on your bill and do not pay for it.

Energy Utilities

On gas and electric bills, be particularly wary of "estimated meter readings," in which the company simply extrapolates usage in prior months to determine your current bill. They are a major form of billing abuse. The Public Service Company of New Mexico has stated that 5 percent of its monthly bills are wrong due to faulty meter reading. One customer of Brooklyn Union Gas was billed $33 because of an estimated meter reading on an apartment which happened to be vacant during that month.

Also, watch carefully for other types of creative billing scams: a customer of Commonwealth Edison in Chicago noted that the company underreads his meter in the month prior to rate increases; his bill jumped 25 percent when the utility billed for the full usage at the new, higher kilowatt hour rate. Similarly, a Florida couple realized that their local utility company billed in longer periods (i.e., 32 days) during peak usage seasons so that the extra days would push the customers into the expensive, second-tier level.

Always demand that your utility company explain every charge on your bill. Many states provide specific procedures for disputing a utility bill; follow these to prevent the company from terminating your service. Watch out for late payment charges or interest fees on erroneous charges. If the problem appears to be widespread, contact state utility officials and your state legislators about the matter. ❖

Low-Cost Solar Heat
Keeping The Solar Flame Alive After Tax Credits
BY CRAIG CANINE
RODALE'S *NEW SHELTER*, DECEMBER 1985

WILL THE MARKET for solar water- and space-heating systems dry up when tax credits expire? Researchers at the Solar Energy Research Institute (SERI) in Golden, Colorado think so—unless the cost of solar heating systems comes down dramatically.

The SERI researchers haven't found the definitive low-cost system, but they have identified some promising approaches to reducing costs without sacrificing performance. Their investigations so far have focused on three areas; drainback systems, integrated collector storage (ICS, or "breadbox") systems, and low-cost collectors.

The drainback system—so called because its collector fluid drains back into a storage reservoir whenever the pump goes off—is the leading low-cost candidate because of its simplicity, reliability, and performance. SERI believes that the cost of a fully installed drainback system could be brought down to $25 per square foot of collector area—a significant reduction from today's cost of more than $50 per square foot for a typical residential solar water- or space-heating system.

But drainback systems have a few disadvantages, too. As with other kinds of solar heating systems, corrosion is a potential problem. One straightforward solution is to seal and pressurize the collector loop in order to eliminate oxygen (which must be present for corrosion to occur). If the system is sealed, however, all components in the loop must be capable of withstanding fairly high pressures—a requirement that raises material and manufacturing costs.

The use of plastic (polybutylene) pipe instead of copper can greatly reduce both materials and installation costs. Per foot, polybutylene pipe costs about half as much as copper and is much easier to install. But plastic piping can't withstand sustained temperatures above 200 degrees Farenheit. Fortunately, SERI tests have identified some simple ways to hold system temperatures below the melt-down level.

Even with installed costs of $25 per square foot of collector area, drainback systems are more expensive than SERI's $15-per-square-foot goal. The only system that rivals the drainback for potential cost savings is the integrated collector storage (ICS) system. ICS systems—in which water heats up while it's stored in a glazed collector box—are even simpler than drainback designs, since they don't need pumps or controllers . But because the storage tank is outside, exposed to the weather, nighttime heat losses significantly detract from overall efficiency and raise the possibility of freezeups.

So despite its relatively low initial cost, an ICS system may not pay for itself any sooner than slightly more expensive (but also more efficient) drainback system. SERI is running experiments and calculations to determine which system performs most economically for various heating loads and climates.

SERI's researchers have come a long way toward finding ways to reduce the installed costs of solar heating systems. But SERI points out that research alone is not enough; with the possible end of tax credits in sight, the entire solar industry must aggressively tackle the low-cost challenge to prevent an eclipse of its market.

SERI engineers also point out that the best low-cost solar system may not have been invented yet. If you have any new ideas you'd like to share with them, write to Chuck Kutscher at the Solar Energy Research Institute, 1617 Cold Blvd., Golden, CO 80401. Your ideas may help rekindle the solar flame. ❖

The Well-Heated House

RODALE'S *NEW SHELTER*, FEBRUARY 1985

ON A CHILLY winter's night, few of us value anything more than our heating systems. Yet while we depend on our furnaces, heat pumps, woodstoves, and boilers, we needn't be slaves to them and the fuel bills they rack up. The articles in this section put you in charge of your well-heated house.

.... "Cutting Your Losses" compares the cost and value of insulation alternatives.... "More Heat For Your Dollar" takes you through the steps of tuning up your gas furnace. "The New Furnaces" introduces you to cutting-edge heating systems that can be more than 90 percent efficient. And if that's not good enough, read "High-Efficiency Heat Pumps"; these devices can achieve efficiencies far above 100 percent....

Cutting Your Losses

Suppose you get your water from a well, and the pipe springs a leak. Which do you do first: A) fix the leak, or B) install a more efficient pump? Naturally, the answer is "A."

Finding the Leaks

Back in physics class, you probably learned that heat always flows downward in temperature, from warm to cool, in winter, if flow from the warm inside of your house to the cool outside, and in summer from the warm outside to the cool inside. It flows through what engineers call the "thermal envelope," the collection of building surfaces surrounding and separating the interior heated or cooled space from the outdoors.

A typical thermal envelope includes: ceiling, walls, windows, floors, foundation walls, and basement or crawlspace floor. Sometimes, the top of the envelope is the roof (a cathedral ceiling) or the bottom is a floor (slab-on-grade or a floor over unheated space), but the principle remains the same: Energy is lost through every surface separating hot and cold areas.

Fortunately, we have an ally in our battle against air leakage and energy loss: insulation.

Which Insulation?

Commercial insulations are simply materials designed to trap air in tiny pockets and render it relatively motionless. Although all materials resist heat flow to some degree, insulations have a higher thermal resistance (R-value) per inch than most other building materials. For an R-10 wall, we would need only two inches of foam insulation but 10 feet of concrete!

When choosing insulation, there are several factors to consider: strength, fire resistance, ease of installation. Taking these factors into account, here's where I'd use each type.

Fibrous blown-in insulations, such as chopped fiberglass, mineral wool, and cellulose (shredded newsprint) are best for filling the irregular cavities of older attics and walls. To avoid settling, all must be installed at manufacturer's recommended densities. Although it's treated to repel water, cellulose shouldn't be installed in walls or attics subject to ice dam flooding or wind-driven water. My choice for retrofits: short-fiber fiberglass such as Certainteed's Insulsafe.

Fibrous batts come in long rolls or four-foot lengths and in widths of 15 and 23 inches. These dimensions allow the batt to fit standard stud cavities.

Some batts come with a foil face. In my experience, the foil adds little to $-value, hides heat-robbing gaps in the insulation, and is generally insufficient as a vapor barrier. For new construction, I use carefully placed unfaced batts covered with a continuous six-mil clear polyethylene vapor barrier.

Loose-pour pellets are relatively expensive and good only for filling the gaps between batts already placed in an attic.

Rigid foams include molded or loosely fused polystyrene beads (generally white), water-impervious extruded polystyrene (usually blue), and open-celled polyurethanes and polyisocyanurates (yellow or tan and paper- or foil-faced).

Nowadays, foams are often substituted for plywood wall sheathings because they add R-value at a low cost. Water-impervious extruded polystyrene is also used below and above ground to insulate the outsides of foundation walls.

How Much?

When homeowners try to figure how much money to put into insulation, they generally calculate the number of years it will take to pay back the purchase price.

A more sensible way of looking at cost is to regard energy conservation as an investment, giving a tax-free rate of return. By dividing the energy dollars saved by the cost to insulate, you'll discover that a six-year payback becomes a six-year investment with a tax-free interest of 16 percent.

Let's take, for example a typical two-story, 1,556-square-foot wood-frame house with a heated basement in a northern climate of 6,000 heating degree-days. Built before 1950, it has no insulation, no storm windows or doors, and leaks air at the rate of 1.5 volume changes per hour.

If the heating system in this house operates at 70 percent efficiency, and the fuel to run the heater is either oil at $1 per gallon or gas at 70 cents per 100 cubic feet, the heat would cost $1 per 100,000 Btu, or roughly $2,332 for a single year's heating season. "Free" heat from occupants, lights, appliances, and the sun would contribute 37 million Btu per year, or $370. The total cost to heat the house would be $2,332 minus the $370, or $1,962 annually.

If you were to insulate the attic and walls, add new storm windows and doors, and caulk and weatherstrip the major air leaks, you could cut that fuel bill in half. After construction costs, the rate of return on the investment would be 38 percent.

That's an impressive rate of return, but if you're planning on building or buying a new home, you can do even better. By comparing the costs of construction with the costs of heat loss over the lifetime of the building (assuming a lifetime of 30 years and fuel costs rising at a rate equal to the general inflation rate), we can find out what $-values will bring us the lowest lifetime cost of owning and operating the house.

With R-25 walls, an R-49 ceiling, basements walls insulated to $-12 above ground and $-15 below, energy-conserving Heat Mirror windows, and an insulated door, you could get an additional return of 17 percent on your investment on that first-rate thermal envelope. These optimum $-values for the sample house exceed current industry standards, but still fall short of "superinsulation."

Plugging Hidden Leaks

You already know about insulating attics, floors, and basements, and the importance of caulking and weatherstripping to keep out that chilling (and expensive) draft. But after taking care of these basic weatherization needs, you may still find a room that is always cold or an annoying draft that seems to come from nowhere.

Here's some advice to help you trouble-shoot hard-to-find heat leaks especially common in older homes.

Dropped ceilings are found in homes of all ages and come in all sizes and shapes. (Kitchen ceilings, for example, are often dropped to meet cabinet tops.) These drops can often be seen from the attic, since they are seldom covered with insulation. Cold air sinks into these areas and produces uncomfortable drafts.

Interior wall cavities can produce similar openings. They result in drafts at the wall outlets. Foam outlet gaskets, available at any hardware store, can help stope the symptoms but aren't a cure for the problem.

Pocket doors can create a similar problem. Common in the early part of the century, these large doors slide open into specially built wall pockets. Unfortunately, the hollow pockets are sometimes open at the top or bottom, allowing cold air to find its way into the living space.

Your best bet is to stop any of these elusive drafts at the source. Seal attic or crawlspace openings with wood or heavy plastic and cover with insulation.

Built-in bathtubs, where the tub is recessed into a hollow wall cavity, are another potential trouble spot. The drainpipe hole may open to the unheated crawlspace, allowing cold air to blow in around the entire tub. Whenever possible, insulate the back side of the tub and plug any openings to the outside.

Second-floor cantilevers are frequently inadequately insulated. They can be a source of cold air washing between the floor joist from one end of the house to the other. The result in the bathroom can be frozen pipes, not to mention chilly bathtubs. Insulate cantilevers wherever possible.

The double-hung window operates with weights on cords to counterbalance the window when it is open. These sash weights slide up and down just behind the side trim of the window frame in a fairly large hollow space that is subject to considerable air leakage.

Caulk along the inside and outside window trim. If you're very ambitious, you may want to consider removing the trim, taking out the weights, and filling the pocket with insulation. Then replace the trim and add spring-loaded pegs to the sash to hold the window in open positions.

A mail slot is an often overlooked source of drafts. Stuff insulation around it and caulk it where it meets the house. Or, replace it with a conventional mailbox.

The kitchen vent can be improved by adding a backdraft damper, which keeps air from blowing back through the vent when the hood fan is off....

More Heat For Your Dollar

If you have a forced-air gas furnace, it probably isn't running as efficiently as it might. Here are nine do-it-yourself adjustments; taken together, they can add up to major savings. (WARNING: Before adjusting your furnace, always turn it off at the main switch.)

1. Set back the thermostat. There's a simple rule of thumb for estimating setback savings. Each daily, eight-hour one degree F. setback will save you one percent on your annual heating costs. A five degree F., all-day setback, therefore, means 15 percent savings

over the course of a heating season.

Turn down the temperature another 10 degrees F every night while you're sleeping, and you'll save an additional 10 percent. Every time you turn down the thermostat, even if only for a short while, you save.

2. Insulate the ducts. (Insulate only if the hot-air delivery ducts are accessible and not in a heated area.) Savings vary with the area of duct insulated, but on the average, insulating ducts in an unheated basement or crawlspace with one inch of foil-backed fiberglass can save about 11 percent on your annual bill.

3. Adjust the anticipator. Many thermostats have an anticipator you can adjust to lengthen furnace cycles and increase furnace efficiency. To find out if your thermostat has one, remove the thermostat cover. The anticipator has a scale of numbers (.1 to 1.0, for example) with a small, adjustable pointer.

Set the anticipator at a number equal to 1.5 times the number of amps (A) printed on the gas valve of the furnace. If your gas valve doesn't have this information, move up the anticipator to 1.5 times its original setting.

4. Tape leaky joints in the ducts and plenum. If the ducts are in an accessible crawlspace, go in and check for leaky or disconnected joints. Use sheet-metal screws to reconnect the ducts, and seal the joints with duct tape. If there's a room or section of your house you don't want to heat, seal it off, close the register, and tape it off completely, so heat can't leak in.

5. Check for air flow restrictions. If the hot-air delivery ducts have dampers, make sure they're wide open to all heated rooms. Keep such obstructions as carpeting or furniture away from cold-air-return and hot-air-delivery registers.

6. Adjust the fan switch. A properly adjusted fan switch can save 5 percent on your annual heating bill. For best efficiency, the fan-on temperature should be about 100 degrees F. and the fan-off temperature about 90 degrees F.

The fan switch is a gray or silver-colored box mounted on the furnace or its hot-air plenum. Remove the plenum cover, and look for a silver disk with numbers printed on it. To adjust this switch, hold the disk still while you adjust the pointers. Move the lower pointer (fan-off) down to about 90 degrees F. and set the other pointer (fan-on) just a little higher.

Turn your thermostat up all the way. The gas will come on first, then the fan. Turn the thermostat back down all the way. The gas will go off, and the fan should go off a couple of minutes later. If the fan stays on, turn up the fan off temperature a little until the fan goes off, and cycle the furnace again to see if it operates properly.

7. Clean and oil the blower once a heating season.

To clean the squirrel cage blower, remove it from the blower compartment so you can get at it with small brushes and a vacuum cleaner.

8. Change air filters regularly. Furnaces are designed to run with a certain amount of air flow; any restrictions will cause the furnace to run less efficiently. Changing the air filter every two months during the heating season will save you 3 percent on your bill.

9. Adjust blower speed. If your blower is belt-driven, the motor will be mounted outside of the squirrel cage with a pulley on its shaft. The V-belt on the two pulleys should be snug but not too tight. (If the belt seems worn or cracked, replace it.)

To adjust blower speed, remove the belt. Notice that the pulley on the motor is in two halves, which can be adjusted to be closer together or farther apart. They should fit together tightly. If they don't, loosen the hexhead set screw on the outer pulley half, and screw it in toward the other half until the halves meet. Then tighten the set screw, and replace the belt. You may need a larger belt to get the belt tension right.

If you have a direct-drive blower, it won't have a belt and pulleys. It may or may not be multispeed, and blower-speed adjustments for direct-drive blowers require changes in 110-volt wiring, a job not recommended for do-it-yourselfers.

Furnace Gadgets—Hype or Help?

Consumers are repeatedly told that their furnaces are inefficient and that the purchase of this or that gadget will save 25, 30, or 50 percent on heating bills. Do these gadgets really save you money? Do they save enough to repay your investment? Are they safe? Here are some answers.

Devices that carry outside air to the furnace may save money, depending on how they're used. Air should be ducted directly into a sealed furnace room, not into the basement itself. The device should also have a heat trap; otherwise, the duct will act like a chimney, allowing heat to escape.

At best, this device will save you about 10 percent a year and only if your furnace is in a heated area (not in a crawlspace or an unheated basement). Because installing an outside-air duct may involve major remodeling, it may be tough to make this option pay off.

Heat exchangers (economizers) installed between the furnace and the draft hood extract heat from furnace flue gases and use it to heat house air directly or to increase the combustion efficiency of the furnace. This type of heat exchanger can bring flue-gas temperatures down by as much as 250 degrees F, and should not be used on any flue with normal operating temperatures below 600 degrees F.

When flue temperatures drop below 350 degrees F., water vapor can begin to condense from the gases, causing corrosion in the flue. (A note of caution: On some flues, temperatures of 600 degrees F indicate that the furnace is not operating properly and should be checked and fixed.)

A reasonable price for a flue heat exchanger, installed, is about $500. On a flue with 600 degrees F flue gases, you can expect the heat exchanger to save about 8 percent on your annual heating costs.

Gadgets that turn the gas on and off during a furnace cycle are sold under names such as Furnace Brain, Sav-it, and Electronic Furnace Controller. Off cycles vary from 90 seconds to 4 minutes. When the gas is off, house air continues to blow through the heat exchanger, taking heat from it and delivering it to the house. The longer the gas is off, though, the more likely that flue-gas products will be brought down to temperatures below 350 degrees F. creating a potential for corrosion. These gadgets will save you 10 to 30 percent of your heating bill, but may shorten the life of your furnace and create a safety problem.

Flue dampers prevent house or basement air from escaping up the flue when the furnace is not on. If your furnace is not in a heated space, you are losing little usable heated air up the flue, and a flue damper would not save you much money. In this case, it's more important to keep heated house air from leaking into the basement and to make sure that all furnace ducts are connected, taped, and insulated.

If your furnace is in a heated space (in a closet next to a family room, for example), heated air is escaping up the flue. A reliable electronic flue damper costs about $150, installed, and saves about 5 percent a year on a 5-inch flue.

Electronic ignitions light the pilot only when the furnace needs to come on. An electronic ignition can save you 6 percent per year, at an installed price of about $250. But you'll also need to factor in an annual maintenance cost for these devices, at 5 percent of the initial cost, or about $13. Savings amount to about 4 percent of your annual bill.

Obviously, it may be years before some of these gadgets pay back your investment. Many states, however, offer tax credits on flue dampers and electronic ignitions that enable you to reap savings sooner. Check with your state energy office for more information.

Upgrade Your Boiler

Replacing your boiler is a major job—and an expensive one. If your only reason for getting a new boiler is your present one's inefficient ways, think

again. Regardless of your boiler's age, you can save 20 percent or more of your heating bill if you take the following steps.

Remove extra radiators. In order for you to get the most from your boiler, the delivery system must put the heat exactly where you want and need it. I've found radiators everywhere—from crawlspaces to sheds outside the house. Removing these useless radiators can save 10 percent of your heating bill.

Install a "Minneapolis steam-control system." Old steam systems are notorious for making one room unbearably hot and another extremely cold. Many times, the culprit is a clogged radiator steam vent that will not allow the air out of the radiator so that steam can come in.

The Minneapolis steam-control system evens out steam distribution. The system's larger main steam vent allows steam to fill the entire system of pipes. A relay holds the boiler on until all the radiators are filled with steam.

Bleed the radiators regularly. In a hot-water system, air becomes trapped in radiators. I t not only cuts efficiency, it also makes a lot of noise. Ideally, you should bleed each radiator at least once a heating season, or whenever your radiator knocks.

Insulate the distribution pipes. Insulating heating pipes reduces heat loss.

Install heat zone controls. In some houses, the hot-water systems consist of 2 or more separate loops of pipe. Each loop can be operated by a separate thermostat and zone valve, set to deliver heat to the area only when it's needed, rather than heating the whole house.

Adjust for efficiency. Old boilers with oil or natural gas burners can be modified to increase their efficiency. The heat exchanger in a gas boiler can be altered to increase the heat flow into the water. This coupled with adjustment of the fuel-to-air ratio can bring your system's efficiency up 20 percent to almost 80 percent. These adjustments should cost about $200.

Replace the burner. Installing a retention head on your oil burner or a high efficiency power burner on your gas furnace can raise efficiency to 80 percent. Cost: about $600, installed.

Lower the water temperature. Steam systems must operate at the boiling temperature of water; hot water systems don't. Many homeowners set the thermostat for boiler water at about 190 degrees F. when in many cases a lower temperature will suffice. The most efficient way to control the hot water is called the "Denver Boiler Time Delay." The DBTD works well in houses with one or more heating zones. It varies the boiler water temperature based on total system demand. This is accomplished by first circulating boiler water without turning on the burner. The burner goes on only if additional heat is required. It costs about $100 to switch over to this system. You can expect to save 13 to 24 percent more than if you had a single control thermostat.

Incorporating these measures in your system can result in very high savings. One homeowner who removed radiators in a crawlspace, added pipe insulation, and a Denver Boiler Time Delay cut his heating bill in half.

The New Furnaces: How Efficient?

If you're in the market for a furnace, you may be thinking about purchasing one of the new, high-efficiency models that have received a lot of press lately. But what exactly are high-efficiency furnaces, and how well do they work?

You can compare furnace efficiencies by looking at the Annual Fuel Utilization Efficiency (AFUE) rating determined by the United States Department of Energy Testing Standards. High-efficiency furnaces have an AFUE rating between 80 and 95 percent, compared with 60 percent for a conventional furnace.

All high-efficiency furnaces, however, are not alike; there are a number of ways manufacturers can alter a furnace design to get those high ratings, and some are better than others. Here's a rundown on the types of "high-E" furnaces out there, and what to look for when you go shopping....

Flue-gas temperatures [can be] brought down to around 100 degrees F. and can be vented using two-inch polyvinyl chloride pipe, which cuts down on installation costs. Furnaces that fall into this category include:

- The Whirlpool Tightfist II furnace and the Duomatic/Olsen Ultramax. These furnaces make conventional technology more efficient by the use of an added stainless-steel-tube, aluminum-finned heat exchanger.
- The Amana Energy Command and the Lennox Pulse furnace. These furnaces use new technologies to burn fuel. The Amana, for example, uses a "Heat Transfer Module" that combines the electronic igniter, gas burner, and a heat exchanger in one unit. two other heating coils transfer heat to the house air.

The Lennox Pulse Furnace ignites a gas and air mixture in a combustion chamber. The force of the explosion pushes the hot gases through the heat exchanger and out a plastic flue pipe.

A pressure pulse from the explosion, reflected back to the combustion chamber ignites the gas and air. In this way, the combustion cycle continues without the use of a spark ignition or a draft blower. Although the Amana and the Lennox use new methods to burn fuel, their high efficiencies are mostly due to decreases in stack losses—the amount of waste heat that would otherwise escape up the chimney. This heat is captured in high-efficiency stainless-steel finned heat exchangers.

No matter which furnace you choose, make sure it's the right size for your needs. An oversized furnace will always be less efficient. And, even with a high-efficiency unit, you'll still need to seal the ducts and jacket of the furnace against air leaks to get the most out of your new heater.

High-Efficiency Heat Pumps

Heat is all around us: In the air we breathe and in the water we pump up form below the ground. Trouble is, the heat is at too low a temperature to adequately warm our homes. What we need is a device that increases the temperature so that it's useful for home heating. Such a device exists. It's called a heat pump.

The most common type of heat pump found in the United States is an air-source heat pump. Air-source heat pumps take heat from inside the house—like an air conditioner in reverse.

The efficiency of this type of heat pump is limited by the climate. In the North, where temperatures fall below 10 degrees F. air-source heat pumps tend to freeze up and are not recommended, unless you're also willing to install a backup heating system. That can be a very expensive proposition for most of us.

A better answer, and one that's increasing in popularity, is a water-source heat pump. Water in nature has less of an annual temperature variation than the air; that makes it an ideal source for heating and even for some cooling in the summer.

There are a number of different water sources that you can use in conjunction with a water-source heat pump. Ground or well water can be an excellent source; it's available in abundance in many locations.

In a well-water system, water is pumped from underground aquifers through the heat pump and back into the ground. These heat pumps typically require approximately 2 to 3 gallons per minute for each ton (12,000 Btu/hr) of heat-pump capacity. One sticky point is that this water must be disposed of in a manner acceptable to local and state codes.

River or lake water is not as warm as groundwater, but it's still much better than air. The water can be used directly—pumped from a lake through the heat pump and discharged back to the lake. It can also be used indirectly through a closed continuous pipe installed along the lake bottom. Such a pipe will register, within a few degrees, the normal lake bottom temperatures. In most cases, the closed loop requires less electrical power to circulate the fluid than an open or direct system does. (But make sure you've got water rights before starting the project.)

City water (i.e., tap water or drinking water) can be used, but it is usually too expensive. A 3-ton heat pump using 9 gallons per minute would use approximately one million gallons for both the heating and cooling seasons. City water may be used in emergency periods when another water supply is interrupted.

The water for any of these water-source pumps must be clean and noncorrosive to pipes.

A third kind of water-source heat pump, called a ground heat exchanger, appears to be the best deal. This type of pump consists of a continuous loop of pipe buried below the earth's surface. Water or an antifreeze solution is circulated in a closed pipe that is warmed in the winter by the surrounding ground. The heat pump removes the heat from the continuously circulating fluid.

These systems can be installed in piping arrangements buried 4 to 6 feet below the ground surface or placed vertically to depths of 100 to 600 feet using a drilling machine. Piping lengths are approximately 400 to 600 feet per ton (12,000 Btu/hr) when buried near the ground surface and 150 to 200 feet per ton of well bore when installed vertically. Piping materials generally consist of high-density polyethylene or polybutylene with heat-fused joints.

The closed-loop/ground-coupled (cl/gc) heat pump system has several advantages. 1) It doesn't deplete the groundwater; 2) there's no water-disposal problem; 3) a noncorrosive fluid for heat pump circuits is guaranteed; and 4) minimal electrical power is required for fluid circulation.

Typically, the cl/gc heat pump system reduces energy consumption approximately 25 to 30 percent compared with air-source heat pumps in the Midwest. In colder climates (including Canada), the savings over air-source units can be larger. A coefficient of performance (COP—the ratio of the amount of energy you get out of a particular heat pump compared to the amount of energy you put in) of 3.0 for water-source heat pumps is not uncommon today with projected values as high as 4.0 with the advent of improved heat-pump designs and heat pump compressors. In comparison, a standard electric resistance heater has a COP of one.

The initial cost of the cl/gc heat pump is as much as $2,000 higher than that of other heat pumps for the average home because of the trenching, drilling, and labor costs. But its clear advantages over the other heat pumps and its superior efficiency may well make it the heating system of the future. ❖

TRAC Tele-Tips
Long Distance Comparison
TELECOMMUNICATIONS RESEARCH ACTION CENTER (TRAC), NOVEMBER 1, 1988

Long Distance Options

Selecting and using a long distance company is not a simple process. Consumers are faced with a dizzying array of choices not only of long distance companies, but also in the ways to use long distance service.

Beginning in 1984, as part of the AT&T divestiture, customers were given the right to choose (that is "presubscribe" to) one of several long distance companies—AT&T, Allnet, US Sprint and others—as their "primary carrier." Thus, by dialing "1" plus the area code and number, long distance calls will be carried by the company you selected. Even after selecting one company for "1" plus or "easy dialing" calling, you can use other long distance companies by dialing the five digit access code, "10" plus a different three-digit number for each company listed on the chart.

Equal access has already come to most areas of the United States. If you haven't chosen already, you will soon receive a "ballot" from your local telephone company with presubscription information, including a list of the long distance companies available in your area. You will be asked to presubscribe to the long distance service you wish to reach with "1-plus" dialing.

No matter which company you choose as a primary or 1 plus carrier, others can be used with what is called "code" dialing. For example, if U.S. Sprint is your primary carrier, but you want to make a call over AT&T, you will be able to do so by dialing "10" plus AT&T's code of "288" before the area code number. Or, if you want to call over MCI, you will be able to dial "10" plus MCI's three-digit code of 222 before your long distance number. Most of these calls can be made without any special arrangements with the carrier (See "Casual Calling" on the chart.).

The Long-Distance Check-Up

Experience over the past few years has shown that it is not enough to select a company or rate plan for easy dialing and then to forget about it. Rates, services and features are changing rapidly. The company and plan you select today as best meeting your needs, might be the least desirable for you just a few months later.

That's why it is important for most consumers to compare their available options periodically. For consumers who spend less than $10 a month, an annual review is probably adequate. But if you spend $25 or more each month, you may want to review the options even more frequently.

Charting Your Long Distance Needs

To sort out which service or services to use, you have to look at your own long distance calling habits. Using recent telephone bills, create a composite or hypothetical bill which is representative of the areas you call most, the time of day and the general length of your calls. See if you make enough calls to qualify for volume discounts. Think about whether you make long distance calls when you travel, or whether you would like a friend or family member in another city to be able to call you through you long distance service; travel features can be used for that purpose.

Remember, there are three factors to consider in making your selection of which company or plan to use most often: Cost—how much it costs to use the service in a typical month; Features—whether the company offers the services and conveniences you need; and Quality—whether the company performs as promised.

Use the features chart to compare the features of the various companies. Use the cost chart as a starting point in discovering the monthly cost of using the different services. There are helpful hints on how to reach each of the companies easily. And remember, you are not limited to using only the company you select as your primary carrier—it will simply offer the most convenient dialing. The other companies are available by dialing their code numbers. And you can always change your one-plus company, but check the chart on how to avoid the fee for such changes. ❖

You may obtain a chart comparing the services of long-distance telephone companies by sending $1 and a self-addressed, stamped envelope to: TRAC, P.O. Box 12038, Washington, D.C. 20005.

The Next Ten Years

BY AMORY B. LOVINS
RODALE'S *NEW SHELTER,* AUGUST 1985

FOR MOST AMERICANS, the "energy crisis" may seem remote. Fuel prices are now steady or falling, glossy ads promise that utility rate hikes will level off, America is importing little oil form the Middle East, and the Organization of Petroleum Exporting Countries (OPEC) is on the ropes. Fuel is abundant, while articles about energy rates—once front-page news—are now buried somewhere back in section C.

But the tranquility is only skin-deep. A few minutes of violence could knock out the main Mideast oil terminals for several years. In an evening's work, a handful of people could cut off three-fourths of the oil and natural-gas supplies to the eastern United States for nearly a year—without even leaving Louisiana. Power grids are similarly vulnerable. And the debt-ridden global financial system could crash at any time. Last year's 30,000 gas cutoffs in Philadelphia alone remind us that many people are still choosing between heating and eating.

Are Americans blissfully ignorant of these problems? Not entirely: two oil shocks helped to ingrain a healthy caution and some new energy habits that are reshaping our homes and our lives. Since 1979, millions of individual decisions to save energy have given this country upwards of one hundred times more new energy than all net expansions of the energy supply put together—and more new energy from renewable sources than from all fossil and nuclear fuels.

On average, American houses use 25 percent less space-heating energy per square foot than they did a decade ago; many new houses use 75 percent less. New building technologies, design methods, and diagnostic tools promise to reduce the energy consumption of homes even further in the next decade.

Superinsulation and related technologies have already shown that they can virtually eliminate heating loads in new buildings. Such efficiency makes houses less dependent on our vulnerable energy supply, at no cost to their livability and comfort. Even in existing homes, superinsulation can drastically reduce heating loads, with a typical payback period of 3-10 years.

Progress in cooling has been similarly impressive. Even in the hottest and most humid areas, the best new homes are using 80-90 percent less air conditioning than the local average. An ordinary 1500-square-foot tract house in Houston, for example, might have a peak summer electrical load of about 6.3 kilowatts. But with a light-colored exterior, an R-38 roof, double glazing with sun-control films, west-window shading, 0.5-air-change-per-hour tightness, and the best mass-produced air conditioner, that peak load could drop to 2.2 kilowatts with a two-year payback for all of the improvements. Efficient lights and appliances, by reducing the internal heat gains, could cut this to 1.0 kilowatt; advanced windows and the best available air conditioner (SEER-16) shave the peak load to half a kilowatt—all with payback periods of five years or less.

Heating and cooling loads aren't the only opportunities for huge savings. Lightbulbs with quadrupled efficiency, super-efficient refrigerators and furnaces, half-gallon-per minute compressed-air shower heads, and simple integral-storage Freon solar panels are part of the growing flood of smart ways to do more with less.

Many electric (and some gas) utilities are emerging as major financiers of energy-saving options. Power companies serving over half the country now offer loans to fix up houses and rebates to buy better appliances, simply because it's much cheaper to save electricity than to make it. Some even prepurchase saved electricity, so you can use the up-front payment to buy the device that produces the saving.

Under a new scheme the Rocky Mountain Institute has developed, a utility could offer contractors a rebate for building highly efficient houses. A rebate of about $5,000 would more than cover the contractor's extra cost for building a house that would require no space conditioning. The contractor would save money up front and could market the house with a guaranteed maximum utility bill or with an offer to pay the energy bills for the first few years.

Under new federal mortgage rules, the lower utility bills would qualify the buyer for a bigger (and possibly cheaper) mortgage. The homeowner would save close to $1,000 a year in energy costs and enjoy a greater resale value. And the utility would save 10 or 20 times the value of the rebate by not having to build and run more power plants. The unpalatable alternative: an all-electric "sieve" can make the utility spend more on capacity to serve it than the contractor pays to build it!

Such ways of allocating capital more efficiently could greatly boost economic development, especially in fast-growing communities. A typical town sends out the equivalent of a tenth its citizens' earnings to buy energy from outside. Plugging that leak would keep more money recirculating locally, multiplying dollars and jobs.

We've already cut our national energy bills by about $150 billion a year through conservation and efficiency measures. But we have a long way to go; if we could become as efficient as Western Europe, we'd save another $200 billion annually—enough to wipe out the federal budget deficit. The cumulative net saving from "best buys first" would by the year 2000 be enough to pay off the national debt.

Whether energy prices go up or down, efficiency will continue to bring big rewards. Here are a few tips that will more than pay for themselves—and help protect you from the vagaries of the unpredictable world energy market.

- Efficiency should be your top priority. If you're a homeowner, your savings amount to tax-free personal income. For an annual pretax return of more than 30 percent, call in a "house doctor" and follow his or her prescription.
- Before you buy any appliance, consult the semi-annual guide, "The Most Energy-Efficient Appliances" (available from the American Council for an Energy-Efficient Economy, Suite 530, 1001 Connecticut Avenue, N.W., Washington, D.C. 20036). If your utility doesn't give rebates for efficient appliances, your area is probably a dumping ground for the inefficient models that don't sell in the other half of the country.
- Lobby your utility and its regulators to help you finance efficiency improvements. "Negawatts" are so much cheaper than megawatts that your utility faces a choice between participation and obsolescence.
- Once you've achieved a high degree of energy efficiency, go for passive and simple active solar systems. Remember that they'll be much smaller and work better the more efficient you are.
- If you're building a house, make it so efficient that it requires no space conditioning. You'll save a lot more by eliminating the furnace and air conditioner than by just downsizing them.
- Keep informed of new technologies that will let you save more energy more cheaply. But don't hold off while you wait for lower prices; there are plenty of wonderful buys today.
- If you don't have the information you need to make a wise energy choice, get it before you buy—it's better than repenting later. Don't be rushed into buying or renting a house without seeing its past energy bills. Find out whether the local power company is about to jack up its rates to pay for a new power plant, and whether the utility will finance your energy-saving invest-

ments or discourage them.
- Tell your state and federal representatives what you want in energy policy. Otherwise, you'll get what the lobbyists for other interest groups want.
- If you learn some new or better way to save energy, write to *New Shelter* and tell the rest of us. Nobody has a monopoly on ideas, and many of the best ones have come from people with no technical training. There is, so far as we know, nothing in the universe so powerful as four billion minds wrapping around a problem. Let yours be one of them. ❖

EXCERPTS FROM

When You Move—Your Rights and Responsibilities

INTERSTATE COMMERCE COMMISSION OFFICE OF
COMPLIANCE AND
CONSUMER ASSISTANCE
SEPTEMBER 1983

IF, AFTER DISCUSSING your move with the mover, you still need information or assistance, you may obtain help from an Interstate Commerce Commission office. Local offices are maintained in at least one major city in each state (except Delaware and Hawaii). Regional offices are located in the following cities: Boston, MA, Philadelphia, PA, Atlanta, GA, Chicago, IL, Ft. Worth, TX, and San Francisco, CA. Telephone numbers for these offices may be found in the telephone directory under the heading UNITED STATES GOVERNMENT. In the Washington, D.C. area call 275-0860....

Points to Remember

- Movers may give binding estimates.
- Non-binding estimates may not be accurate; actual charges may often exceed the estimate.
- Specify pick up and delivery dates in the order for service.
- The bill of loading is your contract with the mover...read it carefully...if you have any questions ask your mover or call the I.C.C.
- Be sure that you understand the extent of your mover's liability for loss and damage.
- You have the right to be present each time your shipment is weighed.
- You may request a reweigh of your shipment.
- If you have moved on a non-binding estimate, you should have enough cash or a certified check to pay the estimated cost of your move plus 10 percent more at time of delivery. ❖

Appliance Life Cycle Costing

From *Play to Win: How to Save Money on Your Utility Bill*

NEW YORK STATE PUBLIC SERVICE COMMISSION, AUGUST 1988

1. Figure the difference in purchase price:

Cost of efficient model	$ 198
Cost of standard model	−160
Purchase price difference	**$38**

2. Estimate the yearly energy savings:*

Operating cost of standard model	$ 148
Operating cost of efficient model	−122
Yearly energy savings	**$26**

3. Figure the total energy savings over the life of the appliance:**

Yearly energy savings	$26
Average life (12 years)	x 12
Total energy savings	**$ 312**

4. Subtract the purchase price difference from the total energy savings to get the net savings over the life of the appliance:

Total energy savings	$ 312
Purchase price difference	−38
Net savings	**$ 274**

5. Divide the purchase price difference by the yearly energy savings to find out how long it will take to recover the difference in price between the two heaters:

Purchase price difference	$38
Yearly energy savings	+ 26
Time, in years	**1.46**

Look! You will recover the difference in price in less than a year and a half!

*In this example, a cost of $.40 per therm is used. Use your local energy rate when figuring Life Cycle Costing.

**Ask your dealer about the average life of the appliance.

Play to Win *is available free from the New York State Public Service Commission. For a copy, call the consumer helpline 518-474-5527, the toll-free number within the state, 1-800-342-3377, or write to the Commission at: 3 Empire State Plaza, Albany, NY 12223.*

FROM *Of Meters and Misfeasance:*
What You Should Know About Utility Metering and Billing Errors
BY BRANDON F. GREENE AND SHOW MAO CHEN
CENTER FOR STUDY OF RESPONSIVE LAW, AUGUST 1986

NATURAL GAS, ELECTRIC and water meter billing errors are not uncommon. A variety of technical and environmental factors may be affecting your meters in ways that result in overcharges. In addition there may be what is euphemistically called "computer errors" that can inflate your utility bill. Some examples illustrate the possibilities.

Alan Morrison is an attorney in Washington, D.C. For years he was accustomed to receiving water bills every six months amounting to $50 or $60. When he left town for an extended period, he anticipated receiving a much lower water bill. His actual bill was $337. Employees with the water department could offer no explanation and asked, "Are you taking in laundry?"....

Mrs. Dorothy Jerome is 60 years old. She supports herself with Social Security checks supplemented by income from a part-time job at a local hospital. She disputed her gas bill from Bay State Gas Company and ultimately won that dispute. However, before it was settled and in the midst of winter, Bay State Gas Company entered her residence without her permission, and locked shut the valves controlling the flow of gas from her meter to her heating appliances....

Karen Steele received a back-bill for $153 from Potomac Electric and Power Company. This was an interesting bill considering that the company had neglected to install a meter at her residence during the backbilling period....

Georgia Clay's bare income required her to enter a budget plan for gas service with Peoples Gas Light and Coke Company. Her payments amounted to $45 per month. However, when the company discovered that two other tenants "tapped" into Mrs. Clay's gas line without her knowing it, the company presented her with a bill for $1,350.34....

In the District of Columbia the Public Utilities Commission is charged with the responsibility for ensuring that gas companies maintain the accuracy of residential gas meters. However, the Commission itself does not perform any tests of these meters. What's more, they do not even insist that the gas company provide test records which reveal whether gas meters have been accurate during operation at the customer's residence.

When it comes to billing for utility service, errors can mean more than coming out a little short in pocket change. Errors can mean enormous bills, years of dispute (including litigation) with the utility company, and the risk of losing essential services (e.g., heat, water). Moreover, billing errors of utility companies are far more difficult for consumers to detect and resolve than, say, the errors at the supermarket cashier. Utility service is metered by devices that most people don't understand. Indeed, in the case of telephone service the actual metering occurs at locations which are inaccessible to consumers. Therefore, problems and malfunctions of metering devices can not be readily detected by most consumers. Other glitches in the billing system are equally difficult to trace. A misread meter dial, a key-punch error at a computer terminal, or a mixup of accounts may begin as trivial errors. However, if undetected they can fester and swell into substantial expenses which companies may try to impose upon the innocent consumer.

Even when the problems are detected, many utility companies can not be depended upon to admit their error and absorb the costs. Some companies will align their formidable legal resources in an attempt to force or intimidate consumers into paying for the very errors which victimized them. In ensuing sections of this guide we will describe the details of cases in which companies committed egregious billing errors but nevertheless attempted to hoist the cost upon the consumers who uncovered the errors.

Therefore, consumers must protect themselves. This guide was prepared to assist in that effort. Cases of billing errors will be described to familiarize you with the variety of ways consumers have been overcharged, either intentionally or unintentionally, by utility companies. The appendices in this guide include information to help the lay citizen detect billing errors traceable to technical faults of metering systems... ❖

Of Meters and Misfeasance *is available for $12 from the Center for Study of Responsive Law, P.O. Box 19367, Washington, D.C. 20036.*

Section Six
LAWNS, GARDENS AND CHEMICALS

❖❖❖

THIS SECTION IS largely under your control to do something about. You really can turn off the chemical herbicides, plant vegetable gardens and fruit trees (trees bearing apples, pears, cherries, apricots and plums have taken root as far north as Montreal), use landscaping to reduce fuel costs and join the growing movement for chemical free lawns or at least proper notification of neighbors when that applicator truck comes. The selections in this chapter embody safety, aesthetics, economic enhancement of home values, healthful hobbies and good, fresh food for the table—in short, the home as renewable CORNUCOPIA. ❖

EXCERPT FROM

A Yard Full Of Landscape Solutions
You Can Add Value To Your Home And Overcome Problems Of A Less-Than-Perfect Site With Good Outdoor Design

HOMEOWNER, JANUARY/FEBRUARY 1988

A GOOD LANDSCAPING scheme provides all the benefits of a well-decorated interior: It gives you pleasant living and recreational space, and increases the value of your home. Landscaping with shrubs and trees also helps to insulate your property from street noises and adds privacy from adjacent yards. And within the wide range of landscape design opportunities and strategies, you'll find solutions to many of the problems that can plague selection and less-than-perfect homesites.

The key to landscaping like a pro is planning. Decide how you want to use your yard by making an overall plan. Should a portion be set aside for outdoor entertaining? Do the kids need a play area? Do you want to add trees, flower beds and shrubs? Do you want to increase the lawn area? Remember, too, that good landscaping should make life easier, not give you a never-ending list of chores. If you're a gardening fanatic, by all means indulge yourself. But if you want to minimize maintenance and still have plantings that look good, you'll find many choices in trees, shrubs, perennial flowers and ground covers. And don't shy away from filling space with low-maintenance walkways, patios or decks.

Getting Started

Draw a plan of your property on graph paper. Indicate the house, garage and all existing walkways, fences, patios, decks, trees and shrubs. Make a few copies of the existing plan so you can experiment with different versions of the new one. Draw in the new features you want, such as fences, patios, retaining walls, a barbecue pit and the like, to determine your construction needs. Make plans for installing underground utilities for lighting or a watering system. At this stage, it's best to work up your ideal plan, because even if doing it all at once would strain your finances or time, it pays to develop a unified plan. You could do parts of it one year and more the next. Consider starting with the irrigation system and major plantings of trees, flower beds and shrubs.

Before choosing plants and lawn grass, deal with problem areas. The two most common are poor drainage and hillside erosion.... ❖

Simple Remedies For Plant Nuisances

BY JOAN LEE FAUST
THE NEW YORK TIMES, NOVEMBER 20, 1988

ONE HOUSE PLANT never satisfies. Those who raise plants to have a little greenery around the house usually start with one or two pots. Soon there are four pots, then five. The house plant syndrome begins. Before long there are dozens of indoor plants to be cared for. The window space becomes crowded by leaves. Everything generally goes well—for a while. But then the little beasties begin to appear.

Some crawl. Some hide on the backs of leaves. Some bite holes in leaves. A few fly off when plants are touched. Others sit on top of the soil and float about when plants are watered.

When these invasions are noticed, one question is often asked. Where do the insects come from? There is no single answer.

The important thing, however, is to do something about the bugs as soon as possible. Unless the initial invasion is met with some control, the warm climate of the house appeals to most insect species, and their multiplication is assured.

What is to be done? First, identify the insects correctly so the proper control measures can be applied. But a bug or two seen on an indoor plant does not always mean a quick dash for the spray can. Sometimes the bugs can be halted quite simply.

The insects most likely to attack house plants are mealybugs, red spider mites, whiteflies, scale and fungus gnats. There are several approaches to bringing these nuisances under control. The easiest involves frequent inspection of the plants and taking care of any problems immediately with simple nonpesticide remedies.

For example, mealybugs often appear on jade plants, gardenias and cactuses. They hide on the backs of leaves or deep in leaf axils and resemble tiny lumps of white cotton. The quickest way to get rid of them is to dip a cotton swab in rubbing alcohol and wipe the mealybugs off the plants. A repeat may be needed every few days to be sure the unhatched young are brought under control.

Another nonpesticide remedy can be used to rid ivy of red spider mites. Ivy is usually allowed to grow wildly and its strands attain great lengths. All too soon the leaves may start to look dusty and dry, turn yellow and drop off. The problem is usually red spider, a tiny mite that thrives on dry foliage.

Since mites thrive in dry, nonhumid climates, the remedy for their invasion is a bath in lukewarm water.

Take the ivy plant to the kitchen sink, fill it with lukewarm water, invert the pot so the strands of ivy reach the water and wash them off gently.

If the simple home remedies don't work, then sprays may be needed. But the use of insecticides is usually a last resort. Sometimes spraying is the only way to knock down serious infestations, particularly of such nuisances as whiteflies.

There are products on the market that have been approved for use on indoor plants; if the label directions are carefully followed these products can be used safely. But spraying must be done gently to prevent splashing on walls, furniture or other plants. Many indoor gardeners prefer to isolate their plants before applying any spray.

Several of these products are sold at garden centers, nurseries, hardware stores, novelty stores and many supermarkets. Here are some of them.

Safer Inc. makes soap-based products from a fatty acid of potassium salts selected for its bug-killing ability. Because the products are soaps, many home gardeners believe that they can substitute liquid dishwashing detergents or laundry soaps. But some of the home products are not even soaps and their use for plants is questioned. Some detergents have been known to damage plants. The Safer line of products designed for use on plants, work by suffocating insects found on plants.

Safer also manufactures TrapStix, traps made of sticky yellow paper and covered with waxed paper. When placed on the plastic holders supplied and inserted in pots, the traps attract many kinds of flying insects, particularly fungus gnats and whiteflies. The insects stick fast and the traps can be replaced every few days.

Schultz Inc. makes an Indoor-Outdoor Insecticide for house plants and gardens that contains pyrethrins and piperonyl butoxide, an ingredient that increases the activity of the pyrethrin. The product comes in a plastic pump-spray bottle. According to the label it controls whiteflies, mealybugs, red spider and fern scale. This company also makes a liquid fertilizer for house plants that is sold with a dropper for adding the fertilizer to water to be put on the plants.

Whiteflies are among the most difficult insects to get rid of in the home climate. These tiny insects fly off in clouds when leaves of host plants, particularly geraniums, Cape primroses, lantanas and fuchsias, are disturbed. A combination of resmethrin (SBP 1382) and a synthetic pyrethroid is considered the best means of control. Pratt-Gabriel, a division of the Miller Chemical Company, manufactures a whitefly spray that contains these two products. If used regularly, it brings the population under control. More than one application is usually necessary, however, to knock down the adults, nymphs and eggs that may exist together on the backs of plant leaves.

A new pest-control product just appearing on the market, made by the Hyponex Corporation, is an encapsulated time-release spray that attacks spider mites, aphids and whiteflies. It also contains pyrethrins. The encapsulation makes the product stick to the insects and remain lethal for weeks instead of a few days. The recommended application is a fast, sweeping motion over the plants with the can held about two feet away.

Hyponex makes another time-release product for mealybug and scale control. It contains an encapsulated form of diazinon, which the company says is less toxic to mammals than regular diazinon, but many home gardeners would rather forego use of this product. ❖

The 60-Minute Garden
Big Yields From a Small Space
BY JEFF BALL
RODALE'S *NEW SHELTER*, JANUARY 1985

EVEN IF THE time and space you have for plant growing is limited, you can still have a great vegetable garden. ...

I've developed a system of gardening that can produce 700 pounds of vegetables in just 200 square feet. And it won't take you more than an hour or two each week to manage your garden.

In my opinion, any vegetable gardener who sets out plants in traditional rows, hoes the patch regularly to keep down weeds, waters with a hose or sprinkler, and uses stakes only for tomatoes is wasting both space and time. Those very common gardening practices happen to be the least productive approach to raising vegetables in a small space. The system I use takes some age-old gardening practices and combines them with some new ideas to create a simple yet extremely productive vegetable garden.

While you can increase your garden's productivity by applying any one of the five components in my system, it's the combination of the parts that makes the garden so successful. Here are those components, along with the increase in yields you can expect from using each one:

Boxed Raised Beds

When you plant a garden in raised beds instead of traditional rows, you can increase the actual growing area for plants by at least 80 percent—you eliminate most of the pathways between rows. Raised beds have other advantages over traditional rows—they drain better, warm up sooner in the spring, and allow for much more intensive plantings. And, after digging the beds properly the first year, the gardener need never dig them again.

When I boxed my beds with 2 x 10s, I put 12-inch-long pieces of 2-inch PVC pipe vertically in the ground along the sides of the beds, one every four feet. The pipes are used as foundations to hold tresses and cloche tunnels, which I can move from bed to bed as needed. All these devices are interchangeable throughout the entire garden.

Growing Tunnels

The polyethylene growing tunnel has been used in Europe for decades to extend the growing season. Such a mini greenhouse can be used to cover an entire bed.

I use flexible 1-inch PVC pipe for the ribs of the tunnels; it slides easily and quickly into the foundations permanently installed in the beds. The panels of clear plastic are easy to mount and are just as easy to take down and store.

You can cover an entire 200-foot garden with growing tunnels each spring and fall. And that sure beats working in the limited space available in most cold frames.

Trellises

When you erect a 6-foot trellis along one side of a raised bed, you increase the growing area of that bed by almost 150 percent. By growing cucumbers, winter squash, mellons, peas, and pole beans on a trellis, you can take advantage of the air space above your beds.

The same PVC foundations that support my tunnels also hold the vertical supports for the trellis system. These supports can be made of wood or PVC pipe. The crosspieces hold up a panel of netting or string used for supporting the plants. A 200-square-foot garden can have 500 square feet of growing area on its trellises alone, giving an enormous boost to the garden's potential productivity.

Drip Watering

Drip irrigation puts water right at the roots of plants with virtually no evaporation or runoff. Not only does this method save water, it also reduces the incidence of moisture-related disease. A drip-watering system uses flexible PVC tubing with small emitters spaced every 16 to 24 inches along the length of the tubing. These emitters allow water to enter the soil one drop at a time. One emitter will release about two gallons of water in a full hour.

Another major benefit of a drip system is that it can be operated by an automatic timer. Liquid fertilizer can be applied through a drip system, giving the plants nutrients that are taken up 20 times faster than from dry fertilizers. The time required for watering and feeding the garden is reduced to a total of only an hour or two for the entire season.

Soil-Management System

The key to soil fertility in an efficient garden is the addition of organic material—an inch of aged manure every spring over the entire surface area of the garden, for example. A 4 x 4 x 4-foot compost pile will produce enough finished compost to cover a 200-square-foot garden with a 1-inch layer. Every three years, add a combination of rock powders to the garden's surface (about 20 pounds for 200 square feet).

The second important aspect of soil management involves actively regulating the temperature of the soil. Soil temperature around plant roots is far more important to the growth and health of plants than is air temperature.

In the spring and fall, plastic mulch (clear or black) can be used to raise the soil temperature to a level (45 degrees to 65 degrees Fahrenheit) that allows plants to grow earlier in the season than usual. When the soil temperature reaches 65 degrees to 70 degrees Fahrenheit, place organic mulches, such as straw, hay, or grass clippings on top of the plastic mulch to cool the soil (its temperature must not exceed 85 degrees Fahrenheit, the temperature at which most vegetables will stop growing). The drip irrigation system will help manage soil temperatures, since it cools the soil for several hours after it's used.

Putting It Together

When you take all of the parts and put them together, your garden year looks something like this.

• Spring: About two months before the last frost, take up the straw mulch that's been protecting the soil from the winter, and set it aside for use later. Lay out the drip-system hoses, and cover them with clear or black plastic mulch. Construct your poly tunnels to warm up the soil.

After a few weeks, it will be time to plant the seedlings you've started in your basement or on your windowsill, as well as seeds for crops like spinach and peas. Use half your tunnels for early crops; save the others to get a jump on such warm-weather crops as tomatoes, peppers, and eggplants.

• Summer: After the danger of frost is past, dismantle your tunnels, and install the trellis devices on the beds. When the soil is warm enough, cover the plastic mulch with about six inches of organic mulch, such as straw. As soon as a plant is finished producing, pop a new seedling into its place. The rate of production will steadily increase into the summer and then tail off a bit in the fall.

• Autumn: When soil temperatures drop to 60 degrees Fahrenheit, remove the organic mulch, and relegate it to the compost pile. About three weeks before first frost, reinstall the tunnels. Many plants, including tomatoes and peppers, will continue to produce well past the first frost.

• Winter: In December, after you've harvested the last spinach, chinese cabbage, and collard greens, lay down a thick layer of new straw mulch to protect the soil from the cold.

The Bottom Line

The system I've described requires an initial investment in money and time to build the time-saving production-enhancing devices. The cost of the boards for the beds, the foundations, the drip irrigation system, and the trellis and tunnel systems will run a bit less than $2 a square—about $350 to $400 for a 200-square-foot garden. But you can grow more than $400 worth of food in that garden in one year, quickly recouping your investment.

Once you've installed the system and gotten your soil into a reasonable shape, this gardening system produces an enormous amount of food (about two-three pounds per square foot) and required virtually no digging or watering, little time for feeding, no weeding, and only a few hours to prepare the soil each year. About all you have to do in this garden is plant the seeds, transplant the seedlings, and harvest the food. Gardening can't get much simpler than that. ❖

Housecalls to Main Street

Doctoring the Nation's Lawns with Chemicals

BY LORENS TRONET

NOT MAN APART, MAY/JUNE 1986

THERE ARE NO accurate figures on the number of people affected by the use of lawn pesticides but some medical professionals known as "clinical ecologists," who study the effects of toxic chemicals on health, estimate that as much as 20 percent of the population is suffering symptoms of pesticide exposure...(The Environmental Protection Agency discontinued its listing of pesticide exposure "incidents," the only compilation program in place at the federal level.)

The $1.5 billion lawn care industry has exploded with growth during the last few years, led by ChemLawn Services Corp., with sales of over $300 million alone. The key to the industry's surge in recent years has been the introduction of the "full service" tanker spray truck. While homeowners have been able to use chemicals similar to those used by ChemLawn for years, they haven't used them as much because of the work and hazards entailed in applying them.

By pre-mixing pesticides and fertilizer in large quantities and applying them from a nozzle, lawn care companies have reduced application time to just minutes per lawn. This enables one person with a tank truck to treat dozens of lawns each day, making spray service price-competitive with do-it-yourself products. But applicators don't stop there. Instead of selling single applications, they sell a season long program of herbicide, fungicide, and insecticide treatments. Like the Book of the Month Club, once you sign up, they keep coming back forever unless you tell them to stop. The success of these companies has resulted in increases not only in the number of lawns treated and the quantity of pesticide used, but also in the number of different pesticides employed and their frequency of application.

Lawn pesticides in common use include chlorophenoxy herbicides such as Mecoprop and 2,4-D (the unbanned portion of Agent Orange, the defoliant used in Vietnam); benzoic acid herbicides such as Dacthal and Dicamba; organophosphates such as Diazinon and Dursban; and pesticides...such as Captan, a potent carcinogen recently banned in Germany. Organophosphates are often called nerve gas pesticides because they are less toxic versions of nerve gas chemicals originally developed as weapons of war.

These pesticides are neurotoxins, meaning that they are poisonous to the central nervous system. They evaporate into the air during and even after application. Although an individual lawn may be sprayed only once every four to six weeks, in a typical community, a great many lawns are sprayed every day of the week during each cycle. Thus pesticides which become airborne either through direct spray drift or post-application evaporation form a constant smog of nerve poison throughout the town—a toxic smog from which there is no escape.

If you find this hard to visualize, imagine instead a community where 80 percent of the homes had a ton of manure spread on their lawns on a rotating cycle every six weeks. The entire town would reek to high heaven. One difference between pesticides and manure, unfortunately, is that pesticides have no readily discernible odor, so their fumes go unnoticed. The other difference is the effect they have on human health.

Just ask Elyse Roberts. It was just after midnight on April 18, 1985. Roberts opened the bedroom window of her suburban Chicago home to let in some fresh air. Less than a minute after she lay down, she became nauseous and chilled and began to shiver. Sharp shooting pains developed in her joints and hips. She rolled over and hugged herself hoping that she could get warm and the shaking would go away. It did not. She woke her daughter who took her to the nearest hospital emergency room.

Earlier that day, she had been in the vicinity of a ChemLawn truck that was spraying Bensulfide, an organophosphate pesticide, for crabgrass control. She had gone home to bed where she fell into a drug-like sleep. She woke later, feeling better, but by opening her window she re-exposed herself to drifting fumes from a neighboring lawn which, unknown to her, had also been sprayed by ChemLawn with Bensulfide that same day.

At the hospital, doctors found her pupils contracted to the size of pencil points. Her blood pressure increased dramatically and fluctuated wildly and she developed an irregular heartbeat and a fever that peaked at 103.5—all symptoms of organophosphate poisoning. She was admitted to intensive care, placed on an ice mattress and treated with atropine sulfate, an organophosphate antidote.

Roberts had been given a complete blood test to establish whether her symptoms could be due to infection, a more readily expected cause. Instead of an increased white blood cell count, as one would find from an infection, doctors discovered that her white cells had actually decreased. This was another symptom of organophosphate poisoning.

While Mrs. Roberts' experience is dramatic, it is by no means unique. What makes it unusual is that her episode was properly diagnosed and treated.

Few laypersons are knowledgeable about the health effects of pesticides. The thought that these chemicals might be producing disease in their families, friends and even themselves has never occurred to most people. For those who do fall ill from pesticides, finding treatment is no easy matter.

Victims of stroke, depression, learning disability, anorexia or those who attempt suicide are never asked, "Is your home, school or office sprayed by the Orkin man?" or, "are lawn pesticides used in your neighborhood?" Yet, each of these conditions may be precipitated by exposure to pesticides.

The average doctor has no familiarity either with the symptoms of pesticide poisoning or how frequently patients are exposed to these toxins. This same doctor probably never even considers the possible impact of pesticide exposure on patient health. For example, the University of Miami Hospital has in the past regularly sprayed the rooms of its lung cancer ward with Dursban. An organophosphate pesticide, Dursban can cause neurological damage and pulmonary edema, fluid in the lungs, and is suspected of causing dysfunctions in the immune system.

Most doctors neither know how to test for the effects of pesticides exposure nor make any attempt to do so. They tend, instead, to diagnose patients complaining of pesticide related illness as psychosomatic and refer them to a psychiatrist. Those few patients that are successful in getting medical help usually find it from a clinical ecologist. These doctors will probably not tell them that they have been poisoned, but that they are suffering from a pesticide "allergy."

Poison control specialists are often less helpful. Presented with a patient who exhibits a list of symptoms, after a known exposure to a pesticide, they will tell you if the pesticide was legally applied there is no connection between the exposure and their symptoms.

The only proper treatment for chronic poisoning is to avoid re-exposure. But wherever victims and other concerned individuals have tried to pass "right to know" laws to give themselves fair warning of pesticide use, the spraying companies have combined to use the courts and the legislatures, at every level to prevent it.

Often victims move into remote areas for all or part of the lawn spray season in order to maintain their health. Some relocate permanently. As you can imagine, such places are hard to find. Managing to earn a living is harder.

The combined effect can put severe strain on personal relationships. Friends and other family members who are not affected, and even those who are may become hostile to poisoning victims. The invisible nature of the antagonist makes it easy and convenient to label victims as crazy. Divorce is common....

Healthy Lawns Without Unhealthy Chemicals

Here are some tips on how to take care of your lawn using natural methods:

Select a species: Bluegrass is popular but unsuited to most areas. Sod (deliberately grown as thatch and laid on unprepared soil) is a disaster waiting to happen. An 80/20 mix of fescue and rye grows well in most areas. Pick varieties that resist drought, disease, need little mowing or fertilizer and are suited to available light and traffic. Consider switching from heavily manicured lawns to alternate groundcovers, especially in dryer areas. Natural landscaping, using hardier plants, is attractive, easy to maintain and encourages native wildlife.

Mowing: Let it grow! Close and frequent cutting stresses grass plants. Weed seedlings need sun. Grass that is two and a half to three inches tall shades weeds out and holds moisture in the soil. Mow when dry and in the evening or the cool of the day. Keep your blade sharp. Leave nitrogen rich clippings behind to degrade into soil building compost. Scatter or rake up any large clumps of clipping and use for compost or mulch.

Fungus: Grows in wet, thatchy, over-fertilized lawns. Drain, dry out, de-thatch, re-add soil bacteria (from compost of Ringer Research—address below) and reseed. Minimize or stop using nitrogen fertilizer.

De-Thatch—but not until late spring or early summer (it stresses the lawn). Aerate twice a year. Compacted soil promotes weeds. Add soil loosener (compost, gypsum) and reseed.

Reseed: Bare spots and thinning lawns. Soak seed (mixed with annual rye) water overnight for quick growth to choke out weeds.

Water: Infrequently, deeply, in evening. Allow grass to dry out thoroughly between waterings.

Test: soil pH, nutrients, composition to determine its condition.

Search: For a lawn company that doesn't use toxic chemicals. They exist but are harder to find. If you do, get it in writing. ❖

Not Man Apart, *the newsmagazine of Friends of the Earth, is available for $18. Published monthly. Address: Friends of the Earth, Attn: Not Man Apart, 530 7th Street SE, Washington, D.C. 20003.*

AVOIDING RESIDENTIAL PESTICIDES
Pesticide Ordinances:
Volatile Issues in States and Counties
BY SANDRA MARQUARDT
NOT MAN APART, MAY/JUNE 1986

EVERY YEAR, MORE and more suburban residents are spraying chemicals on their lawns. But as rapidly as the lawn care industry is growing, so is the movement to prevent potentially harmful exposure to these same chemicals.

The movement, led primarily by groups of suburban residents, concerned parents (often of children who suffer ill side-effects upon exposure) and pesticide reform organizations, has been effective in passing four local ordinances since 1983. Lakewood, Ohio; Milford, Michigan and Montgomery and Prince George's counties, Maryland, require companies to provide some form of notification before or at the time of pesticide application.

Although these local laws differ, these "right to know" ordinances generally require the right to know in advance of a treatment when chemicals would be applied, which they would be, and what their potential health and environmental effects could be. In addition, all ordinances call for posting signs in lawns that have been sprayed. Such information, activists say, is vital not only to the hypersensitive individuals, but to those who wish to avoid unnecessary exposure.

The "movement," rooted primarily in the Northeast and Midwest, began in 1983 with the work of one Wauconda, Illinois mother concerned over the effects of pesticides on her chemically sensitive daughter and by activists who were rapidly learning that a product's Environmental Protection Agency registration does not necessarily act as a standard of safety. Rather, it means that the majority of pesticides are next to untested, their data bases replete with gaps concerning such critical areas as the chemical's ability to cause cancer, birth defects, genetic immune system and neurological damage. Furthermore, pesticides may contain any amount of "inert" ingredients, or carrying agents, which are not so "inert" in the benign sense of the work at all. Some, for example, contain benzene or xylene, which are potent carcinogens.

In an effort to address citizens' growing concerns about pesticide exposure, five state legislatures have recently taken up, or are about to address, the controversial "right to know" issue. Connecticut and New York have passed laws requiring companies to present customers with the label before they spray a chemical. Michigan has passed a "prior notification" bill, while Ohio is considering one. The Maryland legislature defeated such a bill.

The lawn care industry, in the meantime, is collecting its own ammunition in an effort to thwart the ordinance brushfire. They have decried local laws as leading to a "patchwork quilt of regulations" and have vilified "right to know" advocates as "lunatic chemophobic." So successful has the industry been that the Maryland legislature, for example, only barely killed a bill which would have outlawed, or preempted, the right of "political subdivisions" from passing pesticide related ordinances. A similar bill is currently before the Ohio Assembly. Federal law is silent on the issue of the rights of localities to pass laws more stringent that those of the state.

Proponents of notification ordinances insist they are not against lawn care companies but opposed to their "ask no questions" style of chemical use and their failure to promote safe lawn care practices— lawn aeration, planting of hardier types of grasses and improved mowing and watering techniques. ❖

Landscaping to Cut Fuel Costs

CONSUMER'S RESEARCH , JULY 1988

This article is excerpted from a U.S. Department of Agriculture Fact Sheet.

PLANTING TREES AND SHRUBS around your home will help to reduce your heating and cooling costs. How much it reduces costs depends on your choice of plants and where you locate them.

Trees and shrubs also reduce noise and air pollution, and make your home more attractive and more valuable. Therefore, money spent on landscaping your home is a good investment.

An unprotected home loses much more heat on a cold, windy day than on an equally cold, still day. Well-located trees and shrubs can intercept the wind and cut your heat loss.

Up to one-third of the heat loss from a building may escape through the walls and roof by conduction. Wind increases the convective air currents along outside walls and the roof, thus increasing this heat loss.

In addition, infiltration or air leakage can account for as much as one-third of heating losses in some buildings. Cold outside air flows in through cracks around windows and doors, and even through the pores in walls. This produces drafts that may cause you to overcompensate by raising the thermostat to unreasonable levels just to maintain a modicum of comfort. Both windbreaks and foundation plantings can cut down this penetrating power of the wind.

Windbreak Benefits

Studies of windbreaks show that they can reduce winter fuel consumption by 10% to 30%. One study in Nebraska compared the fuel requirements of identical test houses, which maintained a constant inside temperature of 70 degrees F. An identical house sheltered by a windbreak used only 270 kilowatt-hours. The difference in average energy requirements for the whole winter was 34%.

The amount of money saved by a windbreak around a home will vary depending on the climate of the area, location of the home, and the materials used to construct it. A well-weatherized house with adequate ventilation, caulking, and weatherstripping won't benefit from windbreaks nearly as much as a poorly weatherized house.

In addition to reducing the force of the wind, windbreaks also can reduce the wind chill impact on people outside the house. Studies of three-row windbreaks, where trees were 25 feet tall, show the wind velocities and the wind chill index were effectively reduced.

Design and Composition

The height and density of trees determine the amount of protection they will provide. Windbreaks of two to five rows of trees and shrubs generally provide good protection, although low-branching deciduous trees can significantly reduce windspeed. Even a single row of evergreen trees will give some protection.

Windbreaks will reduce wind velocity significantly for a distance of about 10 times the height of the trees. Thus, a windbreak 30 feet high protects an area extending as far as 300 feet downwind. Some protection is provided for as far as 20 times the height of the trees.

For onsite assistance in locating and designing windbreaks, and selecting appropriate trees and shrubs, contact your local U.S. Department of Agriculture Soil Conservation Service office, county extension agent, or farm forester.... ❖

Section Seven
BANDING TOGETHER

THE NINETIES MAY well become the decade when the consumers of America band together in powerful bargaining associations to deal with utilities, home repair companies, insurance firms and other sellers to homeowners. Already the signs are propitious.

Along the East Coast from Boston to Washington, thousands of households are joining buying associations which negotiate agreements with area fuel distributors to provide discount heating oil and other related services to homes, apartments and condos. For example, Public Citizen's non-profit Buyer's Up groups in the Washington-Baltimore-Philadelphia regions invite households to join (around $20 per year in dues) and, even with relatively lower oil prices, manage to save their members about $200 each winter season. Buyer's Up (located at 1751 N Street NW # 401 Washington, DC 20036) handles any complaints members may have with dealers, encourages energy conservation audits and, through its newsletter, offers advice that can save households irritation and money. Buyer's Up's expertise on energy matters also expresses itself in news conferences and testimony to give voice to consumer rights before decision-makers and the media. All the heating oil user has to do is send the annual dues; the oil is delivered directly by the cooperating oil dealer and the various credit emergency, maintenance and other services available as with any other dealers.

Up in Toronto, Canada, the Home Owners Association (HOA) for many years has represented tens of thousands of local homeowners who join for $20 a year. HOA concentrates on improving the quality and fair pricing of home repair and many other service firms by preselecting reliable contractors in over 600 different fields. If the work isn't done right the first time, the HOA assures that the firm returns and does it right without charge, or risk being removed from its approval list. HOA also arbitrates any disputes. As an HOA brochure says: "Of course, the 'real saving' in being a member of Home Owners Association is getting your jobs done 'right' the first time...and in having our emergency services available 24 hours a day, 7 days a week, including Sundays and Holidays." HOA has conditions for firms wanting to be on its approved list; one of them is no portal-to-portal or travel time charges or overtime charges. Taking a cue from the Canadians, a few groups are starting up in the U.S.A., some non-profit, some for profit. But the field is essentially wide open for neighborhood activists to organize their community or area of town.

The third kind of 'banding together' are the non-profit Citizen Utility Boards or CUBs which invite residential utility ratepayers (electric, gas, water, telephone) to join and support a full-time staff of consumer champions to watchdog the companies and the regulatory agencies. CUBs were established during the past decade by state laws in Wisconsin, Illinois, Oregon and by local ordinance in San Diego. Until an unfortunate split Supreme Court decision invalidated the procedure in 1986, CUBS were authorized to have inserted a membership solicitation envelope inside the utility company's monthly billing envelope. Now, beginning with Illinois, an alternative insert right is being pushed to place the membership invitations in major state government mailings to residents. Both Wisconsin and Illinois have large memberships and have won many victories before all three branches of state government on behalf of more reasonable rates and other utility policies.

So this momentous trend toward a buyer's market, for a change, is underway. Such groups, and many other types of group buying which will be formed, can achieve better purchasing values, easier complaint handling and more powerful disciplining of corporate practices and governmental policies. Banding together puts marketplace reality back into the principle of consumer sovereignty.

For more details, send a self-addressed, stamped, large envelope to: "Banding Together," *Number 10, P.O. Box 19367, Washington, D.C. 20036.* ❖

Section Eight
RESOURCES

SAFETY AND SECURITY

Free

Write to the U.S. Consumer Product Safety Commission (CPSC), Office of Information and Public Affairs, Washington, D.C. 20207 for the following fact sheets:

Kitchen Ranges, No. 9
TV and Fire and Shock Hazards, No. 11
Lead in Paint, No. 14
Upholstered Furniture, No. 53
Electrically Operated Toys and Children's Articles, No. 61
Clothes Dryers, No. 73
Furnaces, No. 79

Also from the CPSC:
- *What You Should Know About Smoke Detectors*
- *What You Should Know About Home Fire Safety*
- Smoke Detector Fact Sheet
- *The Nine Lives of El Gatto the Cat,* a fire safety comic book
- *Give a Gift- Give a Smoke Detector*
- *Poison Lookout Checklist*
- *Locked Up Poisons* (safety advice)
- *Which Toy For Which Child?* Two booklets providing criteria to follow when choosing toys, for children aged birth through five years and children six through 12 years.
- *The Safe Nursery: A booklet to help avoid injuries from nursery furniture and equipment*

Hazardous Waste: What You Should & Shouldn't Do, from Water Pollution Control Federation, 601 Wythe Street, Alexandria, VA 22314. Send self-addressed, stamped envelope.

Household Hazardous Waste: A Bibliography of Useful References and List of State Experts. To order copies, call EPA's RCRA/Superfund Hotline at 1-800-424-9346.

Oregon Student Public Interest Research Group (OSPIRG) conducts an annual survey of dangerous toys, published shortly after Thanksgiving. Also available is an eight-page brochure titled *Toy Safety Tips for Consumers.* Send a self-addressed stamped envelope to OSPIRG, 27 SW Arthur, Portland, OR 97201. 503-222-9641.

Write to the Environmental Protection Agency, Public Information Center, PM 211B, 401 M Street, SW, Washington, D.C. 20460 for the following publications:
- *Focus On — Recycling*
- *Discarding the Litter Habit*
- *Recycling—A National Effort*
- *Lead and Your Drinking Water*
- *Removal of Radon from Household Water*

From The Consumer Information Center:

The Consumer Information Center in Pueblo, Colorado, 81002, publishes a Consumer Information Catalog four times per year, available for no charge. Each catalog lists over 200 sources of consumer information available from government agencies for free or for a minimal charge. Please note that if you order more than one free publication from the Consumer Information Center you must pay a $1 handling charge for any extras.

Dennis Takes a Poke at Poison. Dennis the Menace learns about poisons in the home and how to tell if something is safe to eat (1981. FDA).

In the Event of a Flood. What to do during a flood and how to minimize loss of life and property. (1983. FEMA) 579T.

Consumer's Resource Handbook. Comprehensive listing of contacts to assist with consumer problems. Includes corporate consumer representatives, private dispute resolution programs, and federal, state, and local government agencies with consumer responsibilities. (1988. OCA) 582T.

Other Publications

Worst Pills, Best Pills: The Older Adult's Guide to Avoiding Drug-Induced Illness. Send $12 to Health Research Group, P.O. Box 19404, Washington, D.C. 20036.

Consumer Guide to Toxic and Non-Toxic Household Products. For a photo-copy of the original booklet, send $1.50 to: Clean Water Action Project, 186A South Street, Boston, MA 02111.

Waste Not, 82 Judson, Canton, NY 13617. Weekly newsletter promoting sound resource management policy. $25 personal, $15 for students and seniors, $100 for consultants and businesses.

The League of Women Voters of Massachusetts makes available a video and kit of materials giving tips on how to set up household hazardous waste days. Write to the league of Women Voters of Massachusetts, 8 Winter Street, Boston, MA 02108, for a flyer and order form.

Toys that Don't Care, by Edward M. Swartz. Gambit, Inc., 535 Albany Street, Boston, MA 02118, 1971. $6.95.

Toys that Kill, by Edward M. Swartz. Vintage Books, Westminster Distribution Center, 400 Hahn Road, Westminster, MD 21157, 1986. $7.95.

The Childwise Catalog: A Consumer Guide to Buying the Safest and Best Products for Your Children, by Jack Gilles and Mary Ellen R. Fise. Pocket Books, Total Warehouse Services, Radcliff Street, Bristol, PA 19007, 1986. $7.95.

Good Toys, by Debbie Wager and Judy Nygren. National Press, Inc., 7201 Wisconsin Avenue, Suite 720, Bethesda, MD 20814, 1986. $5.95.

"War Toys or Peace Toys: What are You Buying Your Kids," by Rene Riley in *Nuclear Times*, Nov./ Dec. 1987. Back issues are $3.00. Address: 1601 Connecticut Avenue NW, Washington, D.C. 20009.

"Toys," *Buyer's Market*, Volume III, Number 9, November, 1987. For a copy, send $1.00 and a self-addressed, stamped envelope to: Center for Study of Responsive Law (CSRL), P.O. Box 19367, Washington, D.C. 20036.

Organizations

National Coalition on Television Violence
P.O. Box 2157
Champaign, IL 61820

Action for Children's Television (ACT)
20 University Road
Cambridge, MA 02138

Stop War Toys Campaign (SWTC)
Box 1093
Norwich, CT 06360

Institute for Local Self-Reliance
2425 18th Street NW
Washington, D.C. 20009

National Recycling Coalition
45 Rockefeller Plaza
New York, NY 10111

Office of Solid Waste
Environmental Protection Agency
Washington, D.C. 20460

For information on neighborhood crime watches in your area, contact your local police department.

Toll-Free Hotlines

Consumer Product Safety Commission:
1-800-638-CPSC
TTY for hearing-impaired:
1-800-638-8270
In Maryland:
800-492-8104
Receives reports on injuries/deaths from hazardous manufactured products; helps consumers evaluate safety of commercial products.

Environmental Protection Agency Safe Drinking Water Hotline:
1-800-426-4791

Resource Conservation and Recovery Act/Superfund Hotline:
1-800-424-9346
Information on regulations governing hazardous waste. In Alaska, Hawaii and the District of Columbia, call
202-382-3000
Federal Crime Insurance Hotline:
1-800-638-8780
Information and applications for federally-subsidized crime insurance for homes and business in participating states; assists individuals denied burglary/robbery insurance.

In Alaska, Hawaii and Maryland call collect:
301-652-2637

Lifeline Systems:
1-800-451-0525
Information on emergency telephone systems for elderly and handicapped people to maintain a direct line to local hospitals.
In Alaska, Hawaii and Massachusetts call:
617-923-4141

INDOOR AIR POLLUTION

Free

Write to: The EPA Public Information Center, 401 M Street SW, Washington, D.C. 20460, for the following publications:

- *Asbestos in the Home*
- *Asbestos Fact Book*
- *A Citizen's Guide to Radon*
- *Radon Reduction Methods*
- *Removal of Radon from Household Water*
- *The Inside Story: A Guide to Indoor Air Quality*
- *Radon Measurement Proficiency Report*, a listing of firms and laboratories in each state that have demonstrated their ability to accurately measure radon in homes.
- *Directory of State Indoor Air Contacts.* Lists contacts by state and by indoor air problem.
- *Safety Tips for Using Treated Wood*
- *Regulating Pesticides*
- *Termiticides*

Fact Sheet, "Air-to-Air Heat Exchangers," U.S. Department of Energy. Write to: Renewable Energy Information, P.O. Box 8900, Silver Spring, MD 20907.

Formaldehyde: Everything You Wanted to Know But Were Afraid to Ask. Send a self-addressed stamped envelope to: Consumer Federation of America, 1424 16th Street NW Washington, D.C. 20036

Other Publications

Healthy HouseCatalog, Environmental Health Watch and Housing Resource Center, 1820 West 48th Street, Cleveland, OH 44102, 1988. $17.00. A major sourcebook which provides comprehensive listings of products, services, materials and information resources that address residential air and water pollutants.

The Reactor, P.O. Box 575, Corte Madera, CA 94925. A bimonthly publication for the environmentally sensitive. $20 basic and $10 fixed/disability. Susan Malloy, editor.

The Delicate Balance, 1100 Rural Avenue, Vorhees, NJ 08043. A quarterly publication for the environmentally sensitive run by Mary Lamielle, director of the Environmental Health Association of New Jersey. $10 for the disabled and for students, $15 regular and $20 professional.

"Radon Detectors: How to find out if your house has a radon problem," *Consumer Reports,* July 1987. Back issues are $4.00 each from Back Issue Department, *Consumer Reports,* P.O. Box 2485, Boulder, CO 80322.

Your Home, Your Health and Your Well-Being by David Rousseau, W.J. Rea M.D. and Jean Enwright. Hartley & Marks Ltd. , 3663 West Broadway, Vancouver V6R 2B8, B.C., 1987. $14.95.

Organizations

Action on Smoking and Health 2013 H Street, NW Washington, D.C. 20006

Americans for Nonsmokers' Rights 2054 University Avenue, Suite 500 Berkeley, CA 94704

National Coalition Against the

Misuse of Pesticides (NCAMP) 530 Seventh Street SE Washington, D.C. 20003

Toll-Free Hotlines

Environmental Protection Agency
1-800-424-4000
D.C.:
202-382-4977
Radon Hotline:
1-800-334-8571   X 713
or call your state health department and ask for the section dealing with radiation.

National Pesticide Telecommunications Network:
1-800-858-7378
Information on health hazards of pesticides, safety precautions, how to obtain laboratory analysis for a fee to determine toxicity levels in soil samples, garments, carpets, etc.; 24-hour service connects callers to human and animal poison control centers. In Alaska and Hawaii call:
512-399-5352

REPAIRS AND REMODELING

Free

Remodeling Without Worry: HOW's Guide for Consumers, a 20-page booklet on home improvement, and *Protect Your Investment: Home Maintenance Tips,* are available from Home Owners Warranty Corporation (HOW), 2000 L Street, NW, Washington, D.C. 20036.

The Small Homes Council-Building Research Council offers an extensive series of reports, technical notes and other publications on home repair and energy conservation. For a copy of their publicaitons list, write to SHC-BRC, University of Illinois at Urbana-Champaign, 1 East St. Mary's Road, Champaign, IL 61820.

Warranties and *Service Contracts* are two handy brochures that out-

line your rights under federal law. They are available from the Federal Trade Commission, 6th and Pennsylvania Avenue, NW, Washington, D.C. 20580

Other Publications

The Helping Hands Guide to Hiring a Remodeling Contractor, by Leon A. Frechette. C.R.S., Inc., P.O. Box 4567, Spokane, WA 99202, 1988. $14.00 plus $1.45 shipping and handling.

You can get copies of *Maintaining Your Home,* a handy checklist for inspecting your own home and practicing preventive maintenance, and *Wet Basements,* a brochure which details do-it-yourself ways to "fix" wet basements, for $1.00 each by sending a stamped, self-addressed, business-sized envelope to The American Society of Home Inspectors, Brochures, P.O. Box 1769-B, Rockville, MD 20850.

"Repairs," *Buyer's Market,* Volume II, Number 4, April 1986. $1.00.

Home Sense: A Year-round Practical Guide for the Homeowner, by Mike McClintock. Charles Scribner's Sons, 115 Fifth Avenue, New York, NY 10003., 1986. $10.95

BUYING, SELLING, INSPECTING, AND INSURING THE HOME

Free

Write to the Mortgage Bankers Association of America, 1125 15th Street NW, Washington, D.C. 20005 for the following publications:
- *Buying a House*
- *A Home Buyer's Guide to Settlement Costs*
- *How to Shop for a Mortgage*

Many of the state bar associations and attorney general's offices distribute free pamphlets on home buying.

Other Publications

The U.S. Department of Housing and Urban Development (HUD) has printed a number of booklets on buying and renting a home, mortgages, settlements, etc., which are available for a small price from the office of your representative in Congress or from the Superintendent of Documents, U.S. Government Printing Office, Washington, D.C. 20402.

"Money Guide/Your Home: Buying It, Selling It, Improving It," by the editors of *Money* Magazine. Box 999, Radio City Station, New York, NY 10019, 1985. $3.95.

The Complete Book of Home Buying, by Michael Sumichrast and Ronald G. Shafer. Bantam Books, 666 Fifth Avenue, New York, NY 10019, 1982. $4.95 in the U.S., $5.95 in Canada.

Planning Your Retirement Housing, by Michael Sumichrast, Ronald G. Shafer, and Marika Sumichrast. American Association of Retired Persons (AARP), 1909 K Street NW, Washington, D.C. 20049, 1984. $8.95.

"10 Questions Consumers Most Frequently Ask About Auto and Home Insurance," Insurance Information Institute, 110 William Street, New York, NY 10038. Individual leaflets are free, bulk orders are $.10 apiece.

"Insurance," *Buyer's Market*, Volume I, Number I, January 1985. $1.00.

At Your Library

These books are out of print but may be available at your local library.

Home Buyers: Lambs to the Slaughter? by Sloan Bashinsky. Menasha Ridge Press, Route 3, Box 450, Hillsborouth, NC 27278, 1984.

How to Buy Your Home....And Do It Right, by Sue Beck. Evans Publishing Company, P.O. Box 26216, Denver, CO 80226, 1984.

Organizations

National Insurance Consumer Organization (NICO)
121 N. Payne Street
Alexandria, VA 22314

National Association of Home Builders
15th & M Streets NW
Wasington, D.C. 20005

Toll-Free Hotlines

Insurance Information Institute:
1-800-221-4954
Trade association gives pointers on how to shop for auto, homeowner, property, casualty and commercial insurance.

UTILITIES: BEATING THE BILLING BLUES

Free

The Public Benefits of Public Power, American Public Power Association, 2301 M Street, NW, Washington, D.C. 20037.

Energy Information Administration, U.S. Department of Energy, 1000 Independence Avenue, SW, Washington, D.C. 20585. Write for list of publications on energy.

Tips for Energy Savers, U.S. Department of Energy, Washington, D.C. 20585. Offers advice on how to change your habits to keep your utility costs low.

Other Publications

"Utilities," *Buyer's Market*, Volume I, Number 5, May 1985. $1.00.

"Energy," *Buyer's Market*, Volume I, Number 4, April 1985. $1.00.

Power Line, Environmental Action Foundation, 724 Dupont Circle Building, Washington, D.C. 20036. Bi-monthly journal offering examples of successful citizen campaigns to reform utility policies. $15.00 a year. Send $.50 for a sample copy.

Organizations

American Council for an Energy Efficient Economy
1001 Connecticut Avenue NW
Washington, D.C. 20036

World Resources Institute
1735 New York Avenue NW
Washington, D.C. 20006

General Services Administration
18th and F Streets NW
Washington, D.C. 20585

Office of Conservation and Renewable Energy
U.S. Department of Energy
1000 Independence Avenue SW
Washington, D.C. 20585

Toll-Free Hotlines

Conservation and Renewable Energy Inquiry and Referral Service
U.S. DEPT. O F ENERGY:
1-800-523-2929
Information about conservation, solar energy and other renewable energy sources, including wind, photo-voltaic, biomass, alcohol fuels, hydroelectric and ocean thermal. In Pennsylvania call:
1-800-462-4983
and in Alaska and Hawaii:
1- 800-233-3071

LAWNS, GARDENS AND CHEMICALS

Free

Write to *Organic Gardening*, 33 E. Minor, Emmaus, PA 18098 for the following reprinted articles:
• *"Growing an Organic Garden in a Nutshell"*
  • *"Compost"*
  • *"An Introduction to Organic Pest Control"*
  • *"Resources for Organic Pest Control"*
  • *"Organic Fertilizers and Soil Builders"*

• *"Seed, Bulb and Nursery Guide"*

(*Organic Gardening* is published monthly and is available for $14.97 a year at the above address).

BANDING TOGETHER

Organizations

Buyer's Up
1751 N Street NW #401
Washington, D.C. 20036

Toronto Homeowners' Association
2590A Young Street
Toronto, Ontario M4P 2J3
Canada

Citizens' Utility Board (CUB)
108 North State Street, Suite 1202
Chicago, IL 60602

Publications from the Center for Study of Responsive Law

These books, some of them already classics in their field, were written to inform, to involve, and to mobilize. They are designed to change one or more injustices and deficiencies through citizen action and awareness. A higher quality of daily democracy requires a higher quality of daily citizenship. These works can help guide the way toward that delightful commitment.

For the People, by Joanne Manning Anderson, with introduction by Ralph Nader. Addison-Wesley, 1977. A consumer handbook for community action. $5.95.

Company State, by James Phelan and Robert Pozen, with introduction by Ralph Nader, Grossman Pub., 1973. A study group report on Dupont in Delaware. $3.95.

Politics of Land, Robert C. Fellmeth, with introduction by Ralph Nader. Grossman Pub., NY, 1973. A study group report on land use in California. $5.95.

How to Appraise and Improve Your Daily Newspaper, by David Bollier, introduction by Ralph Nader, 1980. A manual for readers. $5.00.

Banding Together: How Check-offs Will Revolutionize the Consumer Movement, by Andrew Sharpless and Sarah Gallup, 1981. $5.00.

Disposable Consumer Items: The Overlooked Mercury Pollution Problem, by John Abbotts, 1981. $5.00.

Energy Conservation: A Campus Guidebook, by Kevin O'Brien and David Corn, 1981. $5.00.

Women Take Charge: Asserting Your Rights in the Marketplace, by Nina Easton, preface by Ralph Nader, 1983. $6.50.

Being Beautiful, prepared by Katherine Isaac, with introduction by Ralph Nader, 1986. Selected readings on cosmetics safety and the beauty business. $10.00.

Return To The Jungle, by Kathleen Hughes, with foreword by Ralph Nader, 1983. How the Reagan Administration imperiled the nation's meat and poultry inspection program. $6.50.

Eating Clean[2], prepared by Steven Gold and Katherine Isaac, with introduction by Ralph Nader, 1987. Selected readings on food safety. $8.00.

The Home Book, A Guide to Safety, Security and Savings in the Home, prepared by Elizabeth Hax, with introduction by Ralph Nader, 1989. $8.00.

To order, make checks payable to:
Center for Study of
Responsive Law
P.O. Box 19367
Washington, DC 20036